MW00675199

SURFiNG
SOUTH AFRiCA by Spike
(STEVE PiKE)

DOUBLE
STOREY

Surfing South Africa

First published 2007
by Double Storey Books
an imprint of Juta & Company Ltd
Mercury Crescent, Wetton, Cape Town, South Africa

ISBN 978-1-77013-114-9

Editor: Jennifer Stern
Designer: Patricia Lynch-Blom
Cover designer: Michiel Botha
Printed in South Africa by CTP

Cover: Barry Tuck; Caption: Sav's Island
Back: Barry Tuck; Caption: Grant Washburn at Dungeons

This book is dedicated to
the surfing community of South Africa,
including Janet, Tyler and Ella.

Captions: Chapter openers

Preface, p. 5: Secret line-up, South Coast, KwaZulu-Natal
Contents, p. 6: Locked in the tube, KwaZulu-Natal
History, pp. 10-11: Big-wave champions Ian Armstrong, left, and Cass Collier
Surfrikan Culture, pp. 30-31: Nic Hofmeyr filming *Taking Back the Waves*
Big Wave, pp. 68-69: Giant swell hits on 30 July 2006, Dungeons
Making Waves, pp. 80-81: Storm swell hits the harbour, Kalk Bay, Cape Town
Men in Grey Suits, pp. 114-115: Great white shark, Gansbaai
On Surfari, pp. 132-133: Jumping in for a surf, New Pier, Durban
Spots, pp. 142-143: Two surfers, two waves, South Coast, KwaZulu-Natal
Surfrikan Slang, pp. 254-256: Surf shop mural, Diep River, Cape Town
Useful Websites, p. 270: Slash back, Paul Canning

Take a bow, the following primary writers, photographers and illustrators:

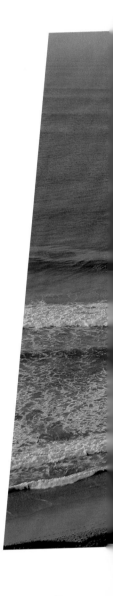

Writers	Photographers	Illustrators
Tom Peschak	Barry Tuck	Andy Mason
Ben Trovato	Harry de Zitter	Tony Butt
Ross Frylinck	Michael Dei-Cont	Chip Snaddon
Gideon Malherbe	Lance Slabbert	
Tony Heard	Tom Peschak	
Tony Weaver	Pierre Marqua	
Jennifer Stern	Brenton Geach	
Darryl Brandreth	Jared Hartman	
Henri du Plessis	Serge Raemaekers	
Meyrick Stockigt	Ant Scholtz	
Dougal Paterson	Ray du Toit	

For comprehensive list of contributors, see Acknowledgements (p.278) and Credits (p.280)

PREFACE

For the love of it.

CONTENTS

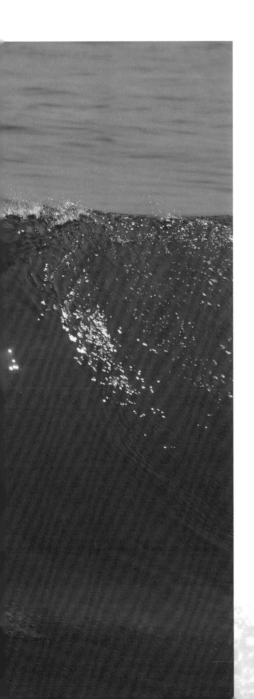

FOREWORD

I can remember that first wave on a board like it was yesterday. It was 1965 at the Bay of Plenty in Durban. I was nine years old. The beach had always been a big part of our family life; my earliest memories are of sitting on the sand with my mom and dad beside me, with a big hamper of food in front of us and an umbrella overhead. My dad would sit in his deck chair with a cigarette and I'd impatiently tug at his arm and say 'Dad, let's go for a tiger, let's go for a tiger.' A swim was called a Tiger Tim, a nod to the Cockney rhyming slang that had made its way to South Africa.

My dad would take me down to the surf, pointing out the dangers of the jellyfish, the stinging bluebottles with their zinging tails and the powerful fast-moving rip tides that ran out beside the piers, stealthily sucking out swimmers. The dangers of sharks he seldom spoke about even though he'd been badly hit less than 20 years before. So I knew about the dangers early but they were all brushed aside and we'd plunge in and swim out to the backline looking for a suitable wave to catch, hoping to find a *broadie*, a wave that would enable us to track across the wall, parallel to the shore. Sometimes we'd just get a *foamie*, a mass of rolling whitewater and we'd body surf straight in, trying to keep our bodies as stiff as possible and my dad would raise one leg while he raced forward, like a rudder in the wind. I don't know what it did and I still don't, but it sure looked good, so I copied that cool style of his.

From body surfing it was a quick progression to *surfoplanes*, a corrugated rubber pillow about a metre long with handles on the front. My brother Paul, cousin Mike and I would battle our way out to the backline and bomb down the dumpers, screaming with the adrenalin rush of the drop. And then my dad got me my first board, a 4'6" Wetteland Surf Rider, a mass-produced pop-out, with red rails and a clear chop mat centre. I had a never seen anything as beautiful before, my very own brand new little surfboard.

That first wave at the Bay – I waxed up with a candle and made my way out through the *shorie*, the impact zone where the waves broke right on the sand. With the world to my back and the horizon ahead, I was truly on my own. The foam rumbled towards me, I swung my board around, dug my little arms hard into the water and paddled. The white water picked me up, shot me forward and I leapt to my feet and stood up. That feeling of stoke instantly imprinted itself on my being; happiness and fear, exhilaration, speed, conquest all melded together into one rush of sensation. And the view, that overview of land, looking over and above it all, racing along on

BACKDOOR HEYDAY: Shaun perfecting his tube skills in 1977.

an invisible band of energy, six centimetres above water, separated by just a sliver of glass fibre, for a brief moment a master of my little universe. Surfing right there, right then, gripped me hard and fast and just never let go.

STILL SHREDDING: Shaun at J-Bay in 2005.

The essence of this book is that feeling that I experienced so long ago, that sensation of being stoked, that excitement that millions of surfers around the world have felt in the self same way. Everything else in surfing is just detail, minutiae floating around in the line-up. Read what Spike has written and you'll get an idea of how it all started in our little surf zone, at the tip of a vast continent. But if you really want to understand what the book is all about, think back through your own history – to your first wave and that feeling of being stoked for the first time. And if you've never surfed before, get a board and paddle out there, look out to that broad expanse of ocean with the world and its worries to your back, and pick that one wave that has been coming just for you from hundred of miles away. Take it and ride it and feel the stoke.

Shaun Tomson

Chapter 1

The sea! The sea!
The open sea!
The blue, the fresh,
the ever free!

Bryan W. Procter, 1837

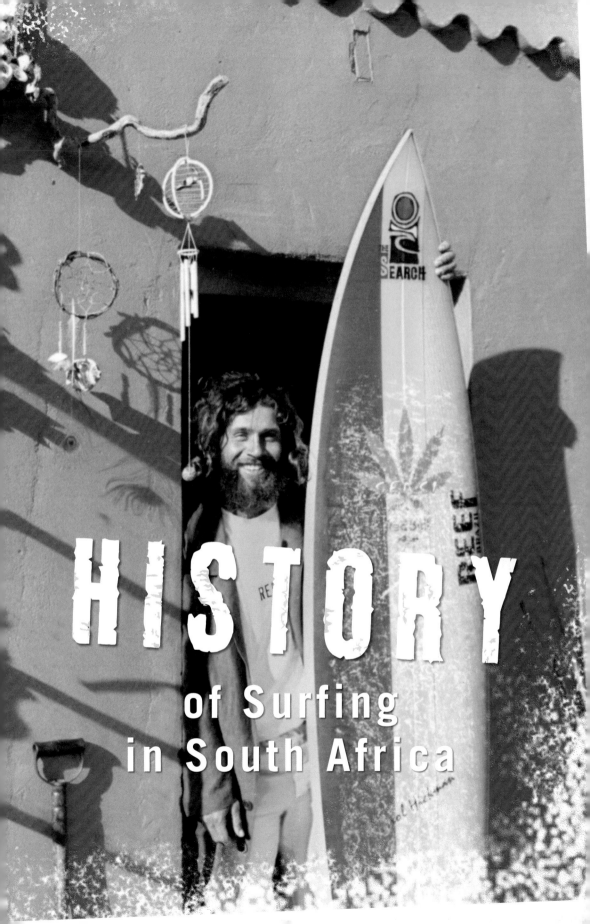

HISTORY
of Surfing
in South Africa

One of the earliest memories of someone standing on a surfboard in South Africa was unearthed in the early 2000s. Cape Town surfer Ross Lindsay was in Zimbabwe visiting his wife's great aunt, Heather Price, who was almost 100 years old. The old lady's face lit up when he mentioned that he was a surfer. She hauled out photographs taken at Muizenberg during the First World War. The pictures showed her surfing with American marines, who had brought their boards with them on US Navy ships stopping off in Cape Town.

There may be other sepia snaps, dog-eared and musty, buried beneath old papers in attics somewhere, but this is the first known experience of surfing in South Africa.

The first contact with surfing came, aptly, over the sea. Wherever ships came to port, the seeds of surfing were sown. At first, surfing was a flirtation with novelty, usually on borrowed boards borne by sailors and passengers disembarking from those old steamers.

The first stirrings of surfing as a regular activity – apart from perhaps one or two lucky recipients of surfboards given to them as gifts – began in the early 1930s. Surfing was restricted to lifeguards – mostly in Durban – riding their heavy 16-foot wooden paddle boards on the way back to the beach.

At the time, surfers were beach sportsmen – lifesavers, divers or spear fishermen. Boards were copied from designs that came from overseas, many from Australia. After World War II, Durbanite Fred Crocker built a light timber-frame paddle boat covered with canvas and impregnated with aeroplane dope. It had paddles tied to the nose. Many people caught their first wave on a Crocker Ski: the rider standing, holding and leaning back on the string and digging a paddle to angle right or left to 'catch a broadie' when the waves were 'play'.

Beach culture began to flourish in Durban from about 1947. Guys like Ernie Tomson and Brian van Biljon were part of the original crew at South Beach. They were the 'older guys' among the younger batch of locals. The 'youngsters' of the day included Cliff Honeysett, George Bell, Wendy Hall, Bruce Giles, Derek and Leith Jardine, Raymond and Anthony Heard, 'Chookie' and Vera Salzman, Jean Baxter, Harry Bold and Shorty Bronkhorst. Margaret Smith was South Africa's first female surfing champion.

'Some women of my early surf years, like Vera Salzman, could handle a "gun",' says Anthony Heard. 'Wendy Hall would ride two-up with adept, angular surfer Bruce Giles – and even stand on her head while white water foamed all around. This – done without leash or skeg or shark nets – is courage.'

Jardine says he rode his first wave in 1948 on a board borrowed from Tomson. In 1951, the South Beach crew founded the South Beach Surfboard Club, the first official surfing club in South Africa.

Meanwhile, the surfing lifestyle was starting to stir in Cape Town. By 1954, perlemoen and crayfish diver John Whitmore, in his early twenties, had built the first foam surfboard from designs he saw in an imported *Findiver* magazine. Carving up a block of newly invented polystyrene foam,

From left, a US marine poses with his board in Cape Town during World War 1; Heather Price and a US marine; and Price rides Muizenberg, the oldest known photograph of surfing in South Africa.

10-foot surfboards

THE LINE-UP: A Crocker ski and assorted South Beach barges, circa early 1950s. From left, Les Ginsberg, Noel Dodd, Cliff Honeysett, Wyndham Woodford, Leith Jardine and two youngsters.

weighing 25kg

CATCHING ON: An advert in *South African Surfer* magazine and, *right*, one of the first Whitmore boards, owned by Derek Jardine, who moved to Cape Town in 1955.

he covered it with muslin soaked in Cascamite glue and sealed it with PVA to stop the coating of polyester resin from eating the foam.

He began building 10-foot surfboards weighing 25 kg in his garage. The boards were used to surf around the Cape Peninsula. News of these 'lightweight' boards spread to Durban, and Whitmore started supplying people like Barry Edwards and Baron Stander. Deliveries to Durban led to Whitmore pioneering surfing in Mossel Bay, Port Elizabeth, East London, Buffalo Bay, Jongensfontein and the beach break at Cape St Francis. He also discovered the break at Elands Bay on the West Coast, first ridden in 1957.

The arrival of epoxy resin – compatible with styrene foam – made glassing easier. According to Harry Bold, he brought the very first polyurethane surfboard to South Africa in 1961. 'It was a beaut nine-foot six inch OLE board by Bob Olson of Seal Beach California. John Whitmore met my ship in Cape Town and invited me to his place, where he made templates. Later the Cape Town boys came to Durban with some pretty close copies.'

A fortuitous encounter with a Californian hitchhiker was to have a profound effect on our history. American surfer Dick Metz arrived after a marathon four-day hitch-hiking trip from Zimbabwe. The driver needed to see his sick mother in Camps Bay, so Metz was dropped him off at Glen Beach. He noticed a lone surfer in the water who had lost his board. Metz retrieved it from the rocks, and the lone surfer, John Whitmore, invited him to stay at their Bakoven cottage. He lived with the Whitmore clan for several months, and they became close friends.

FIRST WAVE: Half the surfing population on a wave.

BUFF OKES: South Africa's early surfers were often lifeguards. Cliff Honeysett, *left*, and Derek Jardine.

STYLING: The scene at South Beach. *From left*, Dux Coetzee, Noel Dodd and an unnamed surfer.

OLD SCHOOL: Cape Town surfers visit their Durban mates in 1961. From left, Arthur Holgate (CT), Brian Wilson, Harry Bold, John Whitmore (CT), Earl Crouse (CT), Peter Hugo (CT), Chuck Salzman and Baron Stander.

Returning home, Metz worked with school friend 'Grubby' Clark, who was moulding surfboard blanks from polyurethane foam. Denser than styrene, they were easier to shape and could be glassed using lighter polyester resin. Metz introduced Whitmore to Clark and by the 1960s, Whitmore was importing Clark foam blanks from California for his thriving Whitmore Surfboards business.

Metz also put him in contact with John Severson, who sent him *Surfer* magazines that were sold in South Africa by subscription.

The trippy era of the 1960s signalled a boom in the surf cult, although it was mostly confined to Australia, California and Hawaii. A perk of Whitmore's job as a Volkswagen salesman was the use of a VW Kombi, and lots of driving along the coast looking for waves. Whitmore owned the first Kombi made in South Africa, and he invented the first roof racks.

He would drive past Jeffreys Bay to the VW factory in Port Elizabeth and see that classic line-up from the road. His tales of perfect waves led Capetonians Gerald 'Gus' Gobel and Brian 'Block' McClarty to the Point, and they became the first humans to surf there. Of course, the real pioneers are the dolphins that have been riding Jeffreys Bay for thousands of years.

Back in Durban, popout foam boards began to appear, based partly on boards brought in from overseas. In the early to mid 1960s, Max Wetteland, George Thomopolous (later Thompson), Ant van den Heuvel and Robert McWade were shaping and surfing. The technology of board riding, tested by the act itself, began to gain momentum. In Cape Town, Whitmore gave up his VW job and started blowing Clark foam blanks.

Filmmaker Bruce Brown arrived in South Africa while filming *Endless Summer*. Metz had told him about Whitmore, and Brown got in touch. Whitmore showed them around and set them up with big game hunter Terence Bullen, who took them to Cape St Francis, where they scored classic two-foot surf they described as 'the most perfect wave in the world'. The film was a hit. Soon, every surfer wanted to visit South Africa.

In 1964, Wetteland, Stander and Harry Bold built the first Safari surfboards in Durban. News came from overseas that South Africa's champion was invited to the first World Surfing Championships at Manly Beach in Australia. But no such event had ever been held in South Africa. Deciding a champion was difficult, but Wetteland got the nod, becoming the first South African to compete overseas. Australian Midget Farrelly won the event.

VOL 3 NO.2
GORDONS BAY CONTESTS
SKIN DIVING
PORT ELIZABETH
AUSTRALIA
40 CENTS

SOUTH AFRICAN SURFER

ORIGINAL MAG: The first *South African Surfer* magazine.

LIQUID LOCAL: Ant van den Heuvel eventually settled in Jeffreys Bay.

Whitmore brought out Brown's movie *Waterlogged*. After selling out shows every day for nine weeks at the Labia Theatre in Cape Town, he took it to Port Elizabeth and East London. Harry Bold put it on in Durban, also to sell-out shows. It was an era that captured the quintessential surfing ethos: a soulful mixture of mythology, brotherhood and travel. After Hollywood's *Gidget* movies and the first Beach Boys album – depicting a surfer riding Hawaii's Sunset Beach – everybody wanted to surf.

The South African Surfriders Association was formed in 1965. Whitmore was chairman. Thomopolous, Van den Heuvel and Wetteland represented the country at the world champs in Peru. Harry Bold became editor of the first surfing magazine, *South African Surfer*, which appeared in 1965. The magazine folded three years later, but it played a critical role in documenting the early days of modern surfing. Some of the older guys, like Derick Jardine and Bold, are the proud owners of every issue – a valuable collection of memories.

The first official South African Surfing Championships were held in Durban in 1966. The event was moved from tiny Wedge to Ansteys, which promptly jacked to a solid 12 feet. A triple overhead wave, ridden by a guy who was free-surfing as a non-contestant, Neville Callenbourne, was immortalised in a photograph by John Thornton, published in *South African Surfer*.

The first official Springbok team was selected from this event, and competed in San Diego, California. Australian Nat Young won the world title. The team brought back the latest board designs, skills and fashions. They also brought back Van den Heuvel, found wandering around Huntington Beach in a drug haze. He became an instant folk hero as surfers 'tuned in' to rock and roll, 'turned on' to mind-altering substances and 'dropped out', mostly in Jeffreys Bay, in true 1960s style.

A breakthrough for surfers, who up until then had had to endure the frigid waters of the Western Cape, came when Gobel imported neoprene from the United States and started making Surf & Ski wetsuits. Zero Wetsuits was born.

Two Australian surfers, John Bachelador and Tony Wright, toured the coastline at the end of 1967. They were riding the revolutionary 'V Machine' boards by Bob McTavish and Nat Young. Suddenly, surfboards over eight feet were obsolete. Nose-riding was history. Square bottom turns, roller coasters and slashing cutbacks were the rage. Boards became shorter and surfers did amazing things on the waves. Surfing changed from riding waves to performing on them.

It was the era of Jimi Hendrix, Led Zeppelin, Cream and The Doors. Bell-bottom and floral-clad hippies flocked to J-Bay, freaking out the locals. The police cited the town as a drug smuggling haven. Some surfers opened Swiss bank accounts to hide the fortunes they accumulated. Durban Poison and Transkei Gold earned a global reputation, and surfing's image took a nosedive into the soup. Older surfers bailed to go fishing, take up golf or other acceptable pastimes.

In 1968, Baron Stander started a daily radio surf report for Durban that was to last for 34 years, a world record. Meanwhile, some of the best surfers in the world were emerging from South Africa.

In 1969, Wetteland, Ernie Tomson and Ian McDonald staged the Durban 500. The first world champion, Midget Farrelly, was invited to give an exhibition. Gavin Rudolph won, but it was a financial failure.

Peter Burness, secretary of the Natal Surfriders Association, took over and found sponsorship with Gunston cigarettes. The Gunston 500 became the world's longest running professional surfing event, ending 30 years later in 1999 when Mr Price took over.

In the seventies, Burness invited top surfers to compete in the Gunston to generate overseas invites for South African surfers. Youngsters Anthony Brodowicz, 14, Shaun Tomson, 15, his cousin Michael Tomson, 16, Gavin Rudolph, 18, and Errol Hickman, 17, were invited to the 1971 Smirnoff Pro Am at Sunset Beach. Rudolph stunned the surfing world by winning the competition in eight- to twelve-foot surf – in only his second session at the fabled break. He thus became the first South African to win a professional event outside the country.

Dozens of foreign surfers began to compete in Durban, doing the mandatory pilgrimage to Jeffreys Bay, where seamstress Cheron Kraak was making boardshorts for surfers on the beach under her label Country Feeling. She was later to take over the Billabong franchise in South Africa, culminating in the 2007 sale of Billabong South Africa back to the parent company for R350 million.

While Cheron was fulfilling her rags-to-riches story, South Africa was becoming a surfing superpower. Shaun and Michael Tomson joined a global brotherhood including Mark Richards, Rabbit Bartholomew, Buzzy Kerbox, Dane Kealoha and the Bronzed Aussies – Ian Cairns, Peter Townend and Mark Warren.

Other world-class South African surfers were Cape Town's big-wave charger Jonathan 'Iceman' Paarman; the king of Jeffreys Bay, Peers Pittard; PE's Gavin Rudolph; the South Coast's Ant Brodowicz; and Durbanites Mike Esposito, Bruce Jackson, Wayne Shaw and Paul Naude, the first goofy foot to win at Sunset Beach.

In 1976, Naude, Doug McDonald and Mike Larmont started *Zigzag* magazine. A group called International Professional Surfers (IPS), was formed in Hawaii by Randy Rarick and Fred Hemmings. Michael Tomson started Gotcha clothing, Shaun started Instinct, and everybody from Aberdeen to Zeerust knew about surfing.

A regular visitor to Hawaii with father Ernie and cousin Michael, Shaun was a seasoned traveller with a clean-cut demeanour and a marketable image. Credited as the world's best tube rider, as immortalised in the movie *Free Ride*, Shaun won six consecutive Gunstons (1973-78). He did more than any other South African to popularise the sport, and dispel its drug-related connotations.

His famous 'pink banana', shaped by a young Spider Murphy back in Durban, blew away the cynics who suggested that the single fin pintail's outlandish rocker was a no-hoper in top-to-bottom Pipeline at 10 feet. Shaun won the 1977 world title, which included first at the World Cup of Surfing at Sunset in Hawaii, after a season of pro surfing that *Surfing* magazine says established 'the single greatest performance gap that has ever existed on the North Shore, surfing virtually a decade ahead, technique-wise, than such luminary contemporaries as Richards, Bartholomew, Cairns and Michael Ho'.

Design innovations included Mark Richards's twin-fin in 1978. Spider Murphy started shaping some of the world's best surfboards at Safari in Durban. Lightning Bolt was 'the' label to ride and wear, and disco ruled, well, until punk took over. Durban's Anthony Brodowicz won the ISA World Championships in East London in 1978.

Everyone was riding twins, including a 14-year-old, Martin Potter, who burst on to the scene, defeating Shaun Tomson in East London on his pro debut and finishing as runner-up to Dane Kealoha in the Gunston and Cheyne Horan in the Mainstay Magnum in his first two world tour contests in 1981.

East London's Wendy Botha dominated women's surfing. Potter and Botha relocated to Australia because of apartheid. Both won world titles, Potter in 1989 and Botha an incredible four times – in 1987, 1989, 1991 and 1992.

Shaun Tomson retired at the end of 1989 after 13 years in the top 16, having achieved a legendary status as South Africa's pre-eminent surfing citizen.

In 1983, Ian Cairns introduced the Association of Surfing Professionals (ASP), which superseded the IPS and was sponsored by surfwear giant OP. South Africa staged four ASP events in 1984,

including the Spur Steak Ranch Surfabout, in Cape Town, and Country Feeling Surf classic at J-Bay. The Spur experienced some of the stormiest weather for an ASP event and J-Bay produced epic eight- to twelve-foot surf for four days. Young prodigy Mark Occhilupo, 18, won. The next year, the finals of the Spur were held in flawless 15-foot surf at Outer Kom, the biggest surf for an ASP event outside Hawaii.

Performance surfing had taken a quantum leap when Simon Anderson introduced the three-fin 'thruster' in 1981. The giant Aussie won events in Sydney slop and 12-foot Bells Beach, and scooped the Pipeline Masters. South Africans converted in droves.

Meanwhile, big-wave surfing was ticking along quietly in Cape Town, with Pierre de Villiers and Peter Button pioneering Dungeons in 1985.

Floaters were the big manoeuvre in 1985. Pottz and Californian Richie Collins managed to catapult themselves along the 'roof' of the wave before freefalling over the whitewater.

But, while every grommet from Long Beach in Cape Town to Dairy Beach in Durban was trying to emulate the radical new moves, the political situation in South Africa was deteriorating. The Cold War was raging in Angola, and boycotts and sanctions hurt the economy. Democracy was fighting for air. The apartheid government

NO WETSUIT: Surfing pioneers were hardy, surfing Cape Town bare-chested or fighting off sharks in Durban.

Goodbye Oom

Former Cape Times editor Tony Heard pays tribute to John Whitmore

About 500 people gathered at Glen Beach on Saturday 12 January 2002 to pay homage to the man revered by many as the grandfather of surfing in South Africa. John Whitmore, 73, died on his farm near Elands Bay, one of many surf spots he pioneered.

They came in their hundreds – from ho-daddies to lighties – to pay their respects, in a unique and watery way, to the legendary surf great. It was a meshing of generations in a single, sad cause and it was duplicated in Durban, where Baron Stander organised a surf wake, and in other spots on the coast. Whitmore died of cancer after a valiant battle, showing the casual courage of someone undaunted by a monster 'backie' heading his way. The beach gatherings were the surfing community's way of saying goodbye. Glen Beach was wilder and more towering than ever – the rip sucked towards the rocks. Nature seemed to add a powerful eloquence to the remembrance of John.

Standing there on the beach were longboarders, goofies, Atlantic-side gremlins, Corner hot-doggers, the heavily dinged from the Kom, and a few survivors of Sunset or Dungeons. The surf community turned out in force early in the morning as a furious summer Atlantic storm made way for a burst of sunlight. And with the active surfers, of course, were the surf widows and widowers and the sons and daughters and the parents, those co-heroes of surfing who now do time onshore while the surf is up – and who take refuge from the southeaster or northwester in the shelter of cars, and flick the car lights when it is really time to go. There were reminiscences by those who had known this remarkable man – stories about how he befriended a Californian surf hitch-hiker in 1959, Dick Metz, who saved John's board from the Glen rocks, and became a guest of the Whitmore's at Glen Beach for months. It was Metz who helped open John's business to the import prospect of Clark foam, branded boards and boogies. Whitmore was able to put surfing on the map with these and other contacts – and always employing his meticulous professionalism and sense of perfection. The rest is history. There was mention of John's indomitable grit and sense of optimism, not only while ill and apparently refusing chemical relief, but how, when told of someone's death, would show no sadness, but would comment that death is just part of life. He had a way of inspiring others. On the beach, the surfers, old and young, stood out in the crowd, with their wide shoulders, as if propped by giant coat hangers. The relative fitness of Whitmore's generation, in their seventies, was obvious. The familiar Cape surf names were in evidence: Paarman, Strong, Menesis, to mention but some.

There was special music, and some tears. And, after the people had time to remember John and what he did for young and established surfers, the time came to commit the wreath to the waves. Towering Jonathan Paarman – whom I shall never forget in the cusp of a massive wave years ago at Kom Outer, his board a shaking leaf in the high wind as he took off right in front of me – gathered the wreath and took it gently to the beach, placed it on his board and 'hit out'. He was followed by a dozen surfers there to join the 'paddle-out'. It was perilous, and the MC and others expressed concern, but these were Glen surfers, he announced reassuringly. They deftly ducked under the pounding white water and made their way far out, past the treacherous rocks. The wreath was consigned to the very waves which, years ago, I had seen John tame, using his powerful style. It was no ordinary wreath. It was bulky, beautiful. It was kelp.

BLACK AND PROUD: The original Wynberg Surf Club, including a young Cass Collier, *left*, and his role-model dad, Ahmed, *front*, at Nine Miles, False Bay.

responded by tightening its grip, and declared a state of emergency in 1985 to combat the 'swart gevaar' (black danger). Black surfers were being chased from whites-only beaches, with the constitution giving legal credence to racism. Surfing evolved along racial lines, one black and one white. Several pro surfers, including Potter, boycotted the Gunston 500. Momentum grew, and at one point, only four of the world's top 30 surfers competed in the Gunston.

Finally, apartheid began to impact on even white South Africans. Visas were hard to obtain for professionals and surfers wanting to explore exotic destinations. Some South Africans pretended to be Australian or English to escape hostile cross-examinations overseas. Later, in the 90s and early 2000s, the sad by-product of this decade came to pass: a dearth in South Africans competing on the World Tour, with only people like Heather 'Fergie' Clark, Paul Canning and Greg Emslie having success. In 2003, Fergie was the only South African to qualify for the world tour.

In 1986, the country's first full-time pro surfer promoter, Paul Botha, organised the Great Western Cooler Classic in Durban, the inaugural event of the South African Surfing Series (SASS) aimed to provide pro-am events that were a local equivalent of the ASP tour. Tommy Lawson won. Greg Swart was crowned the first SASS champion after four events.

In 1988, Craig Sims and Rob van Wieringen took over *Zigzag* magazine. Steve Morton and David Stolk – influential figures in the growth of

black surfing – started *Offshore* magazine and Pat Flanagan started the broadsheet *Wet*, in Durban. Both lasted a couple of years. In 1989, Professor Mark Jury published *Surfing in Southern Africa*, the first comprehensive guide to surfing in South Africa. Sales of the book were slow initially. By the time surfing had begun to proliferate, in the 1990s, desperate surfers trying to get their hands on the book were horrified to discover that the publisher had pulped it after it failed to meet sales targets.

Surf shops were opening in coastal villages, inland cities and shopping malls. The first wavepool contest was staged at Shareworld in Johannesburg.

The 90s kicked off with the release of Nelson Mandela. Never a surfer, despite his presence on wave-rich Robben Island for nearly two decades, the efforts of our master statesman helped to bring democracy to the country in 1994. A surf spot on the ocean side of the island, Madiba's Left, was surfed illegally by a number of courageous surfers, including Cass Collier and Ian Armstrong.

Former *Cape Times* editor and old South Beach local, Tony Heard, recalls his pie-in-the sky plan in the late 70s to help Madiba escape by paddling him on a surfboard into the shipping lane. 'The prisoners would often harvest kelp on the shoreline. I thought, hey, why not paddle quietly through the soup, camouflaged by the kelp, get him to climb on the board and paddle two-up out into the shipping lane to be picked up by a foreign freighter. Anything to get him out of South Africa!'

The plan – also mentioned by former *Daily Dispatch* editor Donald Woods, in his book *Rainbow Nation Revisited* – did not come to fruition. There was uncertainty about Madiba's safety. What if the ship did not see them? What about weather and sea conditions? But it's a nice thought. Imagine the subject matter of a dialogue between a white surfer and Nelson Mandela as they drift silently out to sea off the Cape of Storms.

Heard almost broached the subject with the famous inmate's wife, Winnie. While Heard's illegal interview with banned and exiled Oliver Tambo in 1985 brought him international recognition, failure in the Madiba paddle plan would have brought him a career-ending notoriety. Besides, it was unlikely that Mandela would agree to a 'take-off' into the unknown so willingly. It was a wipeout waiting to happen.

The ASP introduced their two-tiered world tour structure in 1992. Talks between SASA (South African Surfing Association) and the non-racial South African Surfing Union were initiated, and a unified amateur body – the United Surfing Council of South Africa – was formed. Finally, black surfers were officially recognised, although unification on the ground – in the surf – was still to take several years.

In 1993, the Gunston 500 celebrated its 25th anniversary. The first Ocean Africa festival was staged over 10 days on North Beach and Bay of Plenty. An estimated 250 000 people attended.

The concept, devised and coordinated by Peter Burness and Paul Botha, made corporates take notice. The beach lifestyle was booming and surfing was the major attraction.

The South African surfing team was the first sporting code to compete under the new national flag at the world champs in Brazil in 1994. Paul Canning was the first South African to qualify for the WCT (World Championship Tour) in the ASP's new structure. Sharon Ncongo was the first development surfer to represent South Africa in Bali, at the grommet champs. Baron Stander opened the Time Warp Museum (South Africa's first, and so far only, surf museum) in Durban.

The mid to late 90s were marked by the quiet beginnings of tow-in surfing. In 1994, Capetonians Glen Bee and Pierre du Plessis, and about a year later Nico Johnson, started using a rubber duck in parallel to Laird Hamilton's first flirt with 'motor-assisted surfing'.

The first issue of Zigzag

Zigzag magazine grew from humble roots in 1976 to become South Africa's longest surviving and most popular surfing magazine. Under the stewardship of former South African professional surfing champion Craig Sims since 1988, *Zigzag* reached its 25-year milestone in 2001, making it the fourth-oldest surfing magazine in the world.

In 1995, *Zigzag* designer Garth Robinson broke away and launched *African Soul Surfer*, moving away from what he claimed was 'punting contest surfing as a measure of a surfer's worth'. Robinson wanted to provide surfers with 'the choice to read something more cutting edge, which reflects the reality of our lifestyle and not the aspirations of those few who chase money on the "Tour".'

It was a brave stand. However, despite the euphoria of democracy and new-found brotherhood symbolised by the Springboks' Rugby World Cup victory, advertising failed to materialise. Advertisers quietly ignored the provocative young upstart as they would a precocious grom trying to break into the line-up at New Pier. Inclusive thinking has not always been a priority among the tightly knit South African surfing industry.

Innovations in weather forecasting and the rapid rise of the Internet began to impact positively on the surfing lifestyle. The wave prediction model Wavewatch II, and later the third generation version, became the surfer's oracle. In 1998, the Wavescape surfing portal was launched and the first Spike surf report was sent to a small group of surfers.

In 1999, Cass Collier and Ian Armstrong cracked open the stereotype and thumbed their noses at disgruntled conservatives who had baulked at the idea of giving Springbok blazers to two dreadlocked Rastafarians whose lifestyle was so freely anti-establishment.

But the snipes were stifled when Collier and Armstrong stormed to victory in the ISA (International Surfing Association) Big Wave World Championships at Todos Santos in 1999 on their first attempt. They almost won it again in 2000, with Collier a standout. It was a proud moment.

The South African surfing industry was beginning to expand with a battle for supremacy between local affiliates of multi-nationals Billabong and Quiksilver. A hilarious signboard war broke out in J-Bay.

The second Red Bull Big Wave Africa in 2000 saw Sean Holmes win in 20-foot surf, and the surfing world began to take more notice.

South Africa's top-ranked woman surfer after Wendy Botha, Heather 'Fergie' Clark, broke into the 2000 WCT, and promptly won the 2000 Triple Crown of Surfing in Hawaii, the next best thing to winning the world title. Clark, who hails from Port Shepstone, had a string of earlier wins under her belt, including four South African Champs.

In 2001, Chris Bertish made history by being the only guy to paddle-surf Jaws in Hawaii. Bertish also won the XXL paddle awards (sponsored by Swell.com) that year. In a bizarre twist, Mike Parsons – the Biggest Tow-in winner – got the $60 000 prize because Chris could not get to the awards. Bertish got a $100 voucher. In 2004, he rode big Cribber in the UK and got the lead story in newspapers and TV news.

South Africa made a big come comeback in competitive surfing when they won the Quicksilver ISA World Surfing Games, held in Durban in 2002.

Partly due to Heather Clark's exploits on the women's tour, the movie *Blue Crush*, the rise of *Saltwater Girl* – the most successful magazine in the Atoll Media stable – and a general growth in surf schools and sponsored events for beginners, more women took to the water.

Soon, ASP Africa tour competitors such as Tamarys Walters, Tasha Mentasti, Sarah Johnston and Sacha Moller were competing on the WQS (World Qualifying Series), while at home, events like the Roxy Wahine Cup, Roxy Surf Jam and other junior championships began to bear fruit with the development of a crew of hot youngsters such as Tarryn Chudleigh, Nikita Robb, Chantelle Rautenbach and Holly Armstrong.

By 2005, tow-surfing equipment was state of the art, with quieter, more environment-friendly four-stroke wave runners. Durban's Jason Ribbink and tow partner Gigs Cilliers targeted the heaviest surf they could find, including a session in 30-foot Peahi, Hawaii, in the 2005 winter season.

From just one tow crew in the mid to late nineties, there were around 16 crews in 2007, necessitating the formation of Tow Surf South Africa to make, in the words of founder member Ross Lindsay, 'tow surfing a professionally run pursuit with credibility and legal standing'. To be a member, big wave experience, a skipper's licence and lifesaving skills were required.

Meanwhile, in the early to mid 2000s, a hot crop of young competitors, such as Davey Weare, Royden Bryson, Travis Logie, Warwick Wright and

The other side of the coin

The voices of previously unheard members of our surfing community are finally being written into the history books. These are stories about ordinary people who made extraordinary contributions to our society, but were not recognised in mainstream culture determined by white surfers.

Surfer Faeez Abrahams is one such person. During the crazy eighties, apartheid was coming to a head. For many students, tertiary education comprised more than the standard curriculum. Survival 101 was a class you signed up for without knowing it. Rallies and marches opposing the apartheid regime were a regular occurrence, dodging rubber bullets and tear gas the new skills you learned.

However, at Peninsula Technikon, one student was leaving the street for extra lessons. He was learning to surf. Abrahams went for his first surf with a group of mates at Nine Miles, False Bay, in 1984, a dire period in South Africa's history. It was the lead-up to the State of Emergency, announced the next year.

Because racism was institutionalised, it was illegal to surf at whites-only beaches, which made it difficult and often dangerous to explore Cape Town's more challenging breaks.

For Abrahams and many of his friends, a typical day would consist of a mass march, getting shot at and chased by the cops, and then, when the tide started pushing, going for a surf. Their spots were Nine Miles and Blue Waters, also on False Bay.

While the more affluent surfers could access the surf easily from their upmarket suburbs, surf spots where blacks were allowed were few and far between. 'Our spot was Nine Miles. It wasn't much, but it was ours. We owned it. No-one would swear at us there.'

Abrahams and his surfing comrades couldn't surf that well, barring one or two guys, notably Cass Collier who was ripping from an early age, groomed by his dad Ahmed, who had surfed in Hawaii, and was personal friends with Eddie Aikau. 'We looked up to him. Cass was the best of all of us.'

'We had to travel from the townships to get to the surf. It was tough. Once on Vanguard Drive in Mitchells Plain we were nearly stoned by marchers because we had surfboards on our clapped-out old beetle! We hung out of the windows and said, "Hey we are black surfers". They didn't believe blacks surfed. They stopped us and gave us a thorough examination, but let us go. Getting to the beach could be as dangerous as when you got there!'

The only way to surf other spots was to organise themselves and paddle out as a group. They formed the first non-racial surfing club in South Africa. The Wynberg Surf Club included guys from Strandfontein. Later the Two Oceans Surf Club was formed, comprising

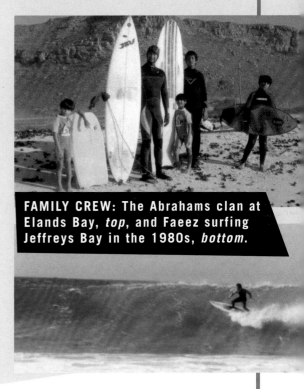

FAMILY CREW: The Abrahams clan at Elands Bay, *top*, and Faeez surfing Jeffreys Bay in the 1980s, *bottom*.

surfers from the City Bowl and Bo-Kaap. Steve Morton and Davey Stolk, two outspoken leaders of their generation, assisted in the formation of the Wynberg club. Steve, now Shafiq, is a respected white journalist and member of the Muslim community.

The founders of Wynberg were guys like Abrahams, Rafiq Bagus, Morton, Stolk and Cecil Solomons. With the formation of non-racial clubs in Durban, PE and J-Bay, they expanded into the SASU (SA Surfing Union) in 1984.

According to Abrahams, as the surfing bug took hold so did the need to spread their wings to more challenging surf breaks – and the sad litany of unsavoury incidents grew. Racism was entrenched in the constitution and they had to beat a path to the whites-only beaches.

'At places like Muizenberg, Long Beach and later J-Bay, the cops would arrive and threaten us with arrest if we paddled out. At Long Beach, we would pretend to leave, then crawl through the bushes around the back and paddle out. But it didn't stop there. Once you were in the water, you had a lot of guys picking fights with us.

'Most of the time it was hostile, seriously hostile, to a point where we had to defend ourselves physically. It was heavy back then. The other surfers didn't want us on the beach. It was illegal for us to be there. They were defending that law – the board that said, "Whites Only".'

Stolk took them on their first trip to Jeffreys Bay to compete in national championships for non-racial surfing clubs.

'We went out for a free-surf at Magnatubes when the cops rocked up and ordered us out of the water with a loudhailer. Davey told them we would not come out. He got into an argument with them on the beach,' says Abrahams.

Ari and Cheron Kraak, the powerful owner of Country Feeling and later the Billabong franchise in South Africa, placated the cops and defused the situation. Cheron backed them all the way. Later she would continue to fight their cause, helping with sponsorship, clothing and setting up their events.

The inaugural trip to J-Bay really opened their eyes to what they were missing. Seeing new levels of surfing and new surf spots made them want to sample more far-flung surfing areas. Unfortunately South Africa wasn't ready for them. Abrahams and his crew, often including Cass, couldn't care less. At one non-racial event in Durban at the Bay of Plenty, there was a fracas on the beach that ended in a local white surfer getting punched. It escalated into a stand-off that included a helicopter gunship and police with machine guns on the beach.

Eventually, change in South Africa spelled an end to apartheid. An uneasy peace broke out with the unification of surfing organisations in the early to mid nineties. It was some time before residual racism was forced into submission. Entrenched attitudes were hard to break down.

'A guy like Cass should have won the SA Champs many times after that but, in my opinion, he was marked down at surf events because of lingering issues from the past,' claims Abrahams.

From being a small, close-knit surfing community, the Nine Miles surfers made the transition to being part of the larger surfing community of South Africa. The old clubs became dormant as their members joined the real world. The rallying calls became muted as the causes faded into the annals of history.

Organised surfing in South Africa is now run by the umbrella body Surfing South Africa, with veteran administrator Robin de Kock having overseen a sometimes tumultuous transition to the new dispensation.

Abrahams says: 'It's great to see all those surfers, young and old, black and white, having fun at Muizenberg these days. But many are oblivious to what went on before, of the blood that was spilled. It's sometimes good to remember, if just for the sake of paving the way for a brighter future for our youth.'

Abrahams, a successful businessmen, still surfs. – *From an original short piece by Darryl Brandreth on www.swellguys.com*

Ricky Basnett cast aside their respect for the older generation by stamping their mark on competitive surfing. They were led by teenage sensation Jordy 'Superfreak' Smith, known for a prodigious surfing talent that drew more than a few parallels with Kelly Slater, not least his birthday.

Amped, a magazine by competitive surfer Peter Nicholson, was launched in 2003 to cater for the young brigade of hot surfers proud of their talents. It lasted a few issues before closing down.

In 2005, king of Muizenberg Corner (now Surfers' Corner), Matthew Moir, won the ASP World Longboard Title with a wonderful mixture of old school nose riding, fancy footwork and carving modern manoeuvres.

The next year – 2006 – was a huge year for South African competition surfing, proof that surfers were clawing their way back up the ranks of the surfing world.

Smith, 18, scooped the men's title at the ISA World Surfing Games at Huntington Beach in California, eliminating several WCT competitors, including 2001 world champ CJ Hobgood. Then he made history at the Billabong Pro at J-Bay in his first ASP World Championshiop Tour event. Entering as a wildcard, Smith made it to the semi-finals, finishing an equal third with Kelly Slater, behind Taj Burrow and Mick Fanning, becoming the highest placed South African at the event in history.

To top off an amazing year for Superfreak, Smith triumphed in Hawaii with a stunning second place at the O'Neill World Cup of Surfing at Sunset Beach, winning the Van's Triple Crown of Surfing Rookie of the Year award.

Not to be outdone, Grant Twiggy Baker scooped the Mavericks Surf Contest in classic 20-foot surf that year. Baker and Smith were among several surfers honoured at the inaugural South African Surfing Awards presented by *Zigzag* in 2007.

A giant session at Dungeons in 2006 saw Californian Greg Long and local tow crews tackle the biggest surf ever seen in Africa, in the same league as huge days recorded at Jaws and the Cortes Bank. Long's giant wave won Biggest Wave at the 2006 Billabong XXL awards, while Marr took second in Best Ride of the Year.

JUBILATION: Travis Logie celebrates South Africa's world title in 2002.

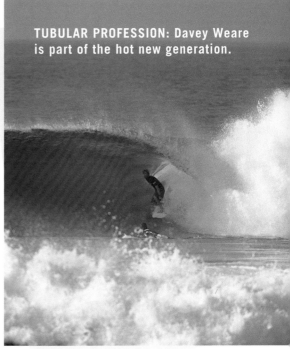

TUBULAR PROFESSION: Davey Weare is part of the hot new generation.

WALL TO WALL: In 2006, 73 surfers at Muizenberg unofficially broke the world record of people riding a single wave.

Rocky the boxing surf dog

The irony is that two days after Rocky died of old age, a massive winter storm hit the Cape and the swell hit levels unsurpassed that year.

Rocky and his owner Rob Abel – a Glen Beach local – were inseparable. If Rob was surfing somewhere in the kelp off Soetwater, the Kom or the Factory, you could be certain that Rocky was lurking about chasing kelp lice or chewing bodyboarders' fins on the beach.

If Rob went out at night to a bar, or a friend's house, Rocky was in tow. On surf trips in other people's cars, you had to have a really persuasive argument to leave Rocky behind. Dog hairs and drool all over the back seat and windows were insufficient reasons to deny Rocky his right to come along.

If you wore a uniform, and Rocky checked you out, you were history. He was obsessed with uniforms. In a split second, Rocky would be transformed from a peace-loving, beach-chilling surf hound into a snarling, snapping beast, jowls flopping up and down like jelly, spittle spattering the car windows.

Perhaps this strange quirk resulted from the time Rocky was savaged by an alpha male baboon in his frivolous youth. A troop of baboons must have grown tired of being chased up and down the mountain at 365 near Kommetjie. One day, the yellow-eyed leader decided it was pay-back time.

Rocky chased a member of the troop into some bushes, snarling and barking in customary Rocky style. His owner claims vehemently that Rocky wouldn't have known what to do once he caught anything. The occasional bodyboarder or petrol attendant might testify otherwise.

Meanwhile, the alpha male baboon had circled back around the fracas and, with his back to the ocean, blocked Rocky's path to his beloved master and attacked with a ferocity that only comes from fang-bared baboons.

Rob heard the screams of pain, and with a blood-curdling cry managed to scare off the baboon. Disembowelled and ripped apart, Rocky escaped death by a whisker and the swift work of a skilled vet.

'It was like the set of *Natural Born Killers*. My car was full of blood. He was in a bad way.'

Rocky was a true surf dog, and lived for the ocean. Rocky, we salute you. Let's hope that dog heaven is populated by plenty of policemen and nurses.

Also in 2006, Muizenberg beach became the unofficial home of the Guinness World Record for the 'Most surfers standing on a single wave' when 73 surfers caught and rode the same wave on a perfect spring day. The event, organised by Dene Botha of the Kahuna Surf Academy, was a substantial improvement on the official record of 44 set by the Lahinch Surf Club in Ireland in May that year. The record was to be broken in 2007 by 84 Brazilians riding a wave at Quebra Mar in Santos, now part of a bigger event – the Earthwave Global Challenge to highlight global warming – which had its roots in the first attempt at Muizenberg in 2006.

Continuing the amazing 2006 run, the South African Masters Team won the inaugural ISA World Masters Champs in Puerto Rico. Competing in the ASP WCT that year were Rosanne Hodge, Ricky Basnett, Royden Bryson, Travis Logie and Greg Emslie, with Smith looking good for a berth in 2008.

In 2007, Smith again stormed into the limelight, taking the Billabong ASP World Junior Championships in North Narrabeen, Australia, with many pundits, including Sean Tomson, predicting a world title for him in the not-too-distant future.

Also in 2007, Durban stalwarts Hugh Thompson and Terry Roderick started *African Surfrider*, a magazine catering more for the older, more discerning surfer, with an emphasis on feature stories.

Later in 2007, big-wave paddle-surfing grew further with the announcement of the O'Neill Raw Courage Awards to reward gutsy performances by local surfers in testing big wave conditions.

With people of all colours, creeds and genders now enjoying the waves of our surf-rich coastline – from the cold-water power of the Western Cape to the perfect point breaks of Eastern Cape to the warm-water tubes of KwaZulu-Natal – South African surfing has much to be thankful for.

OLD SURF SLANG

AGGRESSIVE SURFER
Surfer who pushed the limits. In the 1950s and 1960s, you were called 'aggressive' if you 'attacked' the waves to do moves.

COVER-UP
Surfer rides out of sight behind the lip. 'He got a cover-up'.

BACKIE
A wave that breaks in the area furthest from the shore, where the biggest swells are encountered – the back line.

BROADIE
A wave that breaks with a wall to enable the surfer to track across the wall, parallel to shore.

DRAK
Nasty, horrible or yucky.

FOAMIE
The broken white water of a wave.

GREMMIE
Young, inexperienced or learner surfer. Now known as grommets.

HIT OUT
Paddle out.

KRAAKER
Big, powerful, good wave. The word used nowadays is 'cooker'.

KOOK
Derogatory term for gremmies.

LOCKED IN
Under the lip but not covered up. Riding in the curl of the wave. 'He was locked in.'

LUNCH
Wipe-out. 'Jack was about to get his lunch.'

PEARLED
Nose of the board digs in. 'Chookie caught a kraaker, but pearled when taking off.' The term has since been bastardised. Today a pearler means a perfect wave.

PLAY
Classic, great. 'Let's hit out, the slides are play,' means 'Let's paddle out, the surf is cooking.'

ROOSTER TRAIL
Surfboard wake. Heavier and longer surfboards created a more defined spray. Modern surfers draw a thinner line with lighter, shorter boards.

SKITOOLS
Baggies. A term for the loose-fitting board shorts worn while surfing.

SKEG
Fin.

SLIDE
Wave. The wave at St Francis is a 'right slide'.

SOUP
Broken wave or white water. 'The wave closed out and he rode the soup.'

STOKEY
Someone who is stoked.

TAKES GAS
Wipe-out. More literally, this term referred to a surfer being knocked off his board by the wave.

TOO MUCH
Unreal, radical. Today's equivalent would be 'classic', 'rad' or 'awesome'. That wave was 'too much'.

ZIGZAG
The motion of a surfboard.

Chapter 2

There is a society where none intrudes,
by the deep sea, and music, in its roar.

Lord Byron (1788-1824)

Culture

Ay, bru, I tune you what. Surfers in South Africa don't think they talk funny. This is why our sub-culture has evolved in such happy isolation from the rest of the world, which seems to be driven by the fashions and trends spewed forth from the American-Australian axis.

Never mind apartheid. That is not the only thing that drove a wedge between us and the rest of the world. It is our horrible accent. To mask it, we just started talking faster, using increasingly bizarre and indecipherable words that only an elite few in our surfing tribe can understand. As a result, we have a wonderfully eclectic sub-culture. To give you a taste, here are stories, artworks and photographs from some of South Africa's best cartoonists, artists, writers and photographers. Many of them are surfers who work in the industry. Others are just surfers, while a few don't surf, but love the subject matter.

We have a long and proud history of achievement on the creative front, and it's impossible to do everyone justice. People like Shafiq Morton, Grant Ellis, Karen Wilson, Nic Bothma, Louis Wulff, Lance Slabbert, Alan van Gysen and Barry Tuck have all reached the pinnacle of surf photography, while a guy like Harry de Zitter has cracked the big time on the broader stage of professional photography overseas. Writers and editors like Craig Jarvis, Andy Davis, Will Bendix, Patrick Burnett, Miles Masterson, Byron Loker, Conn Bertish, Hagen Engler and many more have stamped a uniquely South African mark on our creative landscape.

Successful surfing filmmakers are thin on the ground. Only the hardiest have survived toiling for so many years in a barren wilderness devoid of financial support. Among them are Neil Webster, Alan Robb and Jason Hearne. Some great feature documentaries are starting to appear, such as Shaun Tomson's *Pure Line* and Nic Hofmeyr's *Taking Back the Waves*.

Compared to our film-makers, artists are abundant. There are several professional cartoonists whose work stands out, such as Andy Mason, Chip Snaddon and Dan Riding. We have a slew of painters and other artists who either surf, or dabble in surf art as a genre, including Martin Bakker, Paul Cumes, Garth and Yvonne Robinson, Michael Kennedy, Osnat de Villiers, Stephen Bibb, Chris Brehem, Richard Hart and many more too numerous to mention.

In the music industry, balladeer Robin Auld stands at the forefront, while newcomer Farryl Purkiss brings a youthful energy to a laidback style reminiscent of US singer, Jack Johnson.

A driving force in the ebb and flow of lifestyle trends comes from surf brands. An anti-establishment ethos in fashion styles, led by the hands-on design skills of people like Barry Wolins and Cheron Kraak, respective heads of Quiksilver and Billabong, have provided aspirational incentive for mainstream consumers.

Several magazines over the years – including *South African Surfer* (1960s), *Wet* and *Offshore* (1980s), and *African Soul Surfer* (1990s) – have contributed to the milieu in different ways. Although they disappeared, their contribution is imprinted in the collective unconscious. The longest surviving and most established is *Zigzag*. Under the latter-day stewardship of Craig Sims, the *Zag* was able to reinvent itself with the changing whims of a fickle marketplace. More recently, it has catered for youngsters with its brand-driven ethos and primary focus on competitive surfing. An irony perhaps, since the word 'zigzag' as a surfing term is something only the ballies will remember!

Other magazines feeding back into our surfing subconscious have included *Saltwater Girl*, *Blunt*, *Sixty40* and *African Surfrider*, while websites such as wavescape.co.za and swellguys.com have

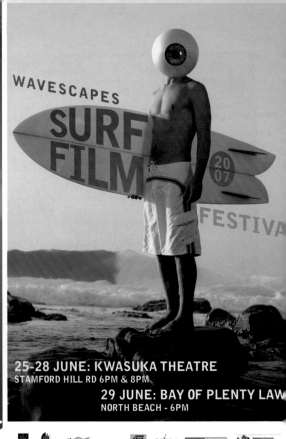

CAPE TOWN
& Western Cape

WAVESCAPES
FILM
SURF '05
FESTIVAL

PRESENTED BY **FIRST NATIONAL BANK**

Showing At **Outdoor and Indoor Venues in Cape Town and Garden Route During December 2005 Holidays**

Plus: SURF ART EXHIBITION   Details At: www.wavescapes.co.za   Infoline: 072 424 69 65

Cape Town Routes Unlimited   CAPE TIMES   GQ   FNB   How can we help you?

WAVESCAPES
SURF
FILM
20 07
FESTIVAL

25-28 JUNE: KWASUKA THEATRE
STAMFORD HILL RD 6PM & 8PM

29 JUNE: BAY OF PLENTY LAW
NORTH BEACH - 6PM

durban international film festival   university of KwaZulu-Natal   CENTRE FOR CREATIVE ARTS   LOTTERY NLDTF   Hivos   DOEN   NATIONALE POSTCODE LOTERIJ   KWAZULU-NATAL

FIRST NATIONAL BANK PRESENTS
wavescapes
surf film festival 2006

**Giant screen
Clifton 4th
Friday 8 Dec**

**Labia Cinema
Brass Bell
Thursday 7 -14 Dec**

infoline 072 424 6965
www.wavescapes.co.za

MALIBU   FNB

THE
WAVESCAPES
SURF ART
EXHIBITION

IN ASSOCIATION WITH
WAVESCAPES SURF FILM FESTIVAL
PRESENTED BY FIRST NATIONAL BANK

Unique Surfboard
ART AND WORK BY
TOP CARTOONISTS,
PHOTOGRAPHERS
& ILLUSTRATORS

FNB
First National Bank

VEO GALLERY
AND ART
WAREHOUSE
28 JARVIS STR
CAPE TOWN
TEL 421-1568

ARTISTS INCLUDE
*Beezy Bailey
Lizza Littlewort
Richard Scott
Cameron Platter
Brett Murray
Richard Hart
M.D Mazin
Brahm van Zyl
Konradski
Rowan Thompson
Sanell Aggenbach
and Zapiro*

CAPE TOWN
& Western Cape

THURSDAY 8 DECEMBER TO **FRIDAY 16 DECEMBER**

Cape Town Routes Unlimited   CAPE TIMES   GQ

PEOPLE'S ICON: Cass Collier

STYLE COUNCIL: Kyle Jacobs

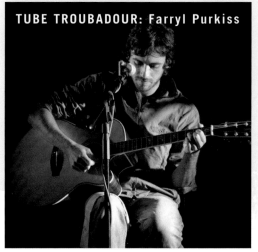

TUBE TROUBADOUR: Farryl Purkiss

BOARD WALK: Lungani Memani, J-Bay

added bytes to the mix. On radio, Deon Bing has added big-personality spice through his Cape Town surf reports laced with humour and surfing slang.

The Wavescapes Surf Film Festival, which includes a surfboard art auction that raises money for the National Sea Rescue Institute and the Shark Spotters, was launched in 2004, showing movies on big screens in Cape Town, Vic Bay and Durban. It was an attempt to recreate the days when John Whitmore and Harry Bold showed films like *Endless Summer* and *Gidget* to packed community halls from Cape Town to Durban.

Many of the individuals and entities have had a wide influence on shaping our subculture, but the whole depends on the sum of its parts: the average member of the community. It is interesting to note that as generations of surfers have grown up, they have begun to infiltrate society.

You'll find tens of thousands of professionals trying to hide their post-surf nasal drip at board meetings (the kind held in a building and not on the ocean), plenary sessions, congregations, corporate headquarters, court hearings, school governing body meetings and even while performing surgery!

Chapter 2: SURFRIKAN Culture 35

ART COLLECTION:
Surfboards decorated
by artists for a
charity auction by
the Wavescapes
Surf Film Festival.

There is also a rich ethnic diversity at many line-ups these days. Okay, you still find your run-of-the-mill silver-spoon WASP, whether English or Afrikaans, but since the transition to a democratic society in 1994, you will also find more and more people of colour in the water, from dreadlocked Rastas and Muslim businessmen to a crop of young, talented Xhosa- and Zulu-speaking surfers, such as Port Alfred prodigy, Lungani Memani, and Springbok longboarder Kwezi Qika.

One of the top glassers in Cape Town is Shahid 'Curly' Heyns. His family-run factory supplies shapers such as David Stubbs and Pierre de Villiers. Then you get guys like 'Sollo' Solomon, a Zulu from Durban who is a skilled ding repairer and glasser, working with shapers like Clayton Nienaber and Peter Lawson.

Ay hundreds bru. Check you in the surf.

So you wanna surf?

In the good old bad old days, learning to surf involved begging, buying, borrowing or stealing a board, and hacking your way into the sport. Nowadays, things are much easier. There are surf schools at almost every friendly break, and you can rent boards almost everywhere so you don't need to risk a jail sentence to figure out whether you like it or not.

To save money on the first two surfing lessons, chalk out a board shape on the floor and practise jumping up and down in the right spot, which is your back foot over where the fins would be and the front foot about two feet in front of the back. If you have a pool, lie on a surfboard and paddle back and forth until you stop rolling off it involuntarily. That will save you another three lessons. Now you are ready to learn to surf.

Approach a surf school, but tell them you want to skip the intro and get straight into the waves. There are many perfect beaches that are good for beginners, including South Beach and Addington in Durban, Kitchen Windows beach break in Jeffreys Bay and Muizenberg Surfers' Corner in Cape Town. If you want to learn about surf culture and language, check out a range of surfing websites and magazines to acquaint yourself with the whole deal. The surfing magzines that are still around include *Sixty40* (bodyboarding), *Zigzag* (core young surfers), *Betty*

STOKED GROMS: Fresh out of the water.

(a girl's surfing lifestyle magazine formerly called *Saltwater Girl*), *African Surfrider* (mature feature-based), Wavescape (e-zine), *Liquid Girl* (core girl surfers), and *Blunt* (general board culture). The actual act of surfing can play a relatively minor role in the lifestyle. Out of perhaps 60 000 surfers in South Africa, how many of them actually surf? For some, it is all about how you look, how you talk and who you're seen with.

Girls just wanna have sun

This article first appeared in the Cape Times *in 2006.*

Surfer girls are walking away from images of airbrushed bodies pimped and preening on the beach. Where are they going? Surfing.

These women defiantly kick sand in the face of girly bling and the pink giggly fluff spewed at them by glamour-mongering media.

They're too busy wolfing down a double thick chocolate shake after a gruelling surf to obsess about their weight.

At night, you'll find them moshing at the gig, or sweating behind a guttural bass guitar on stage. When the surf is flat, you might check them pulling off verts in the half pipe or even carving up the powder. And it's not the powder chopped on a mirror. This powder fizzes from snowboards that fly down frigid slopes.

Scores of women are out in the water along Durban's beachfront, or hanging out at spots like Surfers Corner in Muizenberg. For them,

WHAT IS BEAUTIFUL?
Tammy Lee Smith finds the answer.

bikinis are worn under a wetsuit. Who cares if you look like a frump in sealskin? Who cares that the sea will mess up your hair and streak your eyeliner?

The trend reached maturation in 2006, with the release of a surfing film about South African women called *Beautiful*. The movie came after the death of an anorexic 21-year-old Brazilian model, and underlined the tragic gulf between people weighed down by cruel pressures and those who couldn't give a damn about counting calories. Executive producer John McCarthy, former publisher of *Saltwater Girl*, says the stats justified the project. His magazine had grown from a supplement in male-dominated *Zigzag* surfing magazine to become the top selling youth title in South Africa, with a circulation of 45 000.

The first inkling he had of the new female action generation came a few years earlier. 'I started doing the Duzi Canoe Marathon about 20 years ago,' he said. 'There were no women. A few years ago, during a portage section, this petite girl of maybe 16 years old ran past me. But it wasn't that she was running faster than me. It wasn't even that she had a canoe on her head. She wasn't competing with me. She was trying to catch the girl ahead.'

'*Beautiful* taps into this new consciousness. Women are making a lifestyle choice. They're getting out there. For them, it's the freedom of doing it rather than waiting for it to happen,' he says. 'Life will never be tougher than your teens; that expectation; that pressure to be someone you're not. It causes vast unhappiness. But when you're surfing and being active, you fit in, you find yourself through interaction with the wave. Surfing helps you be who you are.'

It was an unmistakably South African movie that challenged global, money-driven definition of beauty. The irony of it all? A natural by-product of the surfing lifestyle is the healthy good looks deemed so precious by mainstream culture.

Winemakers dip into a few barrels

A special event is held annually to celebrate the perfect blend – wine and surfing.

Stumbling out of my house in Cape Town in dense mist at 5 am, through the foggy soup of a befuddled brain, I am trying to make sense of why, at the age of 41, I am going to drive for 3½ hours, surf in a contest at a quiet point break near Mossel Bay, and drive almost straight back again.

For a start, I think, it is because the people taking part are winemakers, working their magic at boutique cellars such as Beaumont, Boschendal, Bouchard Finlayson, Constantia Uitsig, Coleraine, Conspirare, Fairview, Grangehurst, Lanzerac, Tokara, Villafonte and Villiera. And because, surely, they will flaunt the fruit of their vines – Bacchus dishing out bottles to fauns in a dappled glade. Surely okes built like oaks will fish from the back of their big white double cabs wooden crates of beautifully nosed red cabernets and other varietals with exotic names like syrah and petit verdot.

I am to take part in the Vintners Surf Classic, sponsored by Reynolds Rocha Cork Suppliers and The Bottle Warehouse. This is the sixth year of this special event. I am in the 'Vintage Vintners' age group, otherwise known as 'Veterans', or what they call the 'ballies' or the 'bullets'. You know, old okes over 40. I am told that winemakers, wine sellers and wine marketers make up most of the blend of youth and experience, a mix of the good, the bad and the ugly.

Speaking of blends, I look forward to tasting the annual Big Red, a 1.5 litre limited edition magnum made from the contributions of participating vintners. Only 45 bottles will be made, with each participant taking away a bottle apparently containing a delicious blend of well-known varietals such as cabernet sauvignon, shiraz, cabernet franc, and merlot, as well as ones I have never heard of, such as malbec and mourvedre.

The mist is thick and heavy. The car cuts through a grey curtain woven with water droplets. We drive for hours in the darkness, eyes squinting in the gloom. Eventually we burst through into the sunlight of a bright spring morning, and we arrive at the spot at 9.30 am.

A raucously friendly bunch of burly Boland winemakers mill around the beach. The car park is indeed filled with white double cab 4x4s, but no crates of wine bulge from the back, only wetsuits and surfboards. Out in the water, four surfers in an open-division heat are shredding small two- to three-foot lines rolling sluggishly down the point. Most participants hail from earthy Huguenot stock – buffed and brawny, hale and hearty. Others are shorter and stockier, some slender, and some a little bit gnarled, as though grafted from the vine itself. But they're all here to put their noses in a few barrels, so to speak, while partaking in their other liquid passion.

Everything is very professional. I meet Miles Mossop, friendly organiser and founder of the event. He is the winemaker at Tokara. He tells me how they might take the idea further and hold an international event, attracting surfers from the winelands of California, Chile, Australia, France and New Zealand. But in the meantime, it's locals only. The participants certainly know each other. They're all connected via the Cape wine industry, whether sales people, vintners, suppliers, marketers, cork suppliers, even label designers.

I chat to guys with names like Cobus, Andries, Anton, Gerrit, Willy, Rudi and Pieter. The competitor list reads like a who's who of the wine world (if you know who's who in the wine world).

The tide is pushing in classic light offshore conditions and chunky six-foot bombs are starting to break on the outside. Dries, Cobus and I, having been knocked out of the event, paddle out to the back, beyond the buzz of the event, to where big hooked bowl sections are

BIG RED: Winemakers at the Vintners Surf Classic always make a special blend.

In the open section, the younger guys are popping corks and throwing big spray. They're pulling off vintage moves. The standouts are Pieter Walser and Dane Raath. It's touch and go between the two, but it will be Dane who pulls through in the end, scoring a Stubby board and huge cheers at the prize giving later that day. Organiser Miles Mossop takes third, while fourth goes to Gordon Johnson, winemaker at Newton Johnson and Cape Bay.

The excellent day is topped off with a prize-giving ceremony and a few speeches. The mirth and mayhem, marginally interrupted by Greek salad and pizza, builds inexorably as the drinks flow and the decibels grow. Each table quaffs a bottle of Big Red, and more besides, although it seems that these wine okes prefer rum and coke. Maybe it's like Al Pacino's rule in Scarface: Don't consume your own stash! Maybe they're protecting their tongues and buds for future wine tasting.

But our table is nicely sorted with some great wines, including a delicious pinot noir brought by Jane Ferreira. Her folks, Naas and Jennifer Ferreira, produce a tiny amount of pinot noir grapes at their Wellington farm Klein Optenhorst. Wine writer Kim Maxwell cracks open a bottle of Lindhorst Statement, a red blend from Paarl she has brought. Also at our table, Jeremy Walker, of Grangehurst in Stellenbosch, has brought his tasty cabernet sauvignon/merlot blend.

rearing up double overhead to burp and buckle across a boiling reef before the wall roils across a close-out ledge. You kick out before the take-off zone for the competition.

We return to what is turning into a classic day out on the beach. The bonhomie is buzzing with stoke, and the standard of the surfing is at times red hot. The old ballies are ripping in much improved three- to four-foot waves pushing nicely onto the middle ledge. Anton Smal, the impish vintner from Villiera, does enough and retains his 2004 title. He walks away with a new custom Stubby surfboard. Conspirare's Henry Dowling, married to Lesley-Rae, is second; Robin Marks of Bay Exports is third; and Johan Heckroodt of Lourensford fourth.

After the booze begins to bubble in the bellies of the ballies and their younger brethren, so begins the babbling. Anton Smal, or 'Smallie', is in top form. He is bouncing around like a jack in the box. Our huge host Gerrit Mars – we are staying in his beautiful house melded into the fynbos a badger's spit from the point – regales me with slurred stories while I grin glassily. It was deep and meaningful I'm sure of it.

The next day, it's cooking at the point, four- to six-foot. Nice blend: epic waves and great wine. – 2005

Confessions of a surf addict

By Gideon Malherbe, former owner and operator of the Indies Explorer

Hi. My name is Gideon and I am a surf addict. I have been an addict for 24 years. I can't go without a regular fix. I will do almost anything to surf: lie, cheat, steal and beg. I've quit many jobs. I've lost plenty girlfriends. My career is going nowhere. All because of surfing. And it's getting worse. The addiction has taken over my life so much, I'm living on a boat right next to the line-up. I'm a mainline addict now. I'm mainlining bro. Every day, all day long.

I did the high school and college thing. Kept my addiction in check. There were a few relapses. Extended surf trips that cost me my degree more than once. I fell off the wagon. Big time. A trip here, a trip there. I blew all my cash. Overdosed. Got lost. Lost in Mexico. But I got myself back over the border. Back into my suit and tie. Back on track.

As a young lawyer, I hid my addiction. At first it was easy. My collar masked the wetsuit rash. But the post-surf sinus drip cannot always be controlled – a dead giveaway to other addicts. Things gradually grew worse. I knew it was a real problem when I went surfing on my tea break. Even 15 minutes was long enough. My addiction was a runaway train.

One day, my boss told me that he knew. My addiction was affecting my work performance. Seek help, he said, hoping I would grow out of

TOO FAR GONE: Surf addict Gideon Malherbe adds fuel to the fire.

INDIES EXPLORER: He gave up his law career to build his own boat and feed the addiction of others.

it, develop a resistance, become mature. F*** that. As I watched his lips move, I was planning the next surf. When could I sneak off without being caught? What route should I drive so that my colleagues wouldn't spot me? What excuse would I use? Does this sound familiar?

I was so deep in my addiction, I could no longer function in society. The more I surfed, the more I wanted it. It was not getting better. I was trying to hang in there. I was desperately trying to hold it all together. But my occasional presence at the firm was no longer being tolerated. I knew my time was up when I convinced a colleague to falsify my signature at bar exam lectures so that I could go surfing.

I left the country two months later, a few days before being admitted to the bar. My destination? Indo. I mean, what did you think? That I was going to quit my surfing habit? No way, man. I sold what little I had left and was gone.

Initially I hacked my way overland from spot to spot, crisscrossing the archipelago on motorbikes, buses and ferries. But after a while, I started hooking up with local fishing boat captains. It was a more effective way to satisfy my ever-growing addiction. Eventually I realised that the most direct access to this surf drug was to build my own boat and go directly to the source.

After that I became a dealer. Yes, I'm a dealer now. I know Al Pacino said in *Scarface* that you should never use your own stash, but it's the only way for a hardened addict like me. I sell it now. Package deals. The works.

It's my job to take salivating addicts like you, and make sure you get your fix. I like to think I'm good at this job. Obviously I have no control over my own addiction. I'm a self-confessed connoisseur of what constitutes really good stuff. Only problem is, where do I go from here? Do I need help? But you would be the wrong dude to ask. What would you know? You probably think I have the best job in the world. Which just tells me one thing: You've got a bit of a problem yourself.

Are you too far gone?

1 Do you blow all your cash to surf?
   a. A bit, but I also play golf.
   b. Saving up for my next board.
   c. No job, no cash.

2 Have you broken the law to surf?
   a. What do you mean?
   b. I often speed to the waves.
   c. Multiple summons for
      destruction of property,
      trespassing, squatting and
      speeding.

3 Have you lied to go surfing?
   a. No need. Only surf on Saturday.
   b. Only to avoid fights with
      my partner.
   c. No need. I have no job. I
      live alone.

4 Has surfing made you under-achieve?
   a. No, it fits into a well-ordered
      schedule.
   b. I just managed to pass.
   c. I am 32 and still in matric.

5 Have you rejected a good job
   because it interfered with surfing?
   a. I earn big bucks and surf only
      on holidays.
   b. Didn't get promoted but I live
      on the coast.
   c. I will look for a job when the
      swell drops.

6 Does surfing damage your
   relationships?
   a. Not if we go shopping on
      the weekend.
   b. We understand that swell
      equals surf.
   c. I have no relationships.
      I am alone.

7 Are your friends also surfers?
   a. No, most play golf. One
      plays squash.
   b. A few. Others I see at the
      sports club.
   c. I hate anyone who doesn't surf.

8 Do you stress away from the coast?
   a. Not at all. Life is
      about balance.
   b. Yes, it gets a bit
      quite stressful.
   c. Leave the coast? Are you mad?

9 Do you know what the swell, wind
   and tides are doing?
   a. Well, it's too windy for golf.
   b. I got a tide watch for
      my birthday.
   c. It's a 16-second swell and low
      is 0.3m above chart datum.

10 Do you want to surf right now?
   a. As soon as I've finished
      this assignment.
   b. I'd give my left hand to
      surf now.
   c. I don't need your blessing
      to surf.

11 Do you feel a high when you surf?
   a. Only if it's offshore
      and glassy.
   b. Yes, even in small
      onshore slop.
   c. I'm feeling so kiff right now!

12 Do you flip out without a
   daily surf?
   a. Once a week is enough.
   b. I occasionally get irritable.
   c. I don't know.

Your score: a. = 1 point   b. = 2 points   c. = 3 points

12-15: Highway surfer in flashy car with golf clubs in the back. You're
          confused and should see a doctor immediately. Burn the clubs. Go to
          Indo. Now.
16-20: You're in control. Surfing does not rule your life. You do the right
          thing most of the time. How's the existential void in the pit of your
          stomach?
21-25: You hide the habit, but it flares up often. You are suffering from
          surf suppression syndrome, which makes you moody and a bit of a doos.
          Let it go bro.
26-30: The fight for control is over. You're on the downward slide. Go with
          it. What a relief.
31-36: You are a hardened, reclusive addict with no friends and few
          possessions. Your whereabouts are unknown. The addiction controls
          your life. Can you even read?

Swell-chaser

Be they small glassy curlers folding over a reef, beach-break close-outs, or thundering monsters that stab the surfer in the gut with terror and fry the brain with endorphin-overload, waves have a strong allure.

For some, the softly percolating fantasy of perfect waves fuels a niggling obsession. The distant roar of the relentless sea becomes a soul-call that drowns out the hum-drum drone of the phone, the boss and the incessant murmur of our everyday lives.

John McCarthy has trawled the planet for waves for many years now. He has surfed more hours than many people have slept. At the merest hint of epic waves, he's out of there, and it doesn't matter where – here, or there.

McCarthy, an executive at surfing lifestyle publisher Atoll Media in Durban, cannot be called a professional surfer. He does not number among those paid to surf the world, although he's had his moments. But he probably surfs as much, if not more, than a lot of them.

McCarthy is a family man with a monthly income, a bond and a grocery list. He has a lawn to mow, a car to maintain and a board to report to. Okay, executives to report to.

In his basement lie the tools of his real trade – about 40 surfboards of every conceivable shape and size, most made by Durban shaper Johnno Hutchinson. He has a little slush fund, carefully fed by a strictly enforced surfing tithe.

Every spare moment, once he's (mostly) fulfilled family and career obligations, is spent surfing or planning the next surgical surf strike. Fly in, hire car, drive to surf, surf two or three times, sleep for eight hours, surf two or three times, fly out a broken man.

In some years, his travel miles would rival most high-flying businessmen. Apart from hundreds of short hops to spots north and south of Durban, and to breaks in the city, he's been on numerous surf strikes to places like Mauritius, Jeffreys Bay, Hawaii, Cape Town, Indonesia and Mozambique.

And that's in one year.

– Henri du Plessis

John McCarthy

His quiver

1 x 5' 8" twin (18-year-old Wedge, his first surfboard ever)
5 x 5' 10" variants squash-tail
1 x 5' 11" squash-tail
12 x 6' 0" variants squash-tail
4 x 6' 1" rounded pintail
1 x 6' 2" regular squash-tail
1 x 6' 2" retro single-fin swallow-tail with deep clinkers
2 x 6' 3" pintails
3 x 6' 6" pintails
1 x 6' 10" semi-gun
1 x 7' 4" semi-gun
1 x 8' 2" big-wave gun
1 x 9' 4" Spider hot-dog thruster longboard
1 x 9' 6" classic 1979 single-fin longboard
1 x 9' 6" big-wave gun
1 x 10' 2" Spider rhino chaser
1 x 10' 2" rhino chaser

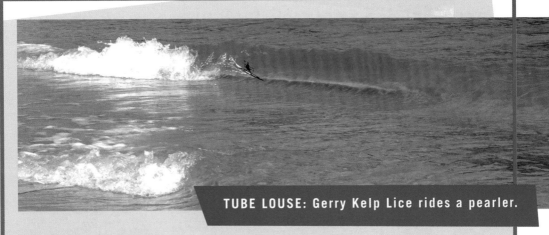

Kelp Lice

The official explanation

These perky isopods (kelp lice) first appeared in the Spike surf report in 1998. Because the surf is often small in False Bay, it 'was only big enough for very small people or kelp lice'. They're mythical insects who live in False Bay. Okay they're not really mythical, only their personification is. You do get kelp lice and sand fleas on the Cape Pensinsula. Sand fleas are amphipods, by the way.

To add some scientific credence: in South Africa, most of the 300 odd isopod species are aquatic. A notable exception is a common 15 mm semi-terrestrial sea louse – *Ligia dilitata* – which swarms over rocks and stranded seaweed along the drift-line. This is our kelp louse. Sea lice are not related to parasitic insect lice, which feed on other animals and humans. On the West Coast, the sand flea *Tylos granulatus* shares the same habitat as the beach hopper – *Talorchestia capensis*.

The main heroes are Gerry Kelp Lice and Vito Sand Flea, as well as Gerry's cousin Bill Bollweevil up in the Eastern Cape at Mellowsands. They are soul surfers who ride wino chasers in 20- to 30-foot Outside Bugdoor or Outer Bog Cabins and sometimes Whyme Bay or Nine Flies Reef. They stick together (especially during mating season).

Sometimes clumps of careening kelp lice can be seen screaming (verbally and with velocity) through the line-up at Outside Bugdoor, towed by bugskis into 36-foot monsters. When it goes flat, normal kelp lice are relieved. Some remember when they had to manually shut Mervyn the Sand Mite's mandibles after his jaw dropped in shock when a thundering 70-foot monster popped at Cork Bay.

In these conditions, many move en masse to the local kelp lice clinic for intensive psycho-kelp-therapy. A day trip across the peninsula to the Crayfish Factory once ended with half the Cork Bay kelp clan taking cover in the swimming pool there, only to be committed to the clinic for psychiatric help.

The core team of big wave riders – Team Kelp Lice – are known to consume Kelpatine (exoskeleton tonal builder), when they prepare for a tow-in sesh at Outer Bugdoor. Gerry Kelp Lice, always the moodier and more solitary, usually waxes his wino chaser alone atop a putrid clump of kelp in a crevice near Whyme Bay.

You get the picture.

Surf-saving

Columnist Ben Trovato blows the lid on lifeguards. This and other advice on staying alive can be found in his Art of Survival.

One of the greatest indignities a surfer can suffer is to be saved by a lifeguard. Lifeguards hate surfers because they won't stay out of the bathing areas. Surfers hate lifeguards because they wear Speedos. However, surfers need lifeguards.

For a start, having a leash means you can surf without learning to swim. But leashes snap. Some people also get into trouble after a bottleneck and a litre of vodka. For most of us, this is the only way we would surf Dungeons. Dropping in on a J-Bay local can also influence your ability to stay afloat.

If you do find yourself drowning, there are two ways to get attention. The first is to put on a blonde wig and scream in a high-pitched voice. Lifeguards rarely bother to save men unless they themselves are gay. I can't speak for you, but I would rather drown than be dragged from the surf by a raving queen in a little red costume and given mouth-to-mouth in front of a rowdy crowd shouting, 'Slip him some tongue!'

The second is to raise your right arm high enough for him to see the R200 note. When he swims out to you, he is going to want to slap you around a bit. This is what lifeguards do to punish drowning people for distracting them from flirting with under-age farm girls. The slapping will make you hysterical. To calm you down, he will punch or head-butt you. It is important to remember that Marquis of Queensbury rules do not apply on the high seas. Retaliate by gouging his eyes, pulling his hair and biting his face. Fight like a girl. Nobody can see you. Adrenalin will course through your body and you will begin to get the upper hand. Your assailant's resolve will weaken and he will try to get away. Go after him. Dive down and swim underwater. He will turn around and think that you have drowned. Sink your teeth into the fleshy part of his leg. He will believe a shark is attacking him and pass out with fright. Flip over on to your back and drag his body over yours. Using one arm to hold his head above water, paddle backwards with your free arm. If he comes round, tighten your grip and cut off his oxygen supply. To crank up the humiliation levels, you may want to remove his Speedo before you get to the beach.

Surfers encounter fundamentalists who warn people not to drink and swim. I have never heard such nonsense. What are you going to do? Lose control on the backstroke and sideswipe a buoy? Burst a water-wing and roll? Have a head-on collision with a jellyfish? The ocean is by far the safest place in which to drink. For a start, it is impossible to fall over. That means no more inexplicable cuts and bruises the next day. There are no roadblocks to ruin your life. No chance of irresponsible sex with someone whose name you can't remember. The only problem I encountered getting my beer diluted with seawater.

Apart from the great white shark and the Congolese man selling beaded flowers, the thing next most likely to ruin your day at the beach is the bluebottle. This little scoundrel is also known as the Portuguese Man o' War, although we are no longer allowed to call them that because the Portuguese say it portrays them as an excitable people who are always up for a fight. I thought that was the whole point of being Portuguese. The tentacles of the bluebottle trail through the water with the aim of snaring plankton and small crustaceans. Whenever I go into the sea, they trail through my baggies with the aim of snaring my testicles. Growing up in Durban, I was stung so many times that my friends called me Welt Boy.

One of the first times I was stung, a friend said the best way to ease the pain was to urinate on the area. Since I had been stung on my back, he helped out. Our friendship was never the same after that.

SURF
Master Series

Chapter 3

A pictorial essay of some
South African personalities

Photographs by

DE ZITTER

Many South Africans have made a mark on our surfing sub-culture. Photographer **Harry de Zitter** has been capturing portraits of them over the years. This is a sample of his work.

If Harry was a cowboy, he'd have been John Wayne. He's shot just about everything and everybody worth shooting: Harley Davidson, Sisley/Benneton, Marlboro, Mack Trucks, Nike, Paul McCartney, Bill Clinton, Bill Gates (three times) – the list is endless. He's been to Argentina alone 52 times. Harry's a big personality. He does nothing in half measures. He is without doubt the most accomplished photographer to shoot his way out of South Africa. Born and raised in the republic of PE where he surfed in the 'early days' with guys like Gavin Rudolph, Harry has homes in Italy and on the Gulf of Mexico. He often visits his motherland.
- *Dougal Paterson*

OLD FATHER TIME

Oom John Whitmore, who passed away in 2001, was a pioneer of South African surfing. The first owner of a VW Kombi in the country, he set many of the big-wave trends. He made the first roof-rack, and was a pioneer in surfboard-shaping. He discovered many of our spots too, including Elands Bay, along the West Coast, his home in his twilight years.

THE ORIGINALS

Ant van den Heuvel (right), pictured here with Bruce Gold. Van den Heuvel spent his last days in his beloved Jeffreys Bay before passing away in 2003. He was a pivotal figure in surfing history, having been selected for the first Springbok surfing team after winning the SA Surfing Championships in 1966. Gold and Van den Heuvel were the original feral surfers in the same mould as Mickey Dora. Gold still lives in J-Bay.

WAVEY STOKE

Davey Stolk, who now lives in Reunion, was one of the first surfers to regularly ride Sunset Reef. A common face at the Red Bull Big Wave Africa event, Stolk is revered for the role he played in the growth of non-racial surfing. He helped pave the way to the new South Africa from a surfing perspective.

THE ICEMAN

Johnny Paarman, from the legendary Glen Beach family, turned heads in Hawaii during the mid 1970s when he posted big results in big surf against the legends of the time, including Peter Townend, Michael Ho, Ian Cairns, Larry Bertlemann and Mark Richards, earning him the moniker of 'Iceman'. Paarman still charges many waves around the Cape, and in 2007 was contest director of the Red Bull Big Wave Africa.

THREE MEN IN A BOAT

Nico Johnson, *left*, Pierre du Plessis and Glenn Bee were the first South African tow-surfers, an evolution that ran parallel to that of Laird Hamilton in Hawaii. In 1994, they conducted early experiments by towing into big waves at Sunset Reef near Cape Town, using a rigid inflatable motor boat and a big-wave gun without foot straps.

FIRST LADY

Margaret Smith, who still lives in Clovelly on the False Bay coast, was an early pioneer of women's surfing. A Springbok who gained her colours after winning the South African Surfing Championships in 1966, Smith, along with people like Sally Sturrock, laid the foundation for a new era of achievement by women surfers.

WATER EXPLORER

Surfboard-shaper Pierre de Villiers, who with Peter Button first surfed Dungeons in 1985, went where no-one had ever been, and the rest followed. Pierre lives in Scarborough on the Cape Peninsula, and continues to shape big-wave guns and ride the challenging surf of the southern peninsula.

LIKE FATHER LIKE KIDS

The Palmbooms, who run a backpackers at Ansteys, on the Bluff in Durban, are the quintessential surfing family. Rudi senior, pictured here with his son Rudi and daughter Heidi, has won accolades around the world for his big-wave temperament and was a regular at the Red Bull Big Wave Africa event. The Palmbooms can often be seen pulling into the deep warm-water tubes of the Bluff.

POCKET ROCKET

Sean Holmes, who hails from Wilderness in the southern Cape, won the 2000 Red Bull Big Wave Africa contest and several other events, including two South African championships. The ultimate competitor – he once out-surfed Kelly Slater, Andy Irons and Cory Lopez as a wildcard entrant to the Billabong Pro at Jeffreys Bay (2002) – he has always kept a deep sense of modesty.

YOUNG GUARD

Kommetjie youngster Michael February's rise to prominence is rapid and sure. In 2007, he dominated the Billabong Junior Series and has been tipped to join a rising number of young South Africans who are spreading their wings in the tough environment of international competitive surfing.

MASTER MARINER

Mickey Duffus is one of South Africa's top big-wave pioneers. He managed the winning South African team at the ISA World Big Wave Championships at Todos Santos in 1999, and is a former winner of the Haleiwa Pro in Hawaii. He is a regular face at the Red Bull Big Wave Africa event and any number of hard-breaking Cape Town spots.

WALKING THE PLANK

Matthew Moir's amazing repertoire of tricks – from old-school nose-riding to modern power surfing – earned him the title of world longboarding champion in 2005. An outspoken regular on the perfect longboarding waves of Muizenberg, Moir is South Africa's most accomplished longboarder.

LOCAL LEGACY

Justin Strong, who hails from Camps Bay, was a child protégé growing up at Glen Beach who took his surfing to professional levels. A seasoned ASP Africa campaigner in the decade before the turn of the century, he won the International Pro Am Surfing title in 1991. Strong has been invited to compete in several Red Bull Big Wave Africa events.

LIQUID MILITIA

Ian Armstrong was part of the team, with Cass Collier and Mickey Duffus, who won the ISA World Big Wave Championships at Todos Santos in 1999. He is a respected shaper, big-wave rider and icon for development surfing. Here he is pictured with his wife, Lee, and children (from left, Ruth, Holly and Max), all of whom are already leaving their surfing imprint on our subculture.

AIR TRAFFIC CONTROLLER

The prodigiously talented Royden Bryson, who hails from East London, hit the world tour in 2007 after several searing performances in a slew of national and international events. He may be light of build, but this goofy footer has been tipped to achieve some major results against the heavyweights of the international circuit.

SHAPE SHIFTER

Tich Paul was part of the crew who discovered many breaks on the Cape Peninsula. Owner of one of the oldest surf shops in South Africa, Lifestyle, in Muizenberg. Tich is a respected surfing judge, who has scored in many events. His phone-in surf report is an institution in Cape Town.

TOP GROM

Another member of the crop of hot young groms, Kommetjie local Mathew Bromley stormed into the limelight when he won the men's and under-16 divisions of the Quiksilver WP Surfing Championships in 2006. Fearless in bigger waves, he has the skill to round off a promising professional surfing career.

RETRO ACTIVE

Cape Town shaper, artist and craftsman Robin Fletcher Evans has an unbelievable eye for detail and a passion for recreating the lost soul of surfing through surfboard models and displays. His surfboards are highly regarded, and he is equally adept at shaping old-school barges and high-performance short boards.

Chapter 4

The earth is rocking, the skies are riven –
Jove in a passion, in god-like fashion,
is breaking the crystal urns of heaven.

Robert Buchanan

BIG WAVE

Until the early 2000s, when big-wave surfing in South Africa finally hauled itself over the ledge of world recognition, it was more of an underground pursuit by a constantly evolving but small cluster of surfers.

According to the founder member of Tow Surf South Africa, Ross Lindsay, the 'official' appearance of big-wave riders from South Africa occurred in the 1960s. The Hawaii charge was led by Durbanites Max Wetteland and Ant van den Heuvel, who were surfing Sunset Beach and Waimea Bay before many of us were born.

Back home, small pockets of surfers around the coast, mostly in Cape Town and Durban, were riding large waves with minimal recognition. The first recorded big-wave photo, taken in 1966, showed a solid 12-foot-plus wave ridden by non-contestant Neville Callenbourne, at Ansteys Beach near Durban, during the first official South African championships.

Lindsay says that the momentum in the early 1960s was slow in South Africa, an isolated backwater mostly unknown to the booming surfing populations of Hawaii, California and Australia.

'Truth be told, big-wave surfing wasn't big in South Africa,' says Lindsay. 'Certainly, it was partly because our big-wave spots were too big and gnarly for the boards that were being ridden at the time; mirrored overseas when North Shore

chargers such as Greg Knoll and Pat Curren were dubious about whether their equipment would prevail at big Waimea Bay.'

In the early 1970s, the advent of lighter surfboards and sleeker shapes brought about better ways to ride big waves, but the social abhorrence of apartheid remained an obstacle, keeping the southern tip of Africa in the dark on the 'Dark Continent'. Surfers went about their business quietly, eschewing the limelight and charging big waves. No news is good news, and no crowds. A nuggety band of young riders in Cape Town were too busy contending with cold water, great white sharks and the brute force of Atlantic Ocean storms.

There were no rescue teams on jetskis to bail out guys like Peter Basford, Jonathan and Mark Paarman, and Peers Pittard when dealing with the gut-wrenching drops at deep-water reefs, such as the Crayfish Factory, the Outer Kom and, later, Sunset and Dungeons.

In the Eastern Cape, an 18-year-old youngster from Port Elizabeth, Gavin Rudolph, was also charging. Rudolph recalls a day at J-Bay that is commonly regarded as the most perfect big surf ever ridden there. Only four people managed to get out as 15-foot-plus waves poured down the point virtually nonstop. Some sets comprised 65 waves. Guys waiting to paddle out from the Supers gulley had to wait 45 minutes. Rudolph, Jonathan Paarman, Pittard and Brad McCaul had the session of their lives.

It was experiences like this that Rudolph could draw from when he won the Smirnoff Pro-am at 12-foot Sunset Beach, Hawaii, in 1971, ahead of legends Bill Hamilton (Laird's adopted dad), Eddie Aikua and Jeff Hakman. Rudolph and Durban's Mike Larmont were invited to compete in the prestigious Golden Breed Expression Session in the same year.

ANSTEYS BOMB:
Neville Callenbourne's wave in 1966.

FREE FALL: Greg Long takes the short route at Dungeons.

BURNISHED GOLD: A giant peak looms at Dungeons, 18 June 2002.

Rudolph's victory was the first major title achieved by a South African. It was as if a psychological doorway opened for South Africans to go large on the North Shore.

Since the mid to late 1960s, a large Durban crew had been sampling big waves generated by tropical cyclones, as had a smaller group of compatriots in the Cape. They hit the North Shore with a vengeance, led by Shaun Tomson, his cousin Michael, Paul Naude, Mike Esposito, Larmont, Robert McWade, Mark Price, Michael Burness, Mark Spowart, Bruce Jackson, Peter Lawson and Pierre Tostee, among many others over the years.

Three years after Rudolph's win, Tomson took the 1974 Hang Ten American Pro, also held in solid Sunset. His cousin, Michael, made it to the final. In 1975, Tomson reached the final at the Smirnoff before making South African history by winning the prestigious Pipeline Masters.

The next year, Paarman – aged 22 – burst onto the scene, clinching a fifth place at the Smirnoff and eighth place at the Duke Kahanamoku Invitational at Sunset Beach. He made the final in both events, surfing in illustrious company that included Peter Townend, Michael Ho, Ian Cairns, Larry Bertlemann and Mark Richards. But it was the hard-earned respect he got for his hell-for-leather approach in Hawaiian surf that was the real prize, far surpassing results in surf contests. The same could be said of Durban's Paul Naude, who came third at the Pipeline Masters in the same year. South Africans were charging.

Guys like Tomson – driven by a competitive camaraderie with Aussie surfers such as Rabbit Bartholomew – were attacking the Second Reef at Pipeline with almost suicidal gusto. People were starting to notice.

Another South African, who relinquished his citizenship in the 1980s, was Martin Potter, also remembered for taking on massive waves, both at the Pipe's second reef in the years before and during his successful campaign to win the world title in 1989.

Other South Africans made their mark elsewhere. Jonathan's brother Mark is still revered by locals at Mundaka, Spain, after his aggressive attack on the grinding sand-bottomed left-hander.

Back home, a second generation of big-wave surfers included Pierre de Villiers, Peter Button and Davey Stolk. They were among a small group of hardened Cape Town locals instrumental in fostering a big-wave brotherhood. According to Lindsay, the 80s were dominated by De Villiers as he relentlessly pursued Sunset and later Dungeons, which he first surfed in 1984 with Button.

'Pierre was shaping the big-wave guns they needed to take the step up, and this early era was dominated by them. It was a case of "We don't need events. We have big waves on our doorstep," Lindsay recalls. He mentions a dog-eared but inspirational image for many South African surfers in the 80s. Taken by Shafiq (then Steve) Morton, the photo depicted Stolk dropping down an 18-foot Sunset bomb.

Other names of the time were Ken Freeland and Glen D'Arcy, both surfer-shapers experimenting with equipment that could cope with big-wave riding.

While the thrash-and-bash generation was just starting to take off – everyone chasing the fluorescent colours of the professional era – the Cape guys quietly stayed underground, riding big waves and staying true to their roots in sometimes arduous conditions, says Lindsay. People like Micky Duffus, commuting from the Strand, were scoring the waves of their lives, and hardly anyone knew. However, an event in 1984 changed all that.

The Spur Surf-about, part of the World Surfing Tour held in Cape Town, took place in perfect big winter surf. The pros were astounded at the power of the Outer Kom, with some competitors undergunned and taking gas in the hard-breaking 12- to 15-foot lefthanders. In free sessions around the event, a 10-foot-plus west swell continued to grind around the peninsula. One particular right-hand reef – a favourite of this writer – was likened by American surfers to Backdoor Pipeline.

In the years after the Spur event, the big-wave scene in Cape Town continued to grow, but slowly.

Things went quiet, mostly because apartheid was peaking. A State of Emergency was called in 1985. Martin Potter, Tom Curren and Tom Carroll boycotted the Gunston 500. Things were heavy, with the infamous Security Branch assassinating activists, and black surfers getting chased from whites-only beaches. Riots were breaking out in the townships and the SADF (South African Defence Force) was engaged in a full-scale war in Angola.

Into the 1990s, Sunset and the Factory – rarely Dungeons – continued to be ridden, mostly by the big-wave underground paddling into the bombs on their big rhino chasers. At the same time, South Africa underwent historic political changes, climaxing in the first democratic elections in 1994.

Under the radar of the political change of the time, in the same year, tow surfing was also undergoing its own quiet revolution.

Courageously but somewhat clumsily – in comparison to the slick equipment in use today – Glen Bee, Pierre du Plessis and, a year later, spearo Nico Johnson pioneered South African tow surfing. Bee and Du Plessis were keen waterskiiers. They would often go 'scurfing' (skiing behind a boat on a wakeboard) when the surf was flat, or too big.

The seed was sown when they looked over to the bombora reef, Sunset, off Kommetjie, and saw flawless 20- to 25-foot waves breaking, with not a surfer in sight. Those glassy A-frames would loom towards the reef, empty and lonely, then convulse into a perfect aquamarine barrel. They could not bear to see such good waves go unridden, so they began to experiment by attaching a ski rope to the

SOWING THE SEED: The famous picture of Davey Stolk at Sunset.

TWO TOW CREWS: Into the 2000s, Sunset was ridden frequently.

boat and pulling into waves around Kommetjie. When friend Craig Yester brought a video back from Hawaii showing tow-surfing pioneer Laird Hamilton and crew experimenting with 'motor-assisted surfing' behind a rubber duck, they knew they were on the right track. The legendary Laird was only about a year into his own learning curve. Seeing what the Hawaiian crew was doing gave the guys a huge boost, and things took off.

For Johnson, the learning curve was rather warped, even inverted. Firstly, he learned to surf at Sunset, not what one would call a beginner's break. Seasoned local Pierre de Villiers would take him surfing out there in return for Johnson taking him spearfishing. Secondly, and more bizarrely, he was tow surfing long before he was a proficient paddle surfer.

The equipment used for the first tow-surfing attempts at Sunset was antiquated compared to the four-stroke wave runners and carefully weighted strap-in short boards of today. Pierre, Glen and Nico mostly rode seven-foot-six guns with no straps behind their rubber duck at Sunset and, later, Dungeons. All three guys are now among South Africa's top jetski safety crews for big-wave surfing.

But the biggest influence comes down to a single surfing competition. The inaugural Red Bull Big Wave Africa (RBBWA) at Dungeons in 1999

marked the turning point. Similar to Mavericks in California, Dungeons is a legitimate, but horrifyingly brutal, big-wave spot that was still to storm on to the world stage. The original event went ahead quietly, with minimal exposure. Dungeons failed to produce the right contest conditions, and photos from the event were sketchy, despite some pretty hard-core wave riding.

The Red Bull came after a crucial breakthrough in 1999, when the Rastafarian duo of Cass Collier and Ian Armstrong – with Micky Duffus as manager – won the ISA Big Wave World Championships for South Africa at Todos Santos, Mexico. The powerful surf of the Cape had given Collier, Armstrong and Duffus the edge over the best in the world, including a number of top surfers from Hawaii, the spiritual home of surfing.

It was testimony to the New South Africa, the talent of her people and the quality and power of the waves. Meanwhile, other South Africans – notably guys like Durbanites John McCarthy and Richie Sills who were surfing the World Qualifying Series – had been campaigning in Hawaii and earning the respect of locals at big Pipeline, Sunset and Waimea Bay. As McCarthy says, 'If you can handle the raw cyclonic power of 10- to 12-foot surf in Durban, you can probably deal with bigger waves elsewhere.'

After the Red Bull event of 2000, which saw 'I am not really a big-wave surfer' Vic Bay local Sean Holmes win the event in classic 20-foot surf, the world started to sit up and take notice – South Africa had legitimate big waves.

A growing number of invited professional big-wave surfers mingled with their South African brethren to create a new mythology around Dungeons, at what the former editor of *Surfing Magazine*, Steve Barilotti, called one of Cape Town's Wagnerian-titled breaks – places that elicit feelings of foreboding and dread.

Recognition brought with it a surge in big-wave cross-pollination. The local crew was exposed to the latest innovations in tow-surfing gear and techniques, and the big-wave scene exploded like a jaw-shuddering Dungeons closeout over the infamous slab. Famous big-wave safety coordinator Shaun Alladio – internationally renowned for her rescue drills in huge surf – was flown in to teach the locals her skills, and help co-ordinate the safety at the Red Bull event. It was her instruction that formed the foundation for the safety certificates now demanded by Tow Surf South Africa, the official body that regulates tow surfing.

Gary Linden, respected big-wave surfer and shaper from California, began shaping tow boards for the local crew. Instead of sporadic trips overseas to get tow boards and learn about the latest techniques, copious quantities of both were coming straight to our doorstep. For the local big-wave guys, it was an intravenous dose of knowledge.

Heather Clark won the 2000 Triple Crown of Surfing in Hawaii, the next best thing to winning the world title, in the same year that she broke into the elite ranks of the World Championship Tour.

In 2001, RBBWA contender and Cape Town local Chris Bertish set out to ride what he believed were the four heaviest waves on the planet: Mavericks, Todos Santos, Waimea and Teahupoo. While surfing big waves at all of the above, he made history by being, at the time, the only guy to paddle into Jaws. Bertish also won the XXL paddle awards (sponsored by Swell.com) that year. Mike Parsons won the Biggest Tow-in. They were each to get a share of the $60,000 prize but, because Bertish was not at the awards (he had no sponsor to fly him there), Parsons got the cheque. Bertish was sent a voucher for $100.

In 2004, Bertish rode some hefty 20-foot bombs at the Cribber in the UK after borrowing a board. It earned him front page news on several national dailies and a slot on BBC TV evening news.

Another milestone along the continuum of the big-wave timeline also occurred in 2004. The inaugural Bayview Big Wave event was held at a squat, ledging monster in Hermanus, near Cape Town. The event attracted a mixture of pro and amateur bodyboarders who were subjected to the biggest surf ever seen for a bodyboarding event

The local crew was exposed to the latest innovations in tow-surfing gear and techniques

DUNGEONS: Waiting for the perfect storm

A confluence of factors is required before the storm-blasted rock slabs beneath the jagged spire of the Sentinel, Hout Bay, can be paddle-surfed. There is more flexibility for tow surfers, who are pulled into waves by jetskis with enough velocity to catch and outrun huge waves moving at speeds beyond the strength of human arms. Tow surfers don't mind wind, onshore or offshore. Their boards are tiny compared to the 10-foot rhino chasers used to paddle into big waves, making tow surfers more aerodynamically compact and less prone to wind gusts and chop when traversing a huge wave face.

Paddle-surfers need big but orderly waves from a single direction to focus on one area – the take-off zone where they wait. The swell must sneak between a pinnacle called Vulcan Rock and a rock ledge called Tafelberg Reef, before refracting around reef slabs off seal-infested Duikereiland.

When the generating storm veers too close, not only is the weather too stormy, but the swell is too wild – large, steep peaks breaking all over the place. Dungeons needs a strong swell to approach in clean lines with regular intervals, with enough submerged energy to push the wave face upwards steeply as it encounters the underwater bathymetry.

Winds that blow too close create a swell with a wide directional spread. The wave peaks shift. This is not fun for surfers scratching around a take-off zone as wide as four football fields. You want the sniper swell from the high-powered storm far enough away to create a focused swell.

However, a storm too far away – despite the right direction – is not always ideal. On 14 June 2002, the perfect swell broke at Dungeons. But the powerful 18-second swell had travelled for three days from a giant storm off the Falkland Islands 2 500 nautical miles away. Mountains of energy had rolled through the deep at great speed – a velocity of up to 100 km/h. The wave height subsided but immense energy was sustained beneath the surface.

When it reached South Africa, it was a thing of beauty, but deceptively dangerous. The few miles from the edge of the continental shelf to the Dungeons reef provided minimal sea floor friction to slow its assault. With nowhere else to go, the submerged power compressed huge volumes of water upwards, the waves rapidly growing in size before contracting over the slab, impacting with fearsome detonations, and causing suicidal surges and suck-downs.

Long waits between sets caused by these long-distance swells – they grow further apart over distance – makes for a jittery surf session as you wait for a beast to loom suddenly, only to discover you've drifted off the peak and it's about to break on your head.

The ideal swell for Dungeons – based on the huge, perfect swell that came through on 30 July 2006 – comes from a peaking storm 900 nautical miles away in an area 240 to 250 degrees west-southwest of Cape Town. The storm needs to be stable and slow moving. Winds need to blow 50 to 60 knots along a narrow, focused fetch for about 700 miles. The resulting swell comes from a single direction with little oscillation in direction. The swell has tight bandwidth dominated by same-sized and same-period waves. In other words, the biggest waves and the average waves were indistinguishable.

Evenly spaced, these swells glide silently through calm seas, unimpeded on their journey to shore. The swells need to occur at medium-period intervals of 13 to 15 seconds, which provides enough power but not the volumes of water that make paddling dangerous. When the swell arrives, you want a calm day between storms, preferably a light variable breeze. Too much offshore wind up the face can stall riders at the top, causing dangerous wipeouts. A light south to southwest onshore wind is not felt on the face.

SATURDAY 3 JULY 2004: Jamie Stirling on a monster.

SATURDAY 3 JULY 2004:
Mikala Jones, same session.

FRIDAY 14 JUNE 2002:
Another suicidal suck-down.

FRIDAY 14 JUNE 2002:
Beautiful, but dangerous.

in South Africa. There was carnage on the first day and the event was called off. Dangerous undertows were caused when terrifying 22-foot bombs exploded on the reef, then surged and richocheted around the bay, before sucking back out to sea. This did not deter the free-surf antics of hardcore mattmen, such as Bayview pioneer Johan 'Tjoekie' de Goede, Brandon Foster, Aadam and Ishmael Grant, Hankus Loubser, Morné Laubser and Wade Harrison. The event was held on the second day in 10- to 15-foot waves, and won by De Goede.

Meanwhile, the Red Bull event was gaining momentum. A steady stream of respected big-wave professionals was arriving annually on our shores, from Cheyne Horan to Ross Clark-Jones. Friendships were forged in the testing waters of Dungeons, Sunset, the Factory and a range of hard-breaking Cape Town reefs, as well as Bayview. Some of the Californian crew took to the Cape surf like ducks to water, notably Grant Washburn and Greg Long. Others who brought their skills, experience and equipment included Peter Mel, Evan Slater, Mike Parsons, Jamie Stirling and Darryl Virotsko.

It should be noted that some of the old-school locals, notably Pierre de Villiers, have always shunned the concept of competing for waves, although the kinship amongst big-wave surfers is noticeably more close-knit than in the numerous neon-tinted thrash-and-bash competitions on the calendar these days. While in the water during the final of the Red Bull event in 2003, the surfers decided unanimously to share the prize money regardless of who won. Greg Long took the win on the podium amidst jocularity and group hugs. Everybody scored a slice of the pie. Big-wave surfers hug each other a lot, mostly due to the camaraderie that bonds individuals in the face of the ocean's might.

Among the growing tribe of South African big-wave surfers, several Durbanites were carving their own niche, including former longboard champion Jason Ribbink, 2006 Red Bull winner John Whittle, and king of Mavericks in 2006, Grant 'Twiggy' Baker. The Red Bull event changed the profile of big-wave surfing, and guys from out of Cape Town who charged hard could now find professional reasons to chase big waves in addition to the benefits of being team riders for their sponsors.

The Durban crew commuted to Cape Town for the Red Bull, and travelled further afield – charging big waves around the world in the northern hemisphere big-wave season, when summer in South Africa brings mostly flat seas.

Ribbink and fearless tow partner Gigs Cilliers procured state-of-the art equipment and began targeting the heaviest surf they could find, including an epic cross-ocean raid to Peahi, Hawaii, in 2005 when they scored 30-foot Jaws to themselves after Gigs made a clever 'gut-feeling' call. The Americans – over-reliant on the techno-gimmickry of wave forecasting – were caught napping that day. Twiggy was also popping up all over the world, as were Sills, McCarthy and others.

Running parallel to the big-wave hype and mounting overseas interest in South Africa, other locals continued to ply their trade in the kelpy waters of the Cape peninsula. The big-wave roll call was growing, with perennial chargers such as De Villiers, Armstrong, Duffus, Collier, Du Plessis, Bee, Johnson, Lindsay, Steve Leonard and Kommetjie hellman, Simon Lowe joined by people like Andy Marr, Mike Schlebach, Dave Smith, Reinhardt Fourie, Jack Smith, Thomas King-Kleynhans and others.

In the early 2000s, with a small group of tow surfers getting huge waves to themselves, it was a matter of time before others began to make the transition from paddle to tow. From just one tow crew in the mid to late 1990s, there were 16 crews by August 2007, which included many of the above surfers, with guys like Kyle Kahn, Greg Bertish and John Henry in Plettenberg Bay.

The increase in surfers, including tow crews from overseas, necessitated the formation of an umbrella body to regulate the sport. There was too much at stake in terms of safety and legal issues around council regulations, marine conservation and coastal management. Founder members of Tow Surf South Africa, Pierre du Plessis and Ross Lindsay, walked a tightrope trying to appease Marine and Coastal Management (MCM), Table Mountain National Park and local residents ignorant of the true nature of the sport.

Armed with video presentations and stats proving negligible noise and other pollution, they had to educate officials about the nature of big-wave tow surfing. By mid 2007, Tow Surf South Africa members were restricted to two breaks, Dungeons and Sunset, but only through a special exemption by MCM that has to be renewed annually.

In 2006, Baker capped a rising big-wave career with a huge fillip for South African big-wave surfing by becoming the first surfer from outside Santa Cruz to win the Mavericks Surf Contest in classic 20-foot surf. His victory was all the more remarkable after securing a wildcard entry via a poll on surfermag.com. A stand-out at RBBWA, he was also an accomplished tow surfer and kite surfer.

In the same year, Jordy 'Superfreak' Smith – at the tender age of 18 – won the Van's Triple Crown of Surfing Rookie of the Year award – a huge feather in his cap after his second place at the O'Neill World Cup of Surfing at Sunset Beach.

Marking another milestone in the progress of our indigenous surfers was the all-South Africa day on the podium at the eighth Red Bull event in 2006. Whittle won, with Marr and Chris Bertish second and third respectively.

But it was the giant 40-foot swell that broke three days later at Dungeons that really got the surfing world going. People gawped at the insane images captured by Shaun Timoney and Al McKinnon at Dungeons on Sunday 31 July 2006. The surf was monstrous, with wave faces approaching 70 feet. Lowe, Schlebach and other tow crews tackled the biggest surf ever seen in Africa.

The day peaked with a giant set that earned the right to be included in the same company as the biggest ever ridden waves at Jaws or Cortes Bank. One wave in that set was ridden by Californian Greg Long. It won him the Biggest Wave title at the 2006 Billabong XXL Awards.

Marr took second in the Ride of the Year award, but not without controversy. Cynical locals pointed at alleged jingoism that denied a relative unknown rider from breaking into the American-centric brotherhood.

In 2007, the O'Neill Raw Courage Awards were announced, the brainchild of Chris Bertish, to reward gutsy performances by local surfers in testing big-wave conditions. Big-wave surfing had taken off in a big way.

MAKING

Chapter 5

Blow, winds, and crack your cheeks. Rage, blow,
You cataracts and hurricanes, spout
Till you have drenched our steeples, downed the cocks.

William Shakespeare

WAVES

Oceanography

1919

'I've picked out as my symbol, surf ... a surfer moving along constantly right at the edge of the tube (is) the metaphor of the highly conscious life. The tube (is) the past and I'm an evolutionary agent. At that point where you're going into the future, you have to keep in touch with the past. There's where you get the power. Sure you're most helpless. But you also have most precise control at that moment. Using the past; the past is pushing you forward, isn't it? The wave is crashing behind you, yeah? And you can't be slow about it or (hands mime a wipeout).'

- Timothy Leary

Surfers like to wax lyrical about surfing. Their clumsy eulogies elevate the tube ride to a cosmic plane perhaps because it is such a fleeting moment, just like the fulfilment we find so elusive in the treadmill of our sorry little lives. But the difficulty of the quest makes the reward of finding the grail that much sweeter. As you can see, surfers struggle with metaphor.

However, they have no problem with fantasy. A seascape is not about sea, sky or land, or seagulls. Just waves. They mind-surf them – chasing the curl, dodging the lip, drawing imaginary speed lines across a synapse-shifting wall.

As Leary proclaims, the tube ride brings surfers to the edge of the universe. That split second in the tube is a fleeting convergence of past, present and future – a snapshot on the space-time continuum where the curving wave extends into the infinite sphere.

Warned you.

Surfers don't agonise over heavy existential issues. There are only two questions: What is the swell doing? What is the wind doing?

Of course there are other profound concerns: Where am I going to surf? How long will I be able to surf for? How long will the wind blow offshore? Will it go onshore? How big will the waves be at my spot? Is the swell direction wrong for that spot? What is the right swell direction for my spot? Will it be crowded? What board should I ride?

Wait until you hear surfers debate swell height versus wave face, or the significance of wave period. Surfers love this stuff. It makes them belong. It also helps them score really good surf now and then. However, where does the information come from?

Licking a finger and pointing it into the breeze is no longer enough. Watching clouds or wind vanes or birds in flight or your auntie's twitching moustache hairs might mean change. The barometer can verify this. When the atmospheric pressure drops, the needle swings towards the stormy part of the dial. It might mean swell. However, crucial details are missing. When will the swell come? How big will it be? What direction will it come from? How long will it last?

The best swells emanate from weather systems far beyond the barometer's scope, despite that instrument's honourable role in seafaring lore. Times have changed. Now surfers surf

EVOLUTIONARY AGENT: Moving along at the edge of the tube, pushed by the past.

Dig a little de

dynamics that

THEORY AND REALITY: A deep-energy swell made conditions tricky at Dungeons on 14 June 2002.

the Internet – the altar of the New Age – to hold council with oceanographic oracles. However, before you try to interpret the swell forecasts, you need to dig a little deeper into the dynamics that govern swell, particularly the mathematical role of wave period, the interval between waves.

A basic understanding of waves goes a long way to boosting your surf experience because it makes it easier to analyse the data to output your own forecast.

In other words, you need to learn how to drive manual before you drive automatic.

Earth the energy engine

Basic school geography tells us that the earth is a giant heat-exchange system. Different regions of the earth, comprising land and sea, absorb and release different amounts of solar radiation. They do it partly because the sun's rays are hitting areas at different angles, and partly because of their chemical and physical make-up. Land absorbs and releases heat a lot quicker then the ocean. Land temperatures oscillate a lot quicker than ocean temperatures, changing from day to night and back to day. The immutable ocean holds steady. Change takes time in Neptune's realm.

Consider that the sun is at its hottest over the equator, because the rays strike the earth more directly there. However, as you follow the curve of the earth away from the equator towards the poles, the sun's rays hit earth at increasingly flat angles, and they must pass through more atmosphere. The equatorial regions are always hot, and the poles are always cold.

The oceans, which cover 70 percent of the earth's surface, are a key factor in minimising these extremes by circulating the energy around our planet. Currents and surface winds between cold and warm areas bring about a more temperate balance.

Seasonal cycles

The area of the equator where the sun is hottest changes from season to season as the earth slowly tilts back and forth on its axis. This heated zone (scientists call it the Intertropical Convergence Zone or ITCZ) oscillates from north to south.

During the summer solstice – the peak of summer – in the northern hemisphere, the sun sits directly over the Tropic of Cancer at 23.5° north. The heated zone has completed its shift to the north, which experiences its longest day. On the same day, usually June 21, the southern hemisphere is having its shortest day. It is our winter solstice. From now on, the heated zone will gradually move back towards us culminating in our summer solstice when the sun is directly over the Tropic of Capricorn at 23.5° south. Then we will enjoy our longest day, usually December 22, just as the people in the northern hemisphere are hunkering down for the shortest day of their year – the winter solstice. Like a pendulum, the tilting movement goes back and forward, slowing to a stop, then slowly moving back, accelerating as it goes. It is interesting to note that the Tropic of Capricorn, which lies 23.5° south, runs through northern Limpopo Province in South Africa, so for certain parts of the year near the summer solstice, the most sun-struck part of the planet includes South Africa.

Under pressure

Warm air is perpetually rising from the over-heated equatorial zone and constantly sinking at the under-heated poles. Warm air rises because it is lighter, and cold air sinks because it is heavier. Simplistically, this heat circulates around the planet across the canopy of the atmosphere from equator to both poles, and back again along the ocean towards the equator as wind.

However, not all the air that has risen from the equatorial belt will reach the poles. Some of it cools along the way and sinks towards the earth's surface. Because of the mild temperature of the ocean, which is releasing minimal heat, the heavier cold air is able to sink in large areas, exerting greater atmospheric pressure on the sea surface. The average pressure on the sea surface is 1013 millibars. A reading above this number indicates higher pressure. A reading below shows lower pressure. A cyclonic system comprises warmer, lighter air and exerts less pressure, hence low pressure. Easy!

The bands of sinking high pressure occur in both hemispheres, the warm air from the equatorial region rising up, flowing towards the poles and sinking between 20° and 35° north and south.

The heated zone shifts north or south, and the whole bang shoot shifts with it. In the southern hemisphere, the movement of the high-pressure zone to the north leaves a void filled by the volatile wind belt of the Roaring Forties, which also moves north. This wild and stormy belt lying between 40° and 50° south is the engine room of the storms that drive most of South Africa's wave action, fuelled by constant conflict between frigid, dry polar air that clashes with warm, moist tropical winds.

SEASONAL SHIFT:
In summer, *below left*, the storms move south.
In winter, *below right*, they move north.

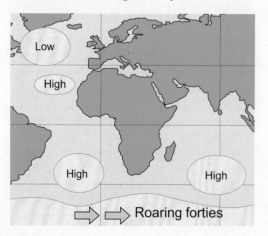
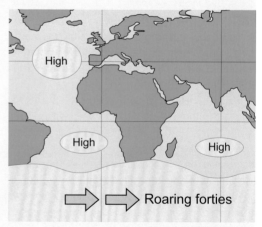

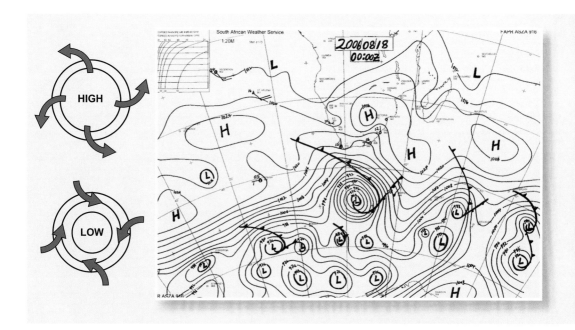

Wind genesis

Because high pressure exerts downward pressure on the sea, surplus air is squeezed outwards along the surface into low pressure areas where rising air has left a void at the surface. The strength of the wind depends on the proximity and strength of high and low pressure systems. The more compressed the gradient between them, the harder the wind blows. The stronger the wind, the bigger the swell. The further the swell travels, the better the surf. Simple as that. Kinda sorta. Take a look at the synoptic chart above.

The snaking contours lines are what you might call an atmospheric pressure map. The numbers on the lines (called isobars) represent units of atmospheric pressure (called millibars). High pressure is indicated by H, higher millibars denoting higher pressure. Low pressure is indicated by L, lower millibars denoting lower pressure. The lines and numbers are like contour lines in a topographical map indicating hills and valleys. Look at that big festering circular clump. It is not a giant koppie in the ocean, but a powerful low pressure storm, with a very low central pressure of 972 millibars. The tightly packed lines indicate a strong pressure gradient and strong winds.

Coriolis

Now we know that gravity dictates the basics of high pressure (sinking heavy air) and low pressure (rising light air). However, there is another powerful force at work. The earth turns on its axis from west to east, creating a continuous, centrifugal force called the Coriolis effect.

In the southern hemisphere, this force causes moving air to deflect to the left. Therefore air moving out from high pressure veers left. The flow around a high is therefore anti-clockwise. Air moving towards low pressure also veers left as it spirals upwards. A low pressure flows clockwise. Get it? Got it? Good.

Fortunately this air flow generally follows the direction of the isobars on the synoptic chart. In other words, generally speaking, wind blows in the direction of the isobars. The old-school synoptic chart indicates where high and low pressure systems are situated, but does not indicate the wind direction and velocity of the air moving between them. Modern wind maps indicate wind speeds and direction superimposed on the synoptic chart, which is hugely beneficial when trying to work out the size and direction of swell.

NORTHERN STORM: Hurricane Floyd rotates counter-clockwise off Florida in 1999.

SOUTHERN STORM: An unnamed tropical cyclone rotates clockwise off Brazil in 2004.

What causes storms

In the northern hemisphere, when a strong cyclonic system deepens sufficiently, it is termed a typhoon (Asia) or hurricane (US). In the southern hemisphere, it remains a cyclone. In the southern hemisphere, cyclones rotate clockwise and track from west to east due to the Coriolis force. Typhoons and hurricanes in the northern hemisphere spin counter-clockwise.

In the vast engine rooms of the oceans, particularly in the mid-latitudes between 30° and 60° south, the warm westerly wind belt collides with cold east winds from the poles and cold fronts form. In the southern hemisphere, cold air moving from the freezing pole (high pressure) veers left due to Coriolis, the centrifugal force of the rotating earth, resulting in cold southeast winds. This cold air under-cuts (moves under) the warmer air of the westerly wind belt, situated in a band around the globe along the Roaring Forties (40° south), the Furious Fifties (50° south) and the Screaming Sixties (60° south). Because cold air is heavier, it moves closer to the surface pushing beneath the lighter, warm air and forcing it upwards, forming a front. As it rises, it cools in what meteorologists call a cyclonic process. Water vapour condenses. Clouds form. It rains. This can result in what surfers regard as the perfect storm – stable and tightly focused. This process is also called cyclo-genesis – meaning creation of a cyclone. Not all cyclones are dramatic enough to warrant being given names like Hilda and Derek.

Swell mechanics

The movement of swell through the open ocean is governed by a set of mathematical rules that are easy to grasp and provide an excellent tool in your quest to accurately predict swell. We've provided some graphics showing the components of swell and how it moves, as well as the basic equations you can use to work out the speed and wavelength of swells. Remember that we are talking about deep-water gravity swells, or groundswell. Once a swell encounters the sea floor, it becomes a shallow-water swell and the mathematical relationships are different.

PERFECT STORM: *Below left*, a cyclone off Cape Town on 29 July 2006 produced the largest waves ridden in Africa the next day. American Greg Long, *below right*, turns off a giant at Dungeons, judged the largest wave ridden in the world in 2006, earning him the Billabong XXL Biggest Wave title.

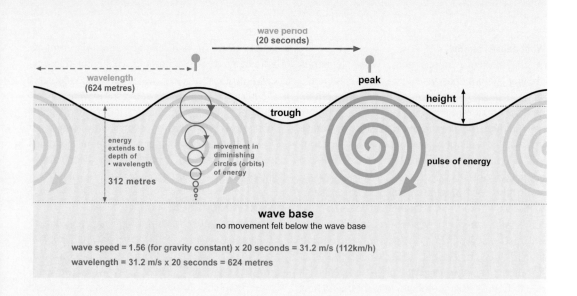

wave period
(20 seconds)

wavelength
(624 metres)

peak

height

trough

energy
extends to
depth of
• wavelength

movement in
diminishing
circles (orbits)
of energy

pulse of energy

312 metres

wave base
no movement felt below the wave base

wave speed = 1.56 (for gravity constant) x 20 seconds = 31.2 m/s (112km/h)
wavelength = 31.2 m/s x 20 seconds = 624 metres

Anatomy of swell

If you had to look at a group of swells from the side, you would see a series of bumps and dents. The tops are the peaks and the dents the troughs. Gravity is counter-acting the energy in the swell, pulling it down between the energised portions of the wave, giving it a simple up-and-down undulating wave shape. Again, in nature, we see the duality – the basic contrast – between yin and yang, up and down, black and white, warm and cool. Hey, like, sjoe bru.

What causes swell

Even the doffest standup, doormat and eggbeater knows that the stronger the wind, the stronger the swell as long as the wind blows over a minimum distance (fetch) for a minimum time (duration). Didn't you? Not to worry. Read on.

When the wind glides over the sea, it rubs against the surface. The velocity and weight of the air exert force, pushing the sea forward and scouring it into crinkles known as micro-ripples or capillary waves. As the wind strengthens, the height of the bumps and depth of the dents increase, becoming wavelets pushed along by the wind. Because the sea surface stretches, the total area increases, causing aerodynamic drag and creating wind stress. On a micro-scale, the bumpy sea surface becomes riddled with turbulent pockets of air that create even

more stickiness for the wind to grip. More grip means deeper scouring. More scouring leads to more friction. The relationship becomes exponential. The wavelets accelerate with the wind, peaks and troughs growing deeper and further apart, in other words, expanding in height, girth and speed.

Up to this point, the process has been slow, momentum gradual. However, with time and distance, the relentless agitation becomes an exponential springboard that catapults the sea from shallow wind waves to deep undulating groundswells travelling at speeds close to the velocity of the wind that created them – as fast as the speed limit on a South African freeway.

When at maximum height and speed, the swells are travelling at just under wind speed. They are fully developed. They have reached maturation – call it saturation – and can't absorb more energy. In turn, the wind has reached peak velocity and can't impart any more energy into the sea.

When the wind exceeds roughly 60 to 70 knots, white-capping occurs, when the crests are ripped apart by the wind. There is a cut-off point where swells get so huge, voluminous and steep, their crests begin to topple, ripped further by the winds, and they can't absorb more energy. A combination of the laws of physics, and the sheer violence of the wind that is tearing them apart, caps or limits their growth.

The best surfing waves generally come from big storms far away. Starting as huge chunks of wind-driven energy, the swells move away from the storm, their ragged steep edges slowly subsiding. The downward pull of gravity results in an undulating form. The younger wavelets and short swells die out or are subsumed by more powerful wave trains. The swells gradually grow more evenly spaced, organising into groups or sets of waves. It should be noted that the swell does not carry the sea with it. Only the energy moves. Each swell is like a pulse of energy undulating beneath the surface of the ocean.

The longer-period swells are the surfer's preference because they have the most energy and can sustain themselves over great distances. They are spaced further apart, and by the time they reach shore, the waves are clean and lined up, with regular intervals between each wave, and a lull between each set (so you can get your breath back after a thick lip breaks on your pip).

In the storm
It should be noted that the originating area is called a sea or wind sea. It refers to a chaotic sea state or wave spectrum containing waves in different stages of development – some big, some small, some short, some long, some weak, some powerful. The shorter-period stuff is raw windswell still absorbing energy from the wind. The longer-period swell is more powerful, and has been around for longer, generated by winds that have been blowing for a longer time. This swell has been pushed along the fetch by the wind, absorbing more energy and increasing in height, length and power. This deeper groundswell grows along the fetch. Energy continually flows from short- to long-period waves. As the sea grows, short waves are being constantly generated. The energy is pumped from one end of the spectrum to the other, piling up at the long-period end before propagating away from the originating area like a package off the production line.

When the wind has blown far enough and long enough (at least 600 nautical miles for eight hours), wind speed becomes the determining variable. An increase in wind velocity brings an exponential increase in energy. A 40-knot wind blows twice as fast as a 20-knot wind yet imparts 16 times more energy into the sea. Fetch and duration are foundation variables, but wind velocity is the determining variable – it dictates the eventual speed of the wave and its power as represented by wave period, or interval.

Working it out
Deep water swell works in a similar way to the basic equation Speed = Distance / Time.

Wave speed is C (Celerity). Distance is L (wavelength). Time is T (period in seconds). $C = L / T$

However, a key ingredient is missing. Ocean swells are gravity waves. The force of gravity is a constant and must be represented. Without going into the complex maths that determines how this constant is expressed, trust me, the number needed is 1.56 (metric). In other words:

$C = 1.56 \times T$
C (speed) x T (period) = L (Length)

How fast is a 20-second swell?
1.56 x 20 s = 31.2 m/s (112 km/h)
Wavelength? 31.2 m/s x 20 s = 624 m

How fast is a 10-second swell?
1.56 x 10 s = 15.6 m/s (56 km/h)
Wavelength? 10 s x 15.6 m/s = 156 m

Tsunami, by Hokusai, c. 1825.

THREE-IN-ONE: Three charts show the same storm in October 2002. *Below*, **a synoptic chart drawn by the South African Weather Service.** *Below middle*, **a US Navy chart showing white capping probability.** *Bottom*, **a US Navy chart showing wave period.**

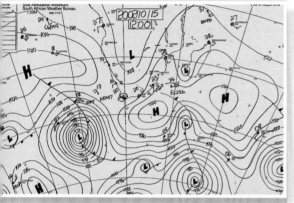

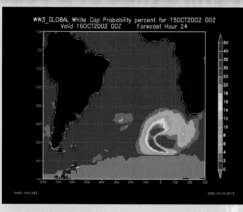

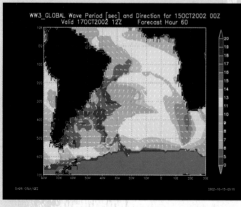

Wave period

Swell interval is the most informing component of swell. Not only does it indicate speed but, more importantly, energy. The stronger a wind blows (if the duration and distance are right), the bigger and more powerful the swell that rolls off the end of the production line. The period, or interval between successive swells, grows longer in stronger winds. Longer-period swells have more energy than short-period swells, because they have longer wavelengths and move faster. These two variables are tied to period by the equations discussed on page 91.

A 10-second swell has a wavelength of 156 metres, moves at just under 60 km/h in the open ocean and is driven by energy that extends to 78 metres below the surface (half its wavelength).

A 20-second swell has a length of 624 metres, moves at 112 km/h and – the clincher – its energy extends to 312 metres beneath it, so it moves a lot more water. Also, a 20-second swell moves at twice the speed of a 10 second swell.

This is why period is so important. A two-metre swell at 10 seconds in the open ocean is hardly a swell at all. It might translate to frequent, but weak two- to four-foot surf. However, a two-metre swell at 20 seconds is a different proposition, with grinding but probably sporadic six- to eight-foot surf with long waits between sets.

Swell height is not always a reliable indicator of what to expect, more so if the swell has travelled a long distance. You need to check the period charts and the height charts when scouring the Internet for forecasts. A nearby storm can build huge windswells at the coast, but these subside quickly because their shorter periods mean shorter wavelengths and shallower energy. There may have been a lot of wind, but without the duration or distance, swells are restricted to short steep waves, as opposed to undulating rollers with a lot more submerged energy. Fully developed swells move from the generating area losing height but retaining a much higher proportion of the energy that can still result in a powerful wave. It is for this reason that reading only a height chart is not enough to accurately predict surfing conditions. In fact, you have a range of charts to look at, including synoptic, swell height, swell period and even white-capping probability charts.

Units of measurement

As a unit for measuring height, the metre is a little too vague for the kind of detail surfers want. One metre occurs every 3.28 feet. Surfers have 3.28 times more ways to describe the size of a wave over a paltry one for the metric system. How doff will you sound saying, 'New Pier is 0.625 metres today, but we're expecting a 1.25-metre pulse this arvie.' Surfers can relate to two foot and four foot a lot easier, because we measure our body height and the length of our surfboards in feet and inches. If the wave face is six-feet high, we know it will be about head high unless you're a lightey in which case it might be double overhead.

The maritime industry – particularly in the US where wave modelling technology originates – relies on the imperial units of measurements. Models depict surface wind over the ocean and the distances they blow in knots and nautical miles. This consistency makes mathematical sense. You know that a swell moving at 25 knots from a storm 1 000 nautical miles away will reach you in 40 hours thanks to the basic equation 'time equals distance divided by speed'. You can't mix metres and knots when there is mathematical relevancy.

However, when it comes to the equations governing swell mechanics, scientists use metric units, such as metres for wavelength. There is a mathematical correlation between speed, wavelength and wave period (the interval between waves expressed in seconds) and there needs to be consistency in these equations.

Trying to use imperial units would be total chaos, according to Professor Tony Butt, a respected oceanographer who enjoys his annual trip to Cape Town to surf big waves. 'Imagine trying to work with pounds, shillings and pence, or yards, rods, cones, perches and poles, gallons and fluid ounces,' he says.

When it comes to wave height, some wave models will give you feet or metres or both, but will rarely mix imperial and metric units. The bottom line is to know some of the basic conversions, not so much for calculating stuff, but to convert data to the unit you are comfortable with.

Conversions

1 metre = 3.28 feet
1 statutory mile = 1.609 km
1 nautical mile = 1.853 km
1 knot = 1 nautical mile per hour
1 m/s = 3.6 km/h
60 knots = 100 km/h

SWELL RADIATION: The digital journey ends in a real-life experience.

WW3_GLOBAL Swell Wave Height [ft] and Direction for 13JUN2002 12Z
Valid 14JUN2002 12Z   Forecast Hour 24

WW3_GLOBAL Wave Period [sec] and Direction for 13JUN2002 12Z
Valid 14JUN2002 00Z   Forecast Hour 12

How swell moves

As swells move from their generating area, they smooth out, stretching into undulating rollers – tubes of energy spreading outwards in giant radial arcs.

As alluded to, short-period swell occurs at a higher frequency, with short wavelengths. The relative steepness of a short swell – imagine a concertina pushed in – makes it more susceptible to decay from opposing winds because there is more drag for the wind to grip. The shallower energy base of the slower-moving short swells deprives them of the stamina to cover the vast distances covered by swells that are more powerful.

The energy in longer-period groundswells erodes more slowly after the initial subsidence (swell loses up to 60 percent in the first 700 nautical miles from the storm). The further swell travels, the less energy is lost. After thousands of nautical miles – like the tip of an iceberg protruding from the sea – only a small manifestation of the energy is evident above the surface. The swell is very long, up to 700 metres, but does not seem very high, maybe only two metres.

A lot more energy exists beneath the hump we see gliding along the surface. The submerged power is realised only when the swell reaches a far shore. The sea floor forces the energy towards the surface, compressing the swell upwards into a wave.

If you look at a swell height chart (above left) that shows swell 3 000 nautical miles from the originating storm, you might see a vague, loosely scattered area of colours indicating uninspiring swell heights of three to six feet. However, look at the swell period chart (above right). Do you see an emphatically shaped arc stretching across the ocean edged by a dark red or purple stripe in front, and a procession of virulently coloured bands behind it in diminishing layers of orange, yellow and green?

The red denotes the longest-period swells out in front, with peak periods of 15 seconds or more, followed by the shorter, and therefore slower, swells behind. If you see that, prepare to get excited. Swell is coming.

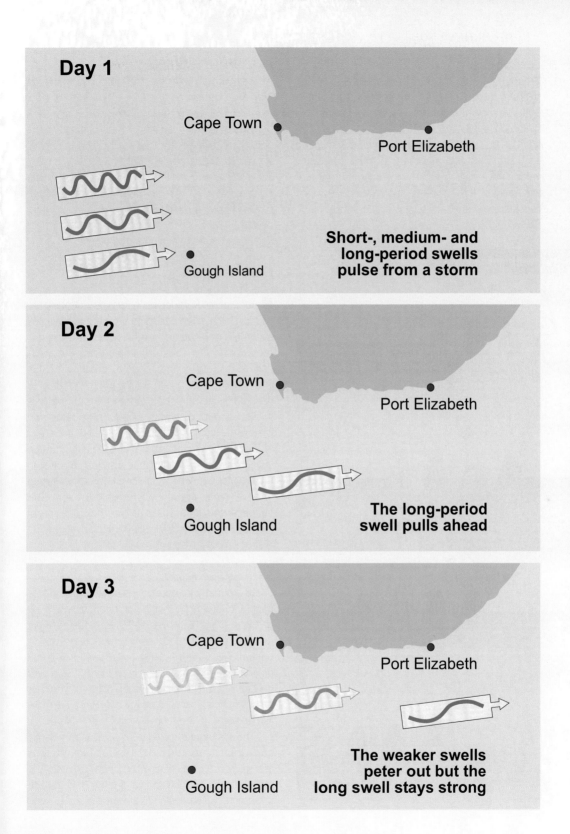

Day 1

Cape Town

Port Elizabeth

Short-, medium- and long-period swells pulse from a storm

Gough Island

Day 2

Cape Town

Port Elizabeth

The long-period swell pulls ahead

Gough Island

Day 3

Cape Town

Port Elizabeth

The weaker swells peter out but the long swell stays strong

Gough Island

Swell trains

Groups of waves travel at half the speed of the swells in them. This quirk of physics means that a 20-second swell moves at 31.2 m/s (112 km/h) in the ocean, but the group only moves at 15.6 m/s (56 km/h). This is due to a conveyor belt effect within each set. You'll find that the front swell constantly fades and a new swell is constantly reforming at the back of the set. This anomaly needs to be considered when making your call, or it will still be flat when you arrive amped for your surf session!

Swell movement

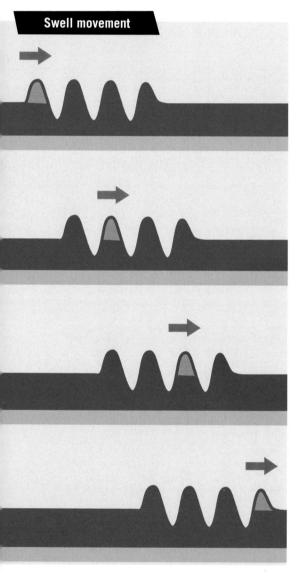

Same height, huge power

A swell with an interval of 10 seconds travels at 15.6 m/s. The speed of a 20-second swell is 31.2 m/s. That is twice as fast. However, there is a bigger exponential variation when it comes to the energy that drives the two swells. The energy of a swell extends to a depth of half its wavelength. For a 20-second swell, this is 312 metres. For the 10-second swell it is a mere 78 metres. Both swells are two metres high, yet one is much more powerful, with exponentially more volume, more speed and more energy than the other.

From swell to wave

After its long journey, a swell approaches the shore. As soon as its submerged energy encounters the sea floor, the swell begins to morph into what will eventually be a breaking wave. Scientists call this process shoaling. The submerged energy of swells begins to drag on the bottom, creating friction and slowing the swell. Swells will bend around headlands, slowing down more where the water is shallower, but not slowing down at the same rate where the water is deeper. This creates the effect of the swell swinging around and breaking on the inside of a point, for instance. In areas of uneven underwater bathymetry, the swell becomes warped and will break unevenly. The best surf spots are characterised by a uniformity in the transition of the sea floor to the shallows, particularly along the reef or sandbar where the wave will break.

Swell vs. wave height

There are many interpretations of wave size. Some people refer to the height of deep ocean swell (peak to trough). Others prefer to measure wave face at a particular location where it breaks (top to bottom) because the same-sized swell will break differently elsewhere. There is even confusion over how to measure swell. Hawaiians famously under-call swell height. A six-foot wave in Hawaii is more like an eight- to ten-foot wave in South Africa.

The confusion is rooted in variables that influence how hard and high a wave breaks. These permutations are made from swell direction (how exposed the break is to the swell), transition of sea floor from deep to shallow, water depth in the impact zone, wind

AT THE SHORE: Numerous factors influence the way a wave breaks.

	Flat	Slope of sea floor	Steep	
Onshore		Wind		Offshore
	Short	Wavelength	Long	

Gently breaking wave

Tubing wave

direction and speed, and wave power (period). Take a long-period swell that has travelled from a storm 2 000 nautical miles away. Height has diminished dramatically, but below the surface, extending more than 300 metres deep, is exponentially more energy than a shallow short-period wave. This submerged energy means bigger waves at the shore. Swells grow larger when they break because this submerged energy is realised when it encounters a shallow reef or sandbar. The wave jacks up. Some waves double – or even triple – in size.

Wind is a factor too. Offshore wind holds up a wave, delaying it from breaking. The wave stands up higher and breaks harder. Onshore winds push the waves forward, making them break earlier and softer.

Beauty and the Beast

At Teahupoo in Tahiti, perhaps the scariest wave in the world, there is a weird disproportion between swell size and wave size. The swell gets bigger, but the wave doesn't seem to. That infamous ocean 'step' just gets deeper. More water sucks off the reef and the lip gets thicker! Powerful deep-ocean groundswells loom suddenly. An unusually rapid transition from deep ocean to shallow ledge does little to cull their power and speed. When they smack that coral slab, we watch transfixed at a Siamese mutation of yin and yang horribly conjoined. Imagine watching *Gone with the Wind* and *The Texas Chainsaw Massacre* on a split screen in a dark room while murderous thieves lurk in the shadows. A hill made of beautiful blue glass shape-shifts into a hump-backed monster squatting and snarling over the reef. In a horrific convulsion, the beast vomits an eight-foot lip that hurtles through the air. The impact is like a ton of TNT detonating. The compression is so intense; a giant spume blasted from the barrel obliterates your view of the wave.

JAW DROPPER: New Zealander Doug Young rides a bomb at Teahupoo, an entry at the Billabong XXL 2006 Awards.

THREE-SIDED COAST: Notwithstanding numerous twists and turns, the South African shoreline faces west, south and east.

The South African coast

The southern tip of the African continent is the meeting places of two mighty oceans, the Atlantic and the Indian. They do not meet at Cape Point, as widely believed, but in a wide area south of Cape Agulhas, where their representative currents, the cold Benguela of the Atlantic and the warm Agulhas of the Indian, mix together. This is the Agulhas Bank, a large slab of continental shelf that extends southward from Agulhas for 110 nautical miles. According to respected marine biologist and photographer Tom Peschak, the two currents divide the coast into 'two contrasting marine ecosystems that rank among the richest, most biologically diverse and oceanographically complex on the planet. The Atlantic Ocean, with its awesome productivity and abundance of animal and plant biomass, borders the subcontinent's western flank, while the Indian Ocean that lies on the east has an ecological signature of great biodiversity.' The total length of the coast is just under 3 000 kilometres.

Continental shelf

The continental shelf is the submerged rim of the continents. The land mass of the continents continues from the shoreline under the sea until a final drop-off at a depth of about 300 metres – the real edge of the continent. The sea floor slopes gradually towards this cliff, then drops towards the abyssal plains of the deep. At some points, the shelf is wider than others. As mentioned earlier, the Agulhas Bank is an example of a wide shelf area. Off the Eastern Cape and KwaZulu-Natal, the shelf narrows dramatically to within a couple of nautical miles in places. The narrowest point is off Point St Johns, on the Wild Coast.

Currents

The cold Benguela current flows up the west coast of South Africa and the warm Agulhas flows down the east coast. Simple. Bear in mind, contrary to common belief, the Mozambique current does not feed into the Agulhas current, except where it mixes with inshore waters along the continental shelf off KwaZulu-Natal. Research in the early 2000s showed that the currents originate differently. The Mozambique originates from the south equatorial current, a huge gyre that sits in the Indian Ocean and circulates water in a counter-clockwise direction towards the east coasts of Somalia, Kenya and Tanzania. The centrifugal force of the earth's rotation (Coriolis) deflects the coastward flow south. However, the 1 600-kilometre-long island of Madagascar cleaves the current into two streams. The Mozambique current flows south off East Africa, and the Eastern Madagascar current flows south off the east side of the island. The Agulhas current, however, originates in the southwestern Indian Ocean sub-gyre. It circulates towards Africa south of Madagascar, and flows down the coast along the continental shelf.

COLD ZONE: Upwelled waters off the West Coast.

Agulhas

The Agulhas Current is warm, between 18° and 28°C, influencing the climate of KwaZulu-Natal. Coupled with warm air masses moving with the current and moisture-bearing northeast winds, KwaZulu-Natal has a sub-tropical climate. Only 60 nautical miles wide, the Agulhas Current flows up to six knots off the east coast of South Africa. Between Durban and East London, it accelerates along the edge of the continental shelf, making it one of the fastest-flowing currents in the world.

Benguela

An icy current that emanates from the Antarctic, the Benguela pushes up the west coast past Cape Agulhas and Namibia as far as Angola. The Benguela is 120 to 180 nautical miles wide. The water is icy, ranging from 8° to 16°C. The current widens further as it flows north into the tropics, up to 400 nautical miles off Angola. In summer on the west coast, there are many days of onshore southwest wind, often as a result of hot inland air sucking cooler air off the sea. These winds worsen later in the day, when the earth radiates more solar energy. When the south Atlantic high is entrenched off the coast, summer southeast trade winds dominate. Despite its seemingly barren aspect, the west coast is rich in marine biodiversity, with these southeast winds upwelling a nutrient-rich cocktail of waters from the Atlantic and Indian Oceans. The western edge of the current is transient, containing temporary and seasonal eddies shed from what scientists call the Agulhas Retroflection.

Where the oceans meet

As the Benguela flows up the west coast, so does the Agulhas flow down the east coast. The Agulhas Current follows the contour of the continental shelf southwards. The Benguela Current flows north, deflected by the western edge of the continental shelf. The two currents don't meet in a definitive way. They mix in a series of eddies spread over a wide area. The area where they mix varies, but generally it's around the Agulhas Bank off the southern tip of Africa. Some of the Agulhas Current flows around the Cape of Good Hope and up the southwest Cape coast.

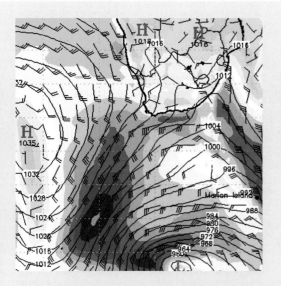
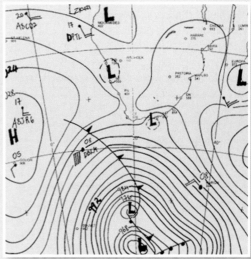

EAST COAST ANGLE: Interaction between a high- and a low-pressure system produces a strong south swell, which is ideal for the east coast, especially the southern Cape.

Coastal orientation

South Africa's coastline faces three directions: west, south and east. The prevailing swell direction is west to southwest – swells that form in the Roaring Forties west or southwest of the country. This is good for the Western Cape, but if there is too much west in the swell, it goes right past the east coast of South Africa. This coastline prefers a south or southeast swell direction.

Many good-quality breaks face away from the predominant swell direction. While the southwest Cape faces the brunt of the westerly or southwest swells that come from the deep, south or southeast swells move past most breaks on the west coast.

The east coast has the same problem with the prevailing west or southwest swell. These swells travel parallel to the coast, and will only swing inwards to break at certain exposed breaks, depending on their exact angle and their energy. Really long-period swells, with a submerged energy reaching as far as 350 metres, begin shoaling right from the edge of the continental shelf, bending towards the coast at certain places.

Bays and headlands

A common surf-spot set-up in South Africa is a large bay, with a point break on the southern end, facing north, and the wild side or southern side of the point facing more directly towards the predominant swell direction, which is southwest. This exposed stretch picks up a lot more swell but only the deeper energy swells make it around the corner to the surf spot. These long-period swells begin shoaling – feeling the sea floor – a lot earlier. They slow down in the shallower water wide of the point, refracting around the shape of the land and sweeping into the break. Only the higher quality waves – those of greater power and cleaner lines – reach the break. We may not be Indo, but our point breaks have built-in swell filtration that approximates that perfection at times.

The mixed-up windswells and mess blown up by the southwester stay on the exposed wild side and do not make it to the break because their energy base is shallow and passes the shoaling area without any refraction. This effect can be seen on all good left- or right-breaking points in South Africa. It also explains why the majority of

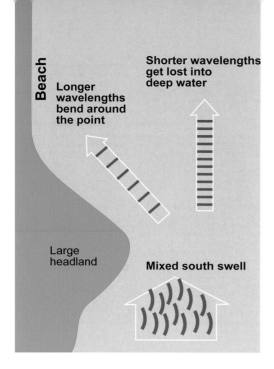

Beach

Longer wavelengths bend around the point

Shorter wavelengths get lost into deep water

Large headland

Mixed south swell

the best waves up the east coast are point breaks that peel to the right, such as Jeffreys Bay, while the west coast offers superlative left-hand points, such as Elands Bay.

Whether swell reaches up the east coast beyond Port Elizabeth and into the Wild Coast and KwaZulu-Natal depends on the speed, angle and intensity of the storm; whether it holds its line as it goes past. If it tracks high enough, it will push swell up and around the east coast as it starts turning a corner at Cape St Francis. At this point, instead of running from west to east, the coastline begins to head northeast. If the storm fades prematurely, or falls to the south or southeast, the swell comes out of the west, and misses the east coast.

West-facing coast

The 850-kilometre coast from the Orange River Mouth down to Cape Agulhas faces the Atlantic Ocean. Primary swell direction for surf spots in this region are west to southwest, with some south-facing breaks preferring more south in the swell. The primary source of swell emanates from storms passing by to the south, or from distant storms off South America that track towards the coast, peaking as they go. This occurs mostly in

winter. The ideal scenario is for a storm to peak 500-1 000 nautical miles from the coast, and then fade or fall away to the south. A secondary source of swell comes from southeast trade winds blowing up the coast, pushing in limited swell to south-facing breaks, notably those in False Bay on the eastern coast of the Cape Peninsula. False Bay faces south to southeast.

South-facing coast

The 650-kilometre coast from Cape Agulhas to Port Elizabeth faces the Indian Ocean but its aspect is more southerly before the coast turns a corner after Algoa Bay and heads in a northeast direction. Primary direction for surf spots is swell with any south in it, preferably from a south-southwest to east-southeast direction. Strong southwest swells refract around the bottom end of the bays, many of which face southeast, and break along the points on their inside northern rim. The primary source of swell emanates from storms passing by to the south, again most active in winter. The ideal scenario is a high-pressure cell chasing a storm passing in the south, and ridging in behind it to the west. This influx of air towards the low often bends the peak wind direction into a more southerly or southeast angle. The originating winds point directly towards the south-facing coast of South Africa.

East-facing coast

The 1 300-kilometre coast from Port Elizabeth to Kosi Bay faces southeast into the Indian Ocean. The primary swell direction for surf spots in this region is south to east, with southeast the best direction for many breaks. The swell originates from a number of sources that work in a seasonal cycle. There is a lot of strong southwest to southeast swell pushing in winter. In summer, northeast to east winds around the northern part of the Indian Ocean high point towards the coast – albeit producing mostly soft windswell, although strong trades can produce big surf on occasion. It is rarely flat on the Wild Coast and KwaZulu-Natal in summer.

The cherries on the top are the fierce tropical cyclones off Madagascar and Mozambique that push in a big east groundswell, also in the summer months.

AIRBORNE: Good snowfalls in the Matroosberg, near Cape Town, were produced by a huge winter front in August 2003.

Seasons

When South Africa moves into winter, the westerly wind belt begins to move north. Storm systems – which are always moving west to east in the southern hemisphere – track closer to South Africa. Considering that Cape Agulhas is only five degrees from 40 ° south, this is not far to go. When the winter storms veer near the coast, many surf spots, particularly those in the Western Cape, are lambasted with storm swell from a west or southwest direction. Bad weather strikes for days on end as cold fronts move in, sometimes stacking up behind one another like squadron after squadron of bombers, bays loaded with water-based munitions. Huge bands of cloud are swung far to the north like a slingshot from a giant vortex. The stormy conditions emanate from the epicentre of each storm, and sweep over the land as the low-pressure cells move south of the country.

As the southern hemisphere reverses its oscillation away from winter, the sun begins to rise higher in the sky and the westerly storm belt retreats south. High-pressure systems become dominant on both sides of Africa once more, acting like buffer zones to the southern storms. Summer cold fronts are occasional and brief. The swell comes and goes quickly, the weather reverting to dry, sunny and hot in the Western Cape as prevailing southeast trade winds return. On the east coast, the prevailing northeast onshore trade wind returns, pushing in soft, mushy surf, and the weather becomes wet, hot and humid once more.

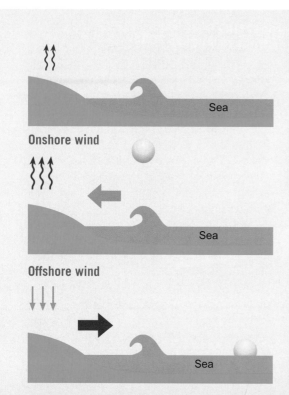

Onshore wind

Offshore wind

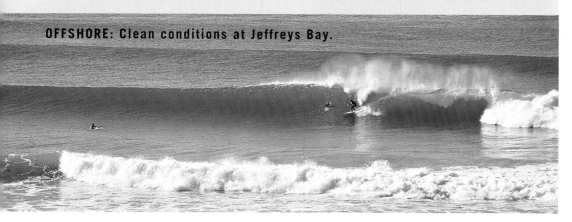

OFFSHORE: Clean conditions at Jeffreys Bay.

Land and sea breezes

Coastal winds in South Africa blow in seasonal cycles, as well as in diurnal cycles, due to the differences in absorption and release of solar radiation on the land and the sea from day to night. The ocean absorbs and releases heat a lot slower and more steadily than the land, which absorbs heat from the sun during the day but quickly loses it at night (see diagram above), particularly when there is little or no cloud cover. By morning, a high-pressure area of cold air sits over the land, while the ocean continues to release gradual heat, resulting in a mild low-pressure system offshore. The air moves off the land towards the ocean, and you have your common-or-garden morning land breeze. Once the sun rises, the reflected solar radiation off the land soon overtakes that of the sea, and the effect is reversed. The onshores gain momentum, blowing at their strongest at the peak of the land's release of heat.

The berg wind blows down from the slopes of inland mountain ranges towards the sea. Momentum grows during the night as the land cools further. As it approaches the coast, the air is sucked towards the sea by slowly rising warm air off the temperate ocean. The compression of the sinking cold air down the mountains, coupled with its journey across the warmer coastal plains, warms up the air. It arrives as a dry, warm breeze feathering the waves into that sublime offshore perfection. In KwaZulu-Natal, despite its sub-tropical climate, this air can be freezing cold in winter because it flows down from the snow-covered Drakensberg Mountains at night.

Berg winds are directly offshore at many breaks. This makes the wave hold up for longer, and creates a smooth wave face. However, it depends on the geographic location of the spot. Jeffreys Bay, for instance, is cross-shore in a northwest berg wind. Generally, however, the berg wind is a sought-after wind.

Rogue waves

Freak waves occur more often than previously thought, according to studies by a scientific collaboration launched in 1980 called MaxWave. Oceanographers and other experts teamed up with the European Space Agency, the German Aerospace Centre and other research bodies to conduct a satellite census of waves around the world. In three weeks, 10 waves at least 82-foot high were measured.

Most surfers know that the east coast of South Africa is a renowned hot spot for abnormal waves that have sunk ships and damaged many more. But why?

The basic explanation boils down to a combination of swell and current. The Agulhas Current – strongest just seaward of the continental shelf in a band roughly 50 nautical miles wide – surges down the coast at six knots. The current flows into deep ocean swells generated in the roaring forties to the southwest. Groups of these powerful swells, with periods of 14 to 18 seconds and wavelengths up to 600 metres, are moving at speeds of up to 30 knots. As the current flows into the oncoming rollers, they slow down. As they slow, their wavelengths shorten. As they move closer together, they steepen. Instead of a rolling wave, the front sloping in the same proportion to the back, a lopsided triangle forms, the front steeper than the back. Northeast trade winds blowing with the current generate windswell that also runs into the upcoming rollers, amplifying this concertina effect.

However, there is more. When strong cold fronts sweep up from the south, southwest gales blow into the current. If the fetch is long enough, strong winds only need about eight hours to generate wind swell that can reach 40 foot with periods of seven to ten seconds and lengths up to 156 metres. These wind waves are steepest where the opposing northeast current is at its strongest (along the seaward side of the shelf). If the above long-period swell is around, random waves suddenly form as underlying swells momentarily join wind swells, stacking up on each other. This occurs because the faster, more powerful groundswells pass through the slower wind waves. When the peaks are superimposed, they are in phase, absorbing the height of both. When out of phase, swells momentarily diminish (when a peak overlaps a trough). If you had two wave trains with heights of 20 feet, the in-phase swells would be 40-foot high. The phrase 'double-up' is the long and short of it, so to speak, but in some scary cases, triple or quadruple is closer to the truth.

Research has studied other factors behind rogue waves off South Africa. One is the inshore counter current. Southwest gales exert friction on the sea, causing the surface to drift with the wind in the shallow waters inside the powerful opposing thrust of the Agulhas Current flowing off the deep end of the shelf. This gradient current forms a bulge at the transition between the two opposing currents along the shelf. On top of this, sea levels can rise due to the lower isobaric pressure (less atmospheric weight) in passing low pressure storms, accentuating the bulge.

In summary, abnormal waves are formed by a confluence of in-phase swells from different wave trains, the steepening effect of the Agulhas Current and a bulge along the edge caused by the counter current and the passage of low pressure systems. Scientists have calculated their theoretical maximum at 198 feet.

Ships have vanished. Myths linger. However, it remains an unhappy stroke of fate that sees modern ships succumb to such a wave. Freak waves don't last. Within minutes – if not seconds – they subside again. Despite ongoing studies, oceanographers still don't fully understand the phenomenon. It might be difficult to explain why it happens, but what happens is horrifyingly simple. Ship climbs up large swell. Big ship suddenly pitches into an abnormally deep pit – the trough preceding a rogue wave. The bow falls into the trough. Before it has had time to pull free, an 80-foot wave rears above. For agonising seconds, a huge ship becomes a submarine. The superstructure snaps.

Fortunately, it does not happen too often. The SS *Waratah* sank without trace off the east coast in 1909, with the loss of all 211 crew and passengers. Six ships off the east coast reported rogue waves between 1964 and 1973. Five survived to tell the tale. *World Glory* – carrying 49 000 tons of crude oil – snapped like a twig on 13 June 1968 and sank within four hours. The Norwegian tanker *Wilstar* was nailed in 1974. She copped a sound structural beating from a rogue wave, but managed to limp to shore.

Skippers have strict instructions to avoid the continental shelf and the area 60 nautical miles seaward. Many ships are steered inside the shelf. Spend time on the Wild Coast of the Eastern Cape, and you will see ships that seem dangerously close to shore. However, it is a safety precaution.

Abnormal waves even occur beneath the surface. In 1963, nuclear submarine USS *Thresher*, while doing deep diving tests off Massachusetts, allegedly encountered an internal wave: a pulse of energy moving along a density discontinuity. The submarine's bow ascended as the wave passed, and the submarine slipped down the back of the wave, sliding deeper than its design allowed. The submarine imploded. All hands were lost.

Wave prediction

While the technology that drives weather-modelling systems has brought about revolutionary changes in our ability to predict the weather, global warming has blurred the picture. Trends that were once constant have become erratic. The behaviour of storms – and therefore the winds that produce swell – has become harder to monitor and track due to increased volatility in the atmosphere. But, climate notwithstanding, the Internet has brought weather prediction into our homes and offices. The emergence of wave models coincided with advances on the Web. Now we can get anything we want in the Internet candy store. Behind that monitor screen lies a maelstrom of binary data – billions of bytes spewing from über-computers endlessly analysing the earth. Swathes from weather satellites swaddle the globe in a digital cocoon of data collection and assimilation. Crisscrossing each other to map the planet's oceans, instruments scope the sea surface and the atmosphere above it. Satellite data and on-site instrumentation from weather stations to drifting buoys are fed in an endless loop of calculation and recalibration into mega-computers with unparalleled processing power. Information is distilled and packaged into formats palatable to humans, disgorged at the other end as hindcasts, nowcasts and forecasts. Not unlike Alice in Wonderland, we get a neat little box marked 'surf me'.

Click through to pictorial, animated, graphic or textual renditions of wave and wind data. Want to know percentage of white-cap probability in that big storm down south? You got it. Need average swell wave height and direction? Of course. Want to watch a radial arc of a perfect, powerful swell expand in glorious 2D animation – a vast red ripple expanding from the generating storm?

You have it, and then some.

Most surfers want the basics: wave height, wave direction and how strong and from where the wind will blow. Some want to know whether there will be a mixture of swells, and what the interval will be between the biggest swells.

Surfers do not care too much about the weather. Rain makes you wet. So does the sea. Who cares? Your average surfer does not want to deal with complex stuff like vorticity.

Thankfully, as surfers proudly proclaim, it is simple. Wind generates swell. Luckily for us, wave models are based on wind predictions from atmospheric models.

Wavewatch III

This amazing piece of software is the cornerstone of surf forecasts on the Internet.

The most reliable surf forecasting system is Wavewatch III, a form of software developed by the American National Oceanic and Atmospheric Administration (NOAA) and the National Centers for Environmental Prediction (NCEP).

Wavewatch processes wind data provided by the Global Forecast System (GFS). GFS gets it from a satellite service managed by NOAA and NASA. Wavewatch extracts from GFS only data that relates to sea surface conditions. It does not need the generic data used in weather forecasting (the biggest client of GFS is the US National Weather Service). See http://goespoes.gsfc.nasa.gov for more information.

The raw GFS data comes from GOES (geo-stationary operational environmental satellites) and POES (polar-orbiting environmental satellites).

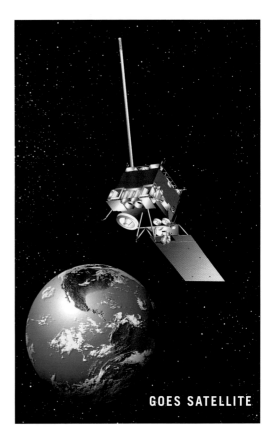

GOES SATELLITE

GOES SATELLITE IMAGE: Hurricane Isabella, off the US state of North Carolina, 2003.

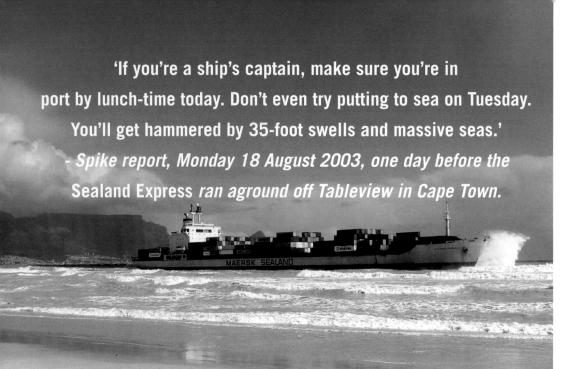

'If you're a ship's captain, make sure you're in port by lunch-time today. Don't even try putting to sea on Tuesday. You'll get hammered by 35-foot swells and massive seas.'
- Spike report, Monday 18 August 2003, one day before the Sealand Express ran aground off Tableview in Cape Town.

SNOWBOUND: Snowboarders enjoyed heavy falls in the Matroosberg from the same storm in August 2003 that caused the *Sealand Express* to run aground.

GOES enables real-time nowcasts. POES enables longer term forecasts (there can't be many South Africans working at NASA).

The raw wind data output by GFS comes from real-time readings from GOES and POES. Gaps in the data are filled in to produce a global picture of wind behaviour on the sea surface. Wavewatch III crunches its selected sea data and outputs chunks of information, which is then harvested by NOAA, the US Navy, Wind Guru, Magic Seaweed, Buoyweather, Wavescape and a growing number of others.

These websites publish the data as swell and wind predictions up to seven days ahead, visible as graphic charts, text tables or animated maps. Different websites might use different colours and styles unique to them, but it all comes from Wave-watch III.

The wave modelling technology originated from nationalistic goals – saving lives, protecting property and last but not least, providing the military with strategic information. You can't invade countries when the swell is huge. The recreational spin-off is bigger than many envisaged, because it has become critical to ocean users' lifestyles.

Here's how it works.

Making the call

Now you should be able to make a call on the next swell to hit your local break. Visit wavescape.co.za and check out the surf forecasting section for websites that offer virtual buoy forecasts, surface wind charts, synoptic charts and many more. This is a DIY section aimed at the novice, or expert, surf forecaster or surfcaster.

Wavescape also runs specialised surf predictions and consultancies to help people with their lifestyle, or surf competition organisers.

All wave predictions come from the data we pick up from the Wavewatch III model. Sometimes we get it right. Sometimes we don't. Certainly, the technology is improving all the time, but nothing beats the constant comparison between what the models said and what you saw or experienced. There are some new advances in science that will impact surfers' quest for the holy grail (perfect, clean, powerful surf). One of these is the directional spectrum. Knowing the main wave interval (period) does not give you a completely accurate assessment of swell quality. It does not show you how spread out or focused the swell is (directional spread) or how many types of swell are in the swell (bandwidth). The directional spectrum indicates how focused and clean a swell might be, as opposed to a messy swell comprising different energies, heights and intervals.

As a rule, a long-range forecast beyond about six or seven days is dodgy. If you're 14 days out, and a model is calling a storm that hasn't even formed yet, hold firm and don't get over-excited. They invariably downgrade as the actual event draws closer. The models tend to overcall the severity of storms, which makes sense because human safety has always been the driving force behind the technology.

If you consider the many steps in the long process towards the eventual outcome – that cranking swell on your doorstep – you would be amazed that the models are so accurate, although this can only be properly experienced once you're three to five days out from the swell's arrival, which usually means the storm is in the early stages of its genesis.

A complex string of events leads to the experience you're striving for at a surf spot. Swell comes from wind that blows in a storm that forms from some-or-other glitch in the jet stream caused by upper-air instability. There's plenty of margin for error when there are so many steps involved.

ON THE MONEY: It's a good feeling when you get it right.

SEPTEMBER 2001

AGROUND: The *Ikan Tanda* at Misty Cliffs, near Cape Town.

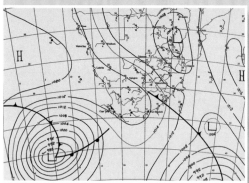

2pm, 4 September 2001

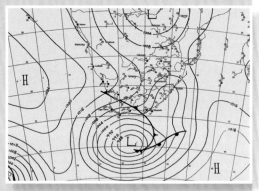

2pm, 5 September 2001

One of the fiercest storms in Cape Town occurred early on Wednesday 5 September 2001. A storm surge, coupled with a huge spring high tide and swells of up to 60 feet, caused widespread damage in Cape Town, and claimed the 10 000-ton iron-ore carrier

Ikan Tanda, which ran aground at Misty Cliffs. Wind speeds of 160 km/h and swells of up to 17 metres were recorded off Kommetjie. It was the result of a cut-off low that deepened rapidly only about 500 miles southwest of Cape Town 36 hours earlier.

MARCH 2007

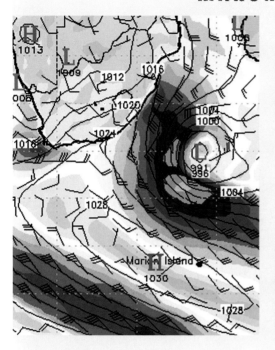

AWASH: Cave Rock on the Bluff, Durban.

The prediction

'By Sunday, the southwest is screaming through and there's chaos out to sea, with gale-force, extremely strong winds hammering the east coast and smacking the soft east swell into oblivion. Any swell out there is being wind-blasted into oblivion, but a new groundswell is in the offing, locked in the cyclo-genesis, with 50-knot-plus winds starting to angle towards the coast several hundred miles out to sea. KZN is hammered by the wind around the storm Sunday and Monday, with HUGE SURF AHEAD on Monday and Tuesday. A dik south to south-southeast swell is jacking late Sunday, getting seriously big Sunday evening and overnight. Monday morning is fresh to strong westerly and the surf is GIANT! Expect DIK wide-banded south to southeast swell 15- to 20-foot grinding in moderating winds while off the continental shelf, it's heaving 30 to 40 foot.' - *Spike surf report, Friday 16 March 2007*

What actually happened

'Extraordinary scenes of mayhem as the South Pier in Durban gets pummelled by giant marching battalions of 20-foot-plus southeast swell. The pier keeps disappearing underwater. Giant slabs of concrete are being shoved with impunity as dubus storm swell smacks banana-land with a swell of stupendously ginormous girth. The southwest buster is still howling after a VICIOUS peak yesterday up to 50 knots. The sea is HEAVING. There are 50- to 60-foot swells lurching off the continental shelf, creating maximum extremities for boats triangulated from Durbs to the Wild Coast to Southern Madagascar to Maputo. Okay quadrulated. Tow ous with screws loose are strapping in and casting jetskis off. Other ous can but gawp at tsunami foam-balls bathing the promenade with Davy Jones' washing. A spring high tide at three in the morning didn't help either.' - *Spike surf report, Monday 19 March 2007*

AUGUST 2005

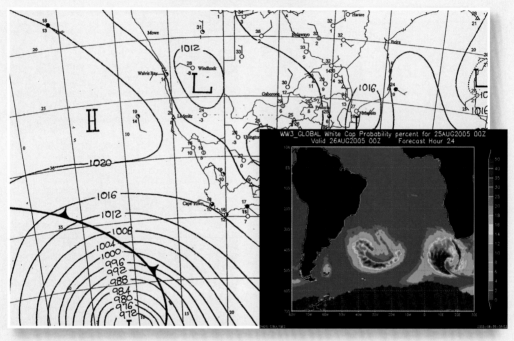

WAVE WARNING: Synoptic chart and US Navy white cap probability chart, 26 August 2005.

'A very intense vortex was located southeast of South Georgia in the Southern Atlantic, with the pressure recorded by two drifting buoys dropping below 940 millibars. The fact that the low was semi-stationary increased the duration factor associated with the wave generation, and in the next four to five days, these waves travelled almost 3 000 nautical miles to reach the Cape of Good Hope by Friday evening, 26 August. They arrived in the form of a long-period swell with peak energy period in excess of 18 seconds (Slangkop Waverider buoy, offshore Cape Town). To complicate matters another deep vortex formed in the interim, much closer to Cape Town on 24 August. This second low – an upper cut-off low – also moved very slowly relative to the speed of a normal mid-latitude frontal trough.

The duration factor for wave generation was also increased. A rough calculation indicates that both wave components would arrive off Cape Town at approximately the same time. The result was a significant wave height of 33 foot – by far the highest since the start of the winter – at around 8 pm. It is a well-known phenomenon in False Bay for long-period swell to be refracted and focused onto certain parts of the coastline. This is particularly the case at the small fishing harbour of Kalk Bay. The harbour master had the foresight to send the trawlers along to the safer haven of Simon's Town. However two tourists inexplicably decided to take a stroll along the breakwater, and both ended up in the sea. Fortunately both were rescued.' - *South African Weather Services forecaster Ian Hunter*

FALSE BAY: A big clean swell wrapped around Cape Point.

STORMS RIVER: A monstrous storm swell pummelled the southern Cape.

JEFFREYS BAY: A handful of surfers dared to tackle 12-foot waves at Supertubes.

MEN IN GREY

Sharks

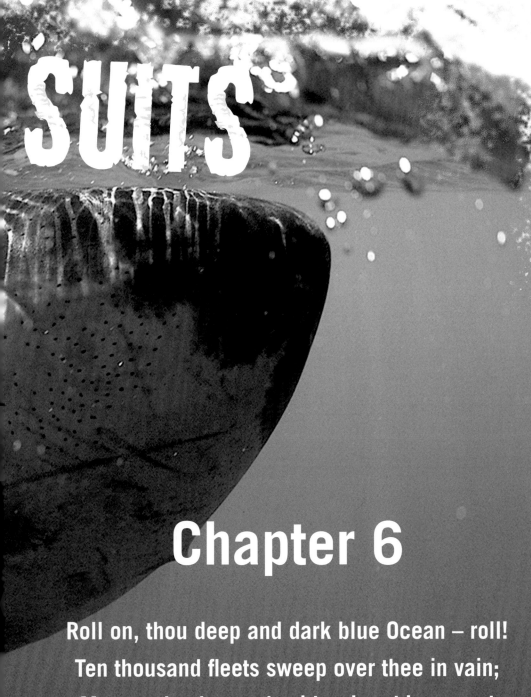

SUITS

Chapter 6

Roll on, thou deep and dark blue Ocean – roll!
Ten thousand fleets sweep over thee in vain;
Man marks the earth with ruin – his control
Stops with the shore

Lord Byron, 1818

Scientists have called for perspective. If sharks wanted to eat us, they say, we'd be in big trouble, yet incidents are few despite increasing numbers of people and sharks. It takes one scary tale to spark a primal terror that boffins insist is not justified, especially with strides in preventive strategies, repellent technology and marine science.

I will never forget the story from my good friend at Rhodes University in the 1980s, Wayne 'Sparky' McMillan. He recalled how one of the country's most infamous shark attacks unravelled before his eyes. His friend Alex Macun was taken by a great white at Ntlonyane on the Wild Coast in June 1982. The shark struck while they were paddling back up the point early one morning after catching an epic wave on a beautiful four- to five-foot day. Sparky was just behind his friend in the line-up when he was hit. He told me how they ran down the point to retrieve their friend's body from the beach break. Despite frenzied attempts to pull him out of the water, the shark came back. They had only a chewed surfboard to take back to his family.

Having grown up in nearby Coffee Bay I was deeply saddened, but it did not deter us from surfing the area, even during the sardine run. Sparky never recovered from that trauma. We once surfed classic six-foot Mdumbe with the Trow brothers from Coffee Bay, but Sparky was taciturn and reluctant. He was out of the water after 20 minutes. A sad irony is that he died, alone in a hotel room, during a spiritual pilgrimage to India almost 20 years afterwards. His death was due to complications arising from dysentery. Like his friend, he too became a rare statistic.

When it comes to statistics and shark attacks, the famous quote by scholar Alfred Housman springs to mind: 'Statistics in the hands of an engineer are like a lamppost to a drunk – they're used more for support than illumination.'

If you visit Thailand frequently, and you always sleep under coconut palms, you are at risk of dying by falling coconut, an overused comparative statistic held up against shark fatalities. But if you don't sleep under palm trees? Well, then the statistics move on – chances of getting cancer, dying in a car crash or being abducted by aliens.

Since avoiding the sea is not an option, the best we can do is reduce the chance of attack when possible.

The debate over why there has been an increase in attacks on surfers in recent years has run hot. Scientists are adamant that chumming is not a factor. They put it down to an increase in surfers, coupled with the rejuvenation of shark stocks due to conservation efforts.

What we know is that humans are not a shark's natural prey. But if we play in their domain, occasionally we will be bitten.

Sharks have far more to fear from us than we need to fear them. Humans kill more than 100 million sharks every year. Fewer than 25 humans are killed by sharks, at a push. That's one person for every four million sharks. However, while some surfers may be comforted by the stats, others will refer you to comedian George Canning's quote: 'I can prove anything by statistics except the truth.'

Being told that we have a minuscule chance of being attacked is not helpful to surfers who regularly surf breaks that are known for shark activity.

Surfers who are addicted to getting good waves as often as they can run a higher risk of attack. Hardened to the many risks, they sometimes push

SARDINE RUN: Cape gannets dive-bomb massive sardine shoals off the East Coast.

KING OF THE HILL: The apex predator of our oceans, the great white shark.

their luck by surfing near shoals of fish, such as sardines or mullet, or when flood-water from rivers deposits organic material in the sea, making the water brown and murky. This is a frequent occurrence in the Transkei and KwaZulu-Natal, when summer rains swell the rivers.

Some surfers ignore bleeding cuts and continue surfing. The author has been guilty of this when surfing on the Wild Coast. In my youth we would often carry on surfing after seeing a shark. Once a large hammerhead cruised past. On another occasion, we watched fishermen catch a two-metre ragged tooth shark off the East Pier, Port Alfred, but we did not abandon our heat in a university surfing competition.

As surfers, if we were to subscribe to every precaution, we might as well take up golf.

On the whole, surfing is a safe sport. To use the statistics as a leaning post, shark attacks are rare, so don't get all wussie about going surfing.

In perspective

Death by shark is a minor statistic when compared to the annual mortality rate among South Africans, such as drowning, snake bite, smoking and and lightning. Scientists claim that the likelihood of a shark attack is minuscule.

Poisonous Snakes	15
Lightning	200
Drowning	408
Burnt To Death	871
Road Accidents	10 000
Murdered	20 000
Smoking	29 000
Aids	370 000 (probably more)
Sharks	Seven in 25 years

Source: Sharklife.co.za

Shark incidents

The introduction of shark nets in the 1960s saw the number of attacks decrease dramatically in KwaZulu-Natal, a traditional hunting ground for the Zambezi and Tiger sharks, two of the liveliest marine predators.

As of August 2007, there had been about 450 reported shark-related incidents in South Africa since 1913. Of those involving wave riders, 11 involved bodyboarders and 82 involved surfers. Of the 93 surfing-related incidents (excluding lifesavers, swimmers, kayakers and divers), eight were fatal. (Source, Global Shark Attack File, Shark Research Institute in Princeton, USA.)

Timeline

- **May 1981** Surfer Simon Hammerton, 24, Ntlonyane, 2.1-metre tiger shark, left leg surgically amputated.
- **June 1982** Surfer Alex Macun, 27, Ntlonyane, 2.4-metre great white, fatal.
- **December 1986** Bodyboarder Richardt Anton Olls, 21, The Strand, 3-metre great white, fatal.
- **July 1994** Surfer Bruce Corby, 22, Nahoon Reef, 4-metre great white, fatal.
- **July 1994** Surfer Andrew Carter, 31, Nahoon Reef, 4-metre great white (moments before Corby's attack), severe lacerations to leg.
- **July 1997** Australian surfer Mark Penche, 25, Ntlonyane, great white, fatal.
- **May 1998** Bodyboarder Neal Stephenson, 22, Keurbooms, 4-metre great white, leg severed.
- **June 1998** Bodyboarder Anton de Vos, 20, Gonubie Point, great white, fatal.
- **July 1999** Bodyboarder Hercules Pretorius, 14, Buffels Bay, great white, fatal.
- **July 2000** Surfer Shannon Ainslie, 15, Nahoon Reef, two great whites, minor injuries – the incident was filmed by a tourist on the beach.
- **August 2003** Surfer Joseph Krone, 16, Jeffreys Bay Point, great white, unharmed – a large bite on his board.
- **September 2003** Bodyboarder Dave Bornman, 19, Dunes, great white, fatal.
- **April 2004** Surfer JP Andrew, 16, Surfers' Corner Muizenberg, 5-metre great white, leg severed.
- **October 2004** Surfer Wayne Monk, 34, Jeffreys Bay, 2-metre ragged tooth, leg lacerations.
- **November 2004** Swimmer Tyna Webb, 77, Fish Hoek, great white, fatal.
- **November 2004** Surfer Llewellyn Maske, 20, Nahoon, ragged tooth, leg lacerations.
- **March 2005** British surfer Chris Sullivan, 32, Dunes, 4-metre great white, leg lacerations – one day after arriving in South Africa.
- **May 2005** Surfer Jay Catarall, 32, Kei River Mouth, ragged tooth, leg lacerations.
- **August 2006** Lifeguard Achmat Hassiem, 24, Sunrise Beach, great white, foot severed.

Some sensible precautions

The ultimate safety measure is to avoid the sea. However, this is not an option. The odds are low that you will encounter a shark while surfing. You might come into contact with one but chances are you will not know that it is there. Great whites can be inquisitive, but are cautious by nature. Usually they will avoid confrontation and swim away, particularly if the so-called prey does not behave as such.

To reduce the rare chance of a shark attack, try to follow the simple rules below, which some people might say is not always possible because of the quality of the waves or other factors.

Don't

▶ surf in murky water near river mouths
▶ surf near a river in flood or where sluice gates have been opened
▶ paddle out with a decomposing seal on your head
▶ piss in your wetsuit
▶ surf with a bleeding wound or when you are menstruating
▶ paddle out before dawn or stay in after sunset
▶ surf alone – great whites in particular are more likely to target a solitary individual as potential prey
▶ surf near where bait or game fish are running or near feeding activity by sea birds
▶ surf near effluent or sewage outlets, or areas used by fishermen
▶ surf in areas with no shark spotters (this will be quite hard, since very few beaches have them)
▶ behave like prey. If you see a shark nearby, don't squeal like a big girl's blouse. Sit tight. Stay calm. Eyeball it. Let it know that you know it's there. Even paddle towards it or dive underwater while facing it. Anecdotal evidence suggests that sharks respond as a predator if the potential prey responds like prey. Standard prey behaviour would be yelping, urinating, splashing in panic or churning up the water in a frantic bid to flee. Behave without fear, and it will treat you as an equal. Easy.

Shark Spotters

The Shark Spotters programme is a community-driven initiative to reduce the chance of shark attacks. Founded in 2004 by Cape Town surfer Greg Bertish, with Rasta Davids, Monwabisi Sikiya, and Surf Shack owners Dave and Fiona Chudleigh, it was initially funded by surfers and friends, with sponsorship by Puma and Reef Wetsuits. The success of the project resulted in funding by WWF through the Table Mountain Fund and the City of Cape Town. O'Neill wetsuits sponsored the non-profit organisation, in 2007. It has since turned into a formalised shark-spotting programme. Spotters, who are from previously disadvantaged communities, are trained, equipped with radios and high-powered binoculars, and employed to watch the ocean near beaches for signs of sharks. When a shark is spotted, they raise the alarm at the beach below by sounding a siren. A shark flag is raised to warn surfers to get out of the water immediately. The aim is prevention as opposed to unnecessary intervention. In this way, great white sharks are treated as equal players in our shared ecosystem, rather than problems that need to be eradicated. The spotting programme came out of a workshop in 2005 that followed a number of attacks. The subject was intensely debated by South Africa's pre-eminent shark experts. Participants reached consensus on policy, ruling out the installation of shark nets as a solution. Instead of approaching

Shark-spotting flags

- A green flag means visibility for the spotters is good and no sharks have been seen.
- A black flag means visibility for the spotters is poor, but no sharks have been seen.
- A red flag means that a shark has been seen recently, but is no longer visible to the spotters.
- A white flag with a black shark, along with a loud siren, means a shark has been sighted and you should leave the water calmly, but immediately.
- No flag means that spotters are not on duty.

SHARK DIVING: Researchers insist that interaction does not lead to attacks on surfers.

the situation in an aggressive and intrusive manner, more ecologically benign action was suggested to prevent further dramatic encounters between great white sharks and people.

The mountainous shoreline of the Cape Peninsula provides ideal vantage points from which to detect great white sharks that approach bathing beaches. Initial areas covered include Monwabisi, Mnandi, Blue Waters, Kommetjie, Glencairn, the Hoek and Noordhoek. Coverage across the Western Cape is being extended. Check out www.sharkspotters. org.za for more information.

Some myths about sharks

Myth: Sharks like the taste of humans
Fact: Not so. Sharks try to avoid us. We are not their prey. Sharks evolved over millions of years feeding on other prey. Most shark attacks on surfers occur as a result of mistaken identity with seals – have you seen a silhouette of a seal? They have a long torpedo body, with two flukes protruding from each side – not unlike a surfer on a board. In most cases, a shark will back off after realising its mistake. Sadly, the damage done during the initial hit can – in rare cases – be fatal.

Myth: Sharks are stupid
Fact: They are complex creatures. Research into the social behaviour of sharks has shown that they are inquisitive, cautious and intelligent. The behaviour of sharks is complex.

Myth: Sharks are virtually blind
Fact: Sharks see a wide spectrum of different colours and have good eyesight, often many times more sensitive to light than human eyes. The great white uses sight as the primary means to 'lock on' for an attack, and can see equally well when its head is protruding out of the water as it can beneath the surface.

Myth: Sharks are feeding machines constantly hunting for food
Fact: According to the National Geographic website, sharks eat only an average of two percent of their body weight each day, which is less than humans typically eat. Most sharks have specific diets. Great whites eat seals, tuna, other sharks, rays and cetaceans (marine mammals such as whales and dolphins), although in the case of the latter, the sharks feed mostly on their carcasses. Some sharks eat plankton, while other sharks will eat only fish. In the False Bay area, great white sharks have been known to exhibit similar patterns to killer whales. When attacking a seal, they have been known to strike their victim from beneath, hitting the hapless mammal into the air. On its way down, the seal is caught in the convulsing jaws of the shark. The great white has the ability to protrude its jaws, giving it more elasticity when devouring prey. During the chase, great whites often leap into the air, as does the mako shark.

The voice of reason

When a white shark bites someone near a surf spot, it can be traumatic. Emotions are unearthed that don't surface after road accidents or disasters. These are primal instincts hard to suppress.

To make it worse, it is nearly impossible for a non-specialist to emerge with an informed opinion after wading through a muddy quagmire of half-truths in magazines, newspapers, websites and TV documentaries. How can one separate scientific fact from falsehood? Fear of the unknown lies at the heart of the issues, and surfers should arm themselves with the truth about the creatures they share the line-up with.

In 2004, there were 560 drownings in South Africa. That's 25 times more fatalities in one year than deaths by white sharks in 83 years. Between 1922 and 2005, 91 people were bitten by great whites, of which 22 were fatal. Surfers accounted for 43 percent.

Yes, white shark bites have increased over this time. Between 1951 and 1970, there were six bites per decade. Between 1991 and 2000 this increased to 22 bites. However, so has the number of people using our oceans, an exponential increase that increases the likelihood of shark encounters.

Why white sharks bite people is the million-dollar question. But I am afraid that there is unlikely to be a definitive answer. Incidences are too infrequent and variables too numerous to postulate an iron-clad mathematical correlation. Despite this uncertainty, there are several theories that at least shed light on shark incidents.

White sharks have roamed the oceans for millions of years. They have evolved their hunting behavior in parallel with their prey: seals, dolphins and tuna. Humans are relative newcomers to the planet. Only in the last 50 years have we begun to spend extended periods of time in the sea. White sharks do not consider us an integral part of their diet. There is only one confirmed account, and a handful of unconfirmed stories, that white sharks actually consumed a person.

Humans send out a different 'sense signature' to fish or seals. White sharks detect sense signatures from far away. However, perhaps when visibility is marginal, or when surf causes background noise and other prey is in the vicinity, a white shark's hunting instinct may be triggered. But taste buds lining its mouth will signal that it has made a mistake. A full bite can snap a person in half, but in most cases people only sustain minor tissue damage suggesting that the shark has not delivered a full bite. Some white shark bites can be linked to curiosity. Sharks don't have hands or paws to investigate with. Unable to satisfy their curiosity with other senses, they will explore by mouthing or biting objects. Injuries are minor because sharks use minimal force. Bites can also have social or defensive reasons – white sharks sometimes communicate by biting. While not territorial, white sharks defend their personal space. When two white sharks meet, one will give way to the dominant individual. If neither backs off, displays of parallel swimming and jaw gaping follow. If this fails then one of the sharks, presumably the more dominant one, will bite or rake its teeth on the other's body. It is plausible that a white shark will treat a human like another shark if there is no response to their body language (withdrawing).

Shark bites are such a rare phenomenon that there is no need to eradicate sharks to surf safely. Neither does one have to stop surfing to be safe. The relative success of humans compared to other species on this planet is largely attributable to our ability to logically process information and make rational and practical decisions. By using this ability wisely and by following a few basic rules (see Precautions on page 120) it is possible to the risk to close to zero, and make the oceans a safer place for humans and sharks.

Since they are often the apex, or top, predators in their ecosystems, the depletion or removal of sharks is likely to affect marine ecosystems and the abundance of other fish species in ways that cannot currently be predicted. Many marine experts believe that sharks are vital in maintaining marine biodiversity, and concern has been raised that some species may become extinct before their ecological role is fully understood.
— sharklife.co.za

Dangerous sharks

There are hundreds of species of sharks in the sea, many of which occur off our shores. However, only a few pose a threat to human beings, or that surfers are likely to come into contact with.

Bull or Zambezi

Carcharhinus leucas

The Zambezi is relatively small – up to three metres long – but it has a wide girth, hence the name 'bull'. This shark has accounted for many attacks in KwaZulu-Natal and the Wild Coast, although shark nets have all but eradicated encounters in KwaZulu-Natal. Common in warm seas, especially around river mouths, it often swims up rivers looking for food, and thrives in shallow waters. Zambezi sharks have been found hundreds of kilometres up the Amazon and the Zambezi Rivers.

Tiger

Galeocerdo cuvier

Perhaps the most dangerous shark in terms of unpredictability, the tiger shark, which grows up to six metres, lives in tropical waters and is common off the coast of KwaZulu-Natal. It is not as discerning as the great white. When a tiger shark has decided to attack it keeps going with voracity, but it rarely attacks humans. They have been known to bite or bump boats. Very few attacks on humans have been recorded by tiger sharks in South Africa, mostly because of shark nets.

Great white

Carcharondon carcharias

The largest accurately measured great white shark was 6.1 metres long, and caught in August 1983 off Prince Edward Island, near the Canadian Atlantic coast. In South Africa, the largest ever landed was 5.9 metres, off Danger Point near Gansbaai. The great white is an elusive and wary fish that feeds on seals, other sharks, rays, bony fish and dolphins, as well as carcasses, especially whales. In South Africa, it is mostly found off the waters of the Cape.

Ragged tooth

Carcharias taurus

The ragged tooth is exactly that. The raggie, as it is locally known, has erratically formed teeth that make it appear ferocious. In reality, it is a relatively docile creature that is only dangerous when provoked.

Most attacks by ragged tooth sharks have resulted from inadvertent contact in a way not dissimilar to our interaction with the lazy puffadder, prone to lying still on open patches of ground or paths in the bush.

Raggies are bulky animals that grow up to about 3.6 metres. They are slow moving, and for that matter, slow growing. Occupants of aquariums have grown to be 16 years old. They have a cone-shaped snout and a long mouth. They are often found near the sea bed, hanging almost motionless. Don't wipe out on one.

BLACKTIP: Many sharks in the sea do not pose much of a threat, such as the blacktip reef shark.

RAGGIE: The ragged tooth is like the puffadder of the sea, lazy and slow, but quick to attack if provoked.

More scared of wipeouts

By Cape Town journalist, Tony Weaver

When Alex Macun was killed by a shark while surfing off Ntlonyane on the Transkei Wild Coast on 29 June 1982, it was the first time that someone relatively close to me had been taken. It was also the last. Alex and I were at school together, and although he was two years ahead of me, his younger brother, Ian, and I were close friends.

That I have only lost one acquaintance to a shark attack is statistically significant (Tyna Webb's daughter and son-in-law are old friends of mine, but I never met Tyna – who was taken by a great white in 2004). The reason I say that is because I have been surfing and diving for over 40 years now. I began diving and surfing not long after I learnt to walk.

Most of that surfing and diving has been either in False Bay, in the Atlantic waters between Kommetjie and Cape Point, and in the waters between Rooi Els and Betty's Bay. Yes, I have seen sharks. Yes, I have had one or two close encounters, but never of the dangerous kind.

I have lost a number of friends to other causes: some were journalists who were killed in the line of fire, others died in car accidents, one was murdered, I lost two friends in one plane crash. But Alex is the only one to have been taken by a shark – and the overwhelming majority of my friends, acquaintances and family members are regular users of the sea.

That is why I was delighted by the way in which the *Cape Times* chose to cover astonishing photographs taken by chief photographer Andrew Ingram. In a helicopter flight over False Bay, Andrew photographed 11 great white sharks within four kilometres of each other. The sharks were concentrated in a stretch that includes some of the Cape's favourite surf spots, including Sunrise Beach, Surfer's Corner and Kalk Bay Reef.

It would have been all too easy to run a hysterical report along the lines of 'False Bay teeming with great whites' and thus fuelling the atavistic fears of regular users of the sea. Instead, the article was a sober and dispassionate piece of reporting, quoting shark experts as saying the high concentrations of sharks and the almost negligible number of attacks was further evidence that great whites do not naturally feed on humans.

My favourite quote was from a shark expert who said: 'If sharks really wanted to attack people, Muizenberg Corner would be a yum-yum factory.' Certainly, taking out a surfer at the corner would be a lot easier for a great white than it would be for your average lion to take an impala at a water hole.

So I will continue to surf, although my diving days are over because of dodgy eardrums. But even in my diving days, I was much more scared of getting tangled up in kelp, or being dashed against the rocks, or getting my arm trapped in a cave in search of crayfish, than I ever was of sharks. And when surfing, it is the catastrophic, unconsciousness-inducing wipeout or the uncontrolled aggression of other surfers that is more of a worry than the sharks.

Even so, like every surfer, there are certain precautions I take: I don't surf near open river mouths or sewage outlets. I don't surf after sunset (well, if the surf's really pumping, I do), and I never, ever, not in a million years, say the word 'shark' when I'm in the water.

Surfers, you see, have this unshakeable belief that to use the word 'shark while out in the backline is inviting an attack. So we talk about 'men in grey suits' or 'Johnnies'. My nine-year-old son learnt this the hard way. We were surfing at Arniston, and it was getting towards sunset.

'Dad,' Zac said to me, 'don't the sharks start feeding near sunset?' I firmly admonished him never to use that word in the water because it was bad luck. He fell silent, then, in a tremulous little voice, said: 'Dad, please can we go in, I'm getting really scared of those things whose name I'm not allowed to mention.'

FEARFUL SYMMETRY: The tiger is confined to the warmer waters of the East Coast.

Sharkman

A 2007 documentary called *Sharkman* marks a cosmic leap in our understanding of this much maligned apex predator. The film by Damon and Craig Foster debunks misconceptions still plaguing people's perceptions – that sharks are stupid killing machines that want to eat every living thing they come across.

In the film, we see Gansbaai free diver Mike Rutzen, known as South Africa's 'shark whisperer', hitch a 70-metre ride on a 1½ ton female white shark by clutching her dorsal fin. We see Rutzen gently wrestle a tiger shark into catatonia, its oven-wide head and tooth-riddled jaw inches from his face. We see Black Tip reef sharks cuddle in his lap after he learns the art of tonic immobility, pioneered by retired US scientist Dr Samuel Gruber by accident during research on shark eyesight. Dr Gruber found that he could induce catatonia in certain sharks by turning them upside down and tickling their sensory area.

But the most remarkable thing, says Craig, was the astounding level of trust shown by sharks during filming. 'To be put into a trance by an alien creature, this wild animal has to approach voluntarily. You can't manipulate sharks. They are too strong. They must want it. To get it, they must approach you. It's the ultimate trust, and a clear sign of how intelligent these animals are.'

Rutzen visits Gruber in the US to learn the secrets of 'tonic' but it is with the 'Shark Lady' of Grand Bahama, Christina Zenato, that he makes the breakthrough. With Zenato's help, he realises that a shark will only allow interaction based on trust, and this level of trust depends on Rutzen's ability and skill. With Zenato, we see Caribbean reef sharks come out of trance, and go back for more. It's almost as though they are seeking human touch for pleasure. One bizarre moment shows sharks vying for his attention. One shark pushes another aside to cuddle, its head nuzzling his lap.

The technique of tonic is knowledge that Rutzen wishes to use on white sharks off Gansbaai, where he had been free diving among them for 10 years by 2007, making him one of the world's foremost white shark divers. The film shows how he uses body language to interact with them. It shows how he uses the current and position of the sun to strengthen his presence in the water. To attract a cautious adult, he curls into a ball to become smaller and less threatening. If they get too close he makes himself big to show that he too is a big predator, without fear. On a good day – but only on those rare days when the visibility is perfect – he spends a long time building trust before hitching a ride on the dorsal fin of a huge adult weighing 1.5 tons.

Sharkman debunks the popular myth of white sharks. It removes the unfair 'Jaws' tag attached to these magnificent creatures. The end result is about changing people's perceptions. The Foster brothers say that this mind shift is critically important because it might stem the horrifying wholesale slaughter of sharks. A new mindset is needed to save not just the white shark, which is protected, but all shark species. Up to 270 000 are killed each day, say the Fosters. This out-of-control slaughter cannot be sustained without fear of total species collapse.

Take out the apex predator, say the Fosters, and there will be catastrophe. The chain of marine life will break, and the cycle will collapse. The ratio between sharks killed by humans and fatalities from sharks is a grim reminder.

Sharks 1 million : humans 1.

In the light of these figures: who is the monster? As Craig says, humans have a primal dread of sharks lodged deep in their psyche. This triggers an illogical fear out of proportion to the threat. 'The bottom line is that they simply are not a danger to us. We have this weird evolutionary trigger that comes from way back but it doesn't make any sense.

'Our film is trying to show that if a guy can communicate on such a profound level with these creatures, then perhaps perceptions will change. When you look at a shark with its menacing stare and teeth, it looks like a machine without intelligence. But we have seen how gentle they can be. They are very intelligent. They are not after humans. They enjoy being touched by humans.'

If this is true, it turns everything we think we know about sharks on its head.

The Fosters have strong views based on their experiences filming *Sharkman*.

'If they were after us, there would be thousands of attacks a day ... and not just by white sharks. They are aware of us all the time. It would be so easy to eat us because we're so slow. The lateral line of a shark is just one sensor in a sensory arsenal. It picks up massive sound pressure waves from activity in the water. This allows the animal to 'touch' us from a distance. Scientists call it the Distant Touch. They pick up beachloads of people all the time. There are literally millions of encounters with sharks,' says Craig.

As humans, we obsess about that millionth encounter, the one that counts.

'Yes, there is that freak occurrence – that one in a million – that does occur. Perhaps the shark is desperate, or hungry or close to death. Perhaps this is combined with a person doing something inappropriate at the wrong time. It's a confluence of factors. There are numbers of things that induce an attack but it remains rare.'

Damon says that predators generally have excellent eyesight because they need to lock onto prey. 'It's the same with sharks. Their vision is 10 times more powerful than a human, particularly in low visibility. It knows about you for a long time before you see it. When it realises you haven't seen it, it becomes more confident. If you suddenly swim away, or paddle into a wave, it sparks a reaction like throwing a ball to a kitten. Bang! It reacts.'

If a human behaves like prey, it becomes prey. 'But if you let him know you have seen him, if you square up to him and eyeball him and let him know you are not afraid, he's more likely to back off. You are bluffing him because he expects prey to act defensively by trying to flee. If you don't, you are probably not prey, and the shark will move on.'

For surfers, he suggests a large eye painted on the bottom of the surfboard, and to make sure nothing glitters or is shiny. But here is the hard part. If a shark does approach and circle you, get off your board and make yourself as big as possible, and keep eyeballing him until he sees you're not viable prey, and moves away.

Sharkman was due for release in early 2007 but post-production never goes quite as smoothly as planned so, hopefully, by the time you read this it will already have been aired – on Discovery Channel as planned. Potential viewership is 200 million people. The power of the media has never been so strong.

'I cannot see any person who sees our film walking away without some sort of profound change in how they see sharks,' says Damon.

SPECIES FIN? If the slaughter of sharks does not stop, scientists say that there could be total ecological collapse in our oceans.

The oceans hold the key to our fate

By Tom Peschak

Southern Africa's coast is the meeting place of two ocean giants – the cold Benguela and the warm Agulhas current. They clash fiercely at the continent's southern tip, dividing the region into two contrasting marine ecosystems that rank among the richest, most biologically diverse and oceanographically complex on the planet.

The Atlantic Ocean, with its awesome productivity and abundance of animal and plant biomass, borders the subcontinent's western flank, while the Indian Ocean that lies on the east has an ecological signature of great biodiversity.

Despite having largely been spared the ravages that marine pollution has wrought upon many of the world's oceans, southern Africa's ocean ecosystems are nonetheless facing severe threats. Today our unique marine biodiversity is severely endangered by over-fishing and unsustainable harvesting. From the near extermination of the southern right whale through whaling, the drastic initial over-fishing of pelagic fish stocks to the rampant poaching of abalone, unsustainable fishing has been wreaking havoc in southern Africa's waters for almost 300 years.

Marine conservation is, however, far from a lost cause. In many instances, South Africa has turned things around to become a world leader. Important sea turtle nesting grounds on the east coast have been under strict protection since the late 1960s. In 1991 South Africa became the first country in the world to protect the great white shark and in recent years even the once depleted southern right whales have made significant comebacks. Nonetheless, the dawn of this new century is not a time for complacency as our rocky reef fish, for example, are in dire straits. The populations of many species have been reduced by more than 90 percent and some are in danger of becoming extinct.

DEAD PETREL: Sea birds are killed in their thousands by fishing nets and hooks.

RARE SEAHORSE: The endangered Knysna sea horse.

Oceans cover more than 70 percent of our planet's surface, yet less than one percent of it is protected in reserves (in comparison, 10 percent of land is protected in parks). This is ironic since marine protected areas (MPAs) are probably amongst the most powerful weapons in our arsenal to protect marine biodiversity. Not only do they promote the good health of species within their boundaries but they can also replenish depleted fish stocks beyond their borders. South Africa currently has the most sophisticated network of marine reserves in Africa and today 18 percent of its coastline is under formal protection. What is still lacking, however, are bigger offshore MPAs that specifically protect habitats under threat from large-scale commercial fishing. Only by giving offshore ecosystems and the important commercial fish stocks that inhabit them protection can we ensure the sustainability of many of southern Africa's fisheries.

The fate of our oceans hangs in the balance. If we continue to exploit wastefully and place economic value only on the volume of protein it provides, then the repercussions will go beyond the species we have destroyed. When entire ecosystems cease to function, the ecological balance will shift, and the impacts will be felt not only at sea, but also on dry land. On the other hand we could choose to begin a new relationship with the sea, where fishing is sustainable and the ocean is valued not only as a place from which to extract protein, but also, and far more importantly, for its cultural and recreational significance. For years tourists have paid handsomely to view Africa's terrestrial wildlife; governments have recognised that lion, leopard and elephant are worth far more alive than dead. The same economic incentive must be adopted in protecting marine wildlife, be it sharks, whales or coral reefs. For in more ways than we care to acknowledge, we depend on a healthy and functioning ocean ecosystem for our own survival.

Useful resources

Sea Shepherd
www.seashepherd.org/south_africa/
The South African chapter of the international activist organisation which offers rewards to people who bring to light the slaughter of marine species.

Apex Predators
www.apexpredators.com
Home of great white shark photographer and conservationist Chris Fallows.

Greenpeace
www.greenpeace.org
Enough said.

South African Sustainable Seafood Initiative
www.wwf.org.za/sassi/
Would you eat that crispy fish fillet if you knew it came from a species over-fished to five percent of its biomass? Would you choose fish caught by a fishery that kills thousands of endangered albatrosses as by-catch every year? SASSI educates the seafood trade – from wholesalers to restaurants to consumers – so they make informed and sustainable choices when buying seafood. Get the guide to see what's cool and what's not. www.wwf.org.za/sassi/downloads/pocket_guide.pdf

World Wild Life Fund South Africa
www.wwf.org.za
Speaks for itself.

Shark Life
www.sharklife.co.za
As a registered non-profit organisation, Shark Life addresses the alarming exploitation of both shark populations and ocean fisheries in South African waters. They actively engage the urgent need for research and protection of many marine species.

The Save our Seas Foundation
www.saveourseas.com
A non-profit Swiss foundation that aims to implement programmes that protect and conserve marine environments around the world.

BORN FREE: Bottlenosed dolphin

KREEF CATCH: East Coast lobster

ALMOST EXTINCT: Abalone

SUBSISTENCE:
Wild Coast boys

ON SURFARI

Travelling
South Africa

Chapter 7

Ye waves
That o'er th' interminable ocean wreathe
Your crisped smiles

Aeschylus

If you're a local, you are so lucky. You have the best surf in the world on your doorstep, and lank other cool activities, destinations and attractions to choose from.

For tourists, travelling around South Africa is easy because, despite the vast expanses of wide open space, wild animals and rustic charm, the infrastructure is First World. The road network is extensive and the roads well maintained, and half-a-dozen airlines compete to carry you from one coastal venue to another. There are many accommodation options in almost every town, and a plethora of coffee shops and restaurants will satisfy even the hungriest surfer.

The surf route

If you're flying in, you can start your adventure in Cape Town or Durban. Many people use Cape Town as their entry point, either direct or via Johannesburg. The city is within one hour's drive of more than 50 breaks, and this excludes numerous spots up the dry, seemingly barren but wave-rich West Coast, as well as spots to the east past Gordon's Bay towards Cape Agulhas (the southern tip of Africa).

The West Coast is rich in marine life, and hosts an abundance of surf spots, many undiscovered. Winding left-hand point breaks often face almost north because they lie on the other side of a coastal headland, such as Elands Bay and spots near Saldanha Bay.

The beach breaks just north of Cape Town can be world class, but they can also be fickle and sensitive to wind. The best time of the year is autumn, when light, warm offshores blow and big groundswells begin rolling in from fronts festering in the southern Atlantic.

There are some extraordinary spots that only work when monstrous storm swells arrive in Cape Town. One spot is aptly called Heaven, although one cannot be sure whether it refers to the quality of the wave, or where you might end up after a brutal wipeout in this powerful, ledging right-hander. A left-hander on the other side of the point is called Hell.

After having your fill of waves, adventure and the laidback lifestyle of one of the world's most beautiful cities, rent a car or join an organised surf tour to sample the warmer waters, epic waves and even more laidback lifestyle of the East Coast.

Taking in the breathtaking mountain scenery along the N2 highway, your next main surfing town is Mossel Bay, four hours away.

Driving for another one and a half hours, you arrive at Knysna, home to indigenous forests, invisible elephants, mountains, neurotically shy leopards, quaint seaside living and plenty of spots. How far to Jeffreys Bay? Only two hours.

The Jeffreys Bay area, incorporating Seal Point and Cape St Francis, is a surfing mecca with quality waves, mostly reefs and points, or combinations of the two.

Jeffreys Bay lies on the southern end of a vast bay, one hour south of Port Elizabeth. The town offers a number of excellent waves, and, surprisingly, a number of spots are still secret. When Supertubes is one to two feet, and hordes of out-of-towners are scrabbling for waist-high close-outs, the locals are blasting four- to five-foot walls around the corner. Heading north, you arrive at the industrialised city of Port Elizabeth (PE). PE gets windy, with fickle surf spots in Algoa Bay, due to a restricted swell window. However, some city spots fire in an east swell (September to April) or a huge south swell (May to August), and the city offers good places to stay, with friendly people. The wild side, which faces south, gets good in summer because the prevailing northeast wind is offshore there. PE is fairly central if you want to surf J-Bay, or head up to East London and the Wild Coast.

PE is near the Addo Elephant Park and other tourist attractions.

Once you're back on the N2, the next main town is Port Alfred, one hour away. This sleepy hamlet boasts a world-class but fickle right-hander.

WIDE OPEN SPACES:
Another uncrowded spot
along a surf-rich coast.

The coastline up to East London (one hour further north) and beyond is riddled with ridiculously uncrowded spots.

People who have lived in East London talk of surfing every day for weeks on end. There is an amazing variety of waves in the area, from beach breaks, river mouths and point breaks to world-class reefs, such as Nahoon, old home to the Gunston 500 (now the Mr Price Pro), the longest running sponsored event on the World Championship Tour.

Just north of East London is the rural Wild Coast, rugged and beautiful. Lush green hills undulate unevenly down to sandy beaches; others are cut away into cliffs, as if chopped by a giant's axe. The jagged cliffs are pounded ceaselessly by wild seas, hence its name, Wild Coast. Many of the hills are dotted with mud huts belonging to communities of Xhosa-speaking people. Rivers snake their way through the terrain.

A typical Transkei surf spot comprises a long sandy beach with a headland, or cliffs, at the far end. This outcrop of rocks is the perfect ingredient for a superlative point break. A river often comes out at the base of the point, depositing sand at the point and to the left of the river mouth.

This combination creates excellent left-hand peaks on the left of the river mouth, and a long walling wave down the point, often joining up with the river-mouth sandbar and freight-training

across the river and on to the beach. Spots like this include Lwandile, Mdumbe and Coffee Bay. Mdumbe can rival Jeffreys Bay in terms of length and quality.

There are plenty of good waves near Coffee Bay (two hours north of East London) and Port St Johns (two hours north of Coffee Bay).

About another three hours from Port St Johns, still on the N2, you cross the border into sub-tropical KwaZulu-Natal near the seaside town of Port Edward, home to some epic spots, such as St Mikes and many others.

The KwaZulu-Natal South Coast is built up, although there are patches of rural coastline near Hibberdene, where you find awesome point breaks. One of them is aptly named The Spot. Befriending a local is likely to be the only way you find this semi-secret gem.

But there are plenty of excellent, easy-to-find beach breaks scattered along beautiful beaches, fringed by palm trees and banana plantations. Some of the beaches tend to be flatter, and often shelve into the sea, making for dumping shore breaks.

Further north, you pass Warner Beach, home to numerous South African chargers. Inland, sugar cane plantations cover the hilly, verdant terrain. In Durban, the hub of the province, there are numerous world-class waves, including the pier breaks in the city, notably New Pier, an awesome right-hander that gets superlative. Past Durban,

There are hikes along the coast, in the mountains of the Western Cape, through the forests of Limpopo, and along the escarpment in Mpumalanga. But probably the best hiking destination is the Drakensberg. These imposing mountains offer hikes from easy, gentle day walks to the hectic Drakensberg Traverse – a 300-kilometre trek along the spine of the steep, high Ukahlamba, as the Zulus call it, the Barrier of Spears.

The Lowveld of Mpumalanga and Limpopo Province offer excellent game viewing. Best known is the immense Kruger National Park, but there are smaller reserves on its flanks, and – the best part – there are few fences separating the different conservation areas. So, whether you choose a budget campsite within the park, or a need-a-second-mortgage stay in a private luxury lodge, you'll get to see an incredible variety and volume of game and birds.

On a less active note, the evidence suggests that humankind evolved in Africa – just outside Johannesburg. The Cradle of Humankind is – as far as we know – the place with the best-preserved fossil remains. It's a good place of pilgrimage if you want to explore your roots. Or just have a fun day in the country, with craft shopping, sightseeing, viewing small game and having a mellow lunch somewhere.

Still on the cultural vibe, visit Robben Island. This island in the middle of Table Bay has a chequered history, but it's best known as the (reluctant) home of ex-president Nelson Mandela. A visit here includes a ferry ride, a tour of the prison and the island. There's a great break just to the north, but you can't fit that in on an official tour.

Even without the historical highlights, South African culture is spectacularly diverse. You could visit a cultural village, do a township tour, opt for a village stay, attend a traditional ceremony, or just hang out in the rural areas to get a glimpse of the traditional and contemporary culture of the extraordinary people that make up our rainbow nation.

And, as you'll probably want to go to Cape Town for the surf, anyway, you should take the short drive to the winelands. With hundreds of wineries, you could spend weeks wandering from cellar to cellar,

and Umhlanga Rocks, you get Ballito Bay and the North Coast. The climate gets hotter and more humid until you're in the tropical zone of Richards Bay and Sodwana Bay. Plenty of secret spots where excellent waves break.

Stuff to do when the surf is flat

There are many options – especially for the wild at heart. You can climb high mountains, paddle wild rivers, fly off into the sunset dangling under a paraglider, jump out of a plane, dodge lions and elephants on horseback, or fly in a supersonic jet. What follows is just a taste.

For a real adrenalin rush, nothing beats jumping off the 216 metre-high Bloukrans Bridge. En route to Jeffreys Bay from the Garden Route, it's the highest commercial bungy jump in the world, sanctified by the *Guinness Book of Records*.

tasting the fruit of the vine, ogling beautiful gabled, white-washed Cape Dutch houses, and enjoying al fresco lunches on shady verandas overlooking green vineyards stretching away to distant blue mountains.

If you're prepared to travel further afield, you will find good surf along the coasts of Namibia and Mozambique. While the former offers freezing water on a rugged desert coast (with some unbelievable, almost unsurfed breaks), the latter is a tropical paradise with long, white coral-fringed beaches, coconut palms and – of course – awesome waves. Mozambique also offers great diving and excellent seafood, usually in the form of fiery peri-peri prawns. Namibia has great wildlife in the north, challenging hikes, horse trails, river rafting on its southern and northern borders, and sand boarding on the highest dunes in the world.

And even though the rest of South Africa's northern neighbours don't have surf, they are worth visiting. Botswana is home to the incredible Okavango Delta, where you can do a floating safari in a traditional dugout canoe, known locally as a mokoro, drifting through limpid, flower-strewn pools between small and large islands filled with game. Or explore the spectacular and game-rich Kalahari Desert.

Victoria Falls, on the border of Zambia and the rather beleaguered Zimbabwe, is a destination of note. While the falls themselves are spectacular, the main attraction is probably the rafting, generally considered to be the best and wildest one-day white-water trip in the world. You can surf several standing waves on the Zambezi. There is good game on both sides of the river, but better in Zimbabwe, and there are lank other activities – bungy jumping, elephant riding, horse trails, gorge swinging, jet-boat trips, booze cruises, scenic flights in a variety of craft, and even walking with lions. You will not get bored here.

Further down the Zambezi, you'll find Kariba, with its great houseboats and fishing (mainly on the Zimbabwean side) and the Lower Zambezi, where you can paddle for days through a true wilderness paradise – either side. While Zimbabwe is in somewhat dire straits, the tourism industry seems to be surviving. And, while you're in Zambia, it's worth visiting Luangwa – one of the best game-viewing destinations in Africa.

Further afield, Malawi has good game viewing, spectacular birding and some great mountain destinations – for climbing, hiking, mountain biking or horse trails. And, of course, the lake is legendary, but you may well query the wisdom of hanging around on a beach without surf. Cute little colourful fish, though.

But you don't have to travel so far. Just pop over the border into Lesotho for the highest commercial abseil in the world, and pony trekking that takes you deep into the rural areas where you travel from village to village spending time with locals and exploring mountain scenery. But if you feel you've grown up to the stage where you prefer to stand on your own two feet, you can hike it, instead. And Swaziland – that tiny little country tucked between South Africa and Mozambique – also has game viewing, hikes, hectic white-water rafting, cultural attractions, and craft shops and studios.

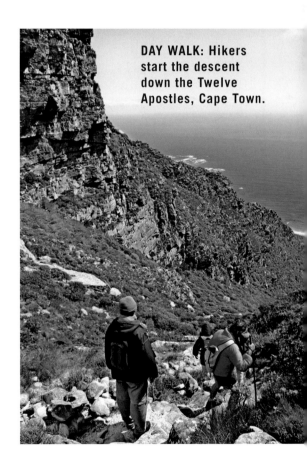

DAY WALK: Hikers start the descent down the Twelve Apostles, Cape Town.

Frequently Asked Questions

When are the seasons?

Summer – November to February
Autumn – March to April
Winter – May to August
Spring – September to October

What is the best time of the year?

There is surf all year, but mostly between autumn and spring. Peak season is winter, but popular breaks like J-Bay are crowded. For the west coast, summer sees strong cross-offshore southeast winds, hot weather, freezing water and small surf. Winter brings storms, bad weather and lots of swell. In 2007, the three peak months of winter in Cape Town brought 48 days of surf six feet or bigger. Only seven days were below four foot. For the east coast, summer sees constant northeast onshore winds, hot and humid weather (Wild Coast and KwaZulu-Natal), warm water and small east windswell, although big east swells occur from mid-summer as cyclones form off Madagascar. Winter on the east coast sees choice surfing options – loads of big south swell and consistent offshores between and during cold fronts. For surf quality – clean lines, nice weather and light winds – autumn is best for both coasts. The winter groundswells are stirring and on the east coast, cyclone swells are still coming. The offshore berg wind – dry and warm – is prevalent. Spring can be excellent. On the west coast, the flowers are out, and you get calm, windless days as storms recede. However, the southeaster is stirring, and by October, it's pumping. Same for the east coast, where the summer northeast lurks.

What wetsuit do I need?

South Africa has many seasonal and climactic variations. Water temperatures vary depending on currents and winds. Boardshorts and/or a chafe vest are applicable in peak summer on the east coast, although you do get cold patches after the northeast blows so include a spring suit or two/three full suit. Take a full suits for all seasons on the west coast. Board shorts, vests or spring suits are adequate for winter on the Wild Coast and KwaZulu-Natal coast, but a full suit is needed occasionally. For the Western Cape, take everything - chafe vest, booties, four/three steamer and spring suit. The waters off the western side of the Cape Peninsula and west coast are cold in summer (12–16°C) and cool (15–18°C) in winter. In summer, upwelling brings water temperatures down to 10°C at times. Upwelling is caused when the earth's rotation deflects sun-warmed surface waters of the cold, upward-flowing Benguela Current out to sea, pulling inshore waters away from the coast. The offshore drift is worsened by the southeaster as water from as deep as 300 metres upwells to the surface. In autumn, the wind dies and the water warms up. A few days of warm berg winds after a strong southeaster can see water temperatures go from a frigid 11°C to a warmish 18°C, which is positively balmy for Cape Town. From Cape Point into False Bay on the east side of the Cape Peninsula, the inverse applies, with warm water in summer (17–22°C), and cold in winter (14–17°C). The further you go up the east coast, the warmer the water in both winter and summer, ending with tropical 26°C in northern KwaZulu-Natal (summer), with only a few degrees variance in winter. The variance between summer and winter is lowest in sub-tropical KwaZulu-Natal.

What surfboards do I need?

South Africa has every conceivable permutation in its surf spots. There is sand. There are rocks. There are reefs. There are point breaks. There are beach breaks. There are river mouths, piers, groins, dolloses (protective concrete barriers), sandbanks and shipwrecks. There are reef/sand and sand/point-beach combinations. Some waves break fast and hard; others are mushy and weak. Some waves offer long, winding walls that grind through like a freight train. Some rear up and spit like an African cobra. Take at least two boards – a short board (six foot four to six foot eight) for average three- to six-foot beach breaks or reef breaks. For those six- to eight-foot days, bring a slightly narrower six foot ten or bigger, depending on your preference. Big-wave surfers know what they need. Tourists save costs and hassle by ordering boards from a shaper and picking them up on arrival. You can purchase a new or second hand board from a surf shop.

don't bring them at all. When you go surfing, use a wetsuit pouch to keep your keys. If you must, find a safe hiding place but make sure no-one sees you!

What about sharks?

Take routine precautions, and you'll be fine. There are sharks in the sea. The great white is found mostly in the Cape, while the tiger, Zambezi and ragged tooth are found on the east Ccast. KwaZulu Natal has shark nets at nearly all beaches. See the shark chapter (page 114) for more details.

	AUTUMN	WINTER	SPRING	SUMMER
WEST COAST	steamer/spring	steamer/spring	steamer/spring	steamer
CAPE PENINSULA	steamer/spring	steamer/spring	steamer/spring	steamer/spring
FALSE BAY	spring	steamer	steamer/spring	spring/shorts
SOUTHERN CAPE	steamer/spring	steamer	steamer/spring	spring/shorts
EASTERN CAPE	spring/shorts	steamer/spring	steamer/spring	spring/shorts
WILD COAST	spring/shorts	steamer/spring	steamer/spring	spring/shorts
KWAZULU-NATAL	spring/shorts	spring/shorts	spring/shorts	shorts

Do backpackers provide double rooms?

Most backpackers have single and double rooms. It's a bit more expensive, but well worth it for the privacy. For the occasional bit of high living, book into bed and breakfast establishments. But all in all, you won't have a problem finding a double room at most backpackers.

How does one get around?

Use your own wheels. Get a group of people together and hire a car. It's affordable, and easier to find waves. Many good spots are tucked away in rural areas, and are hard to find and difficult to access.

What about crime?

Like sharks, there are obvious precautions to prevent attack. Follow global guidelines that you would for, say, Rio de Janiero. Don't be ostentatious and walk around late at night like the proverbial American tourist in Hawaiian shirt, gold chains, and fancy cameras. Most beaches are safe but always lock your car. Hide valuables, put them in the boot or

Is there heavy localism in the water?

Sometimes in peak season, or weekends and holidays. But nowhere near the heavy vibe you can get in Hawaii, California or Australia. Urban growth has led to crowds at many city spots, and some big-name spots out of town. Traditionally, there are flare-ups at places like Glen Beach, Llandudno, Scottborough and Supertubes in J-Bay. In the winter season, Supertubes gets insanely crowded, with up to 100 surfers scratching around in the line-up. It can be a bunfight, with outbursts of aggression. The problem is made worse by out-of-towners with no manners. You do get the occasional local with an abusive personality. However, most of the time, even at the populated beaches, there won't be any issues if you bide your time, act friendly, be polite and wait your turn. If someone threatens you, ignore them. The alternative is to find quiet, lesser-known rural spots, or surf well-known spots on either side of peak winter season (mid-May to the end of July), particularly for the point breaks up the East Coast.

SPOTS

Chapter 8

Hazy from afar,
A dark smudge painted in blue,
Smears the horizon

Spike

I have divided our coastline, which travels for 2 798 km from the Orange River on the brown West Coast to the Mozambique border on the green East Coast, into 14 regions: Namaqualand, West Coast, Table Bay, Cape Peninsula West, Cape Peninsula South, False Bay, Overberg, Garden Route, Sunshine Coast, Wild Coast, South Coast (Hibiscus Coast), Durban, North Coast (Dolphin Coast), and Zululand / Maputaland.

This chapter is a general guide. You won't find detailed maps and directions to spots. Are you mal? Rather buy a map of the South African coast and use it with this book. There are many place names or landmarks that will give you clues. However, unlike other surf guides, we believe in encouraging a spirit of adventure. Going on a surfari is much more fun if you feel like a pioneer. Tough love is good – hardship is character-building. When you're nursing multiple puffadder bites after falling down a snake-infested donga trying to find a surf spot, you'll thank us, serious. Besides, most surf spots are in, or near, large towns, which makes them possible to find. To get to rural surf spots, check out Google Earth, or be nice to the locals. Buy them a bottle of *mampoer*.

Ratings

Each spot has a star rating, based on experience (opinion) and 'heresay' (you should have been here yesterday).

✪ ✪ ✪ ✪ ✪ **Awesome.** Superlative in form, power, consistency and/or length of ride. The berries.

✪ ✪ ✪ ✪ **Classic.** World-class but falling a little short on length of ride or consistency.

✪ ✪ ✪ **Kiff.** Middle-ranked hotdog wave. Fun. Gets good occasionally. Might be unknown.

✪ ✪ **Okay.** Generally a soft wave with marginal form, but easy and fun to ride when at its best.

✪ **Kak.** This wave is weak and just doesn't cut it due to poor shape, inconsistency or ride.

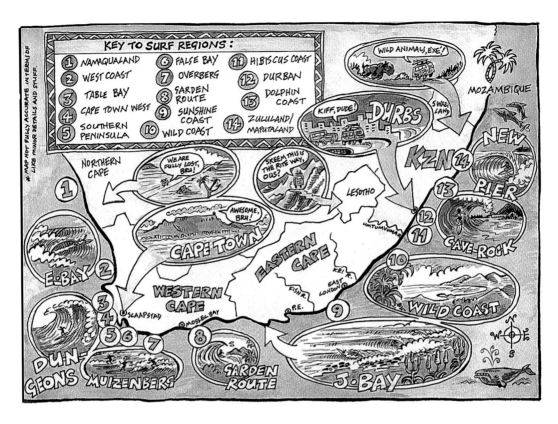

Surf spot names

Surf spots mostly derive their names from geographic or artificial landmarks. The inclination is to name a break after a place – a river, headland, town, street, beach, bay, mountain or other marker, such as a shipwreck. Some spots are named after their physical shape – the way they break. Some are named after, or by, the person who discovered them. Others are named after events. Some are even named after feelings or emotions.

Many surf spots share their names with places that are steeped in a multi-cultural past. Spots along the rugged Wild Coast are known by their indigenous place names such as Mdumbe, Lwandile, Mbomvu and Ntlonyane. In KwaZulu-Natal, there is Zinkwazi, Umhlali, Umhlanga, Umfafazana and Umzumbe, mostly rivers near the break. In Zulu, the prefix 'um' denotes a river. Zumbe is a small brown bean. Umzumbe means Small Brown Bean River.

Legend has it that the name Amanzimtoti in KwaZulu-Natal originated from Zulu King Shaka when he drank water from a river in 1828. 'Kanti amanzi mtoti', he said. 'So, the water is sweet.'

In the 1660s, the Dutch used Schaapeneiland (sheep island) – a grassy headland on the West Coast an hour's drive from Cape Town – to keep sheep traded from Khoi (San) tribes. When the Dutch settlers saw the largest antelope in the world, they used their word for the biggest antelope they knew in Europe, an elk. 'Elands Bay' on the west coast means 'Elk Bay'.

Jongensfontein in the southern Cape is Dutch for 'young man's spring'. One secret surf spot is called Kokkerot (cockroach). When you look at Table Mountain from one west coast suburb, it looks blue, hence Blouberg (blue mountain). A place near Hermanus is named after the restless river nearby, hence Onrus. In the 1700s, a farm south of Cape Town was named Olifantsbos (elephant's bush) after elephant bones that were found in the bush. The surfspot is also Olifantsbos, or Olifants, or The Bos.

Some place-name surf spots – especially prevalent in southern KwaZulu-Natal – have a British colonial past, with places such as Scottburgh, Margate, Brighton, Trafalgar and Hibberdene.

Goukamma, near Knysna in the southern Cape, is Khoi for 'wild fig river'.

Many breaks are named after a bay that is the name of the settlement there. There is Jeffreys Bay (allegedly named after a whale hunter and trader, J. A. Jeffrey, who had a shop at St Francis), Queensbury Bay, Buffalo Bay, Coffee Bay (a ship carrying coffee beans wrecked here), Stilbaai (Quiet Bay), Mossel Bay (Mussel Bay) and Sandbaai (Sand Bay).

Some breaks refer to the point, or cape, where the waves break rather than the bay, such as Seal Point (after a nearby Cape fur seal colony) at Cape St Francis (after the patron saint of sailors) and Shark Point on the Wild Coast (er … go figure).

Sometimes a spot is named after the person who discovered it. Take Lance's Lefts in Indo, named after a feral surfer. A notable example in South Africa is Bruce's Beauties, named after filmmaker Bruce Brown who rode it while filming *Endless Summer*. Farmer Burger's on the West Coast is a fun right-hander that occurs on the land of a local farmer named Gerrit Burger. Kelly's Beach in Port Alfred was first named after the Kelly family before it was a surf spot, but now both beach and spot are Kelly's Beach. The holiday village of Betty's Bay was named after Betty Youlden, daughter of the first developer in the area, while nearby Pringle Bay takes its name from Rear Admiral Thomas Pringle, commander of Simon's Town naval base from 1796 to 1798.

Tramps in Durban refers to hobos who loitered on the grass near trampolines in front of Addington Hospital after receiving treatment at the outpatients: two reasons to call it Tramps.

Vetch's Reef in Durban is named after the pier that Captain James Vetch of the Royal Engineers designed in the early 1900s. He never

Elk Bay

Long Beach

went to Durban but devised the structure from his office in London. Needless to say, it didn't work. The ruins of the pier lie submerged in a 500-metre arc out to sea. When a rare northeast cyclone swell breaks, Vetch's is the longest wave in Durban.

What happens when different people think they are the pioneer of a spot? One spot in the Boland has many names, including Virgins, Secrets, Off the Wall, Ledges and Off the Mountain. Big-wave surfer Micky Duffus says that if you apply the 'original guy gets right of way' principle, then Steven 'Rio' Middleton's name Off the Mountain should stand, unless someone can prove they surfed it before the early 1980s.

Sometimes the stories change in the telling. Cape Town spot 365 was apparently named because it broke 365 days a year. It does not, but that is beside the point. It was apparently first surfed in the late 1960s by Roger Bain. However, veteran surfer Tich Paul says that his crew gave 365 its name from the shape of the wave, which was so round, it was 360 degrees plus five.

Shipwrecks give several spots their name. *Kakapo* in Cape Town is a wreck immersed in dry sand on Noordhoek Beach. *Thermopylae* in Mouille Point, Cape Town, breaks off the boiler of the ship that wrecked in 1899. A wave at Kommetjie is simply The Boiler. The Wreck at Plettenberg Bay is named after the *Athena*, while a sandbar named Shipwrecks near Scarborough on the Cape Peninsula refers to a ship, the *Ikan Tanda*, that briefly ran aground there in 2001 before it was refloated and towed away.

A clump of round white boulders like cannonballs was enough to earn Cannonball Reef, on the way to Llandudno from Cape Town, its name.

There are at least four breaks called Black Rock or Black Rocks, including two in northern KwaZulu-Natal, one on the Cape Peninsula, and another in the Eastern Cape near East London. Crayfish Factory breaks off a crayfish factory. Outer Kom is the outside reef near the town of Kommetjie, an old Dutch word meaning Little Bowl. There are places near pebbles called Pebbles or settlements near periwinkle shells called Periwinkles.

The wave at Kowie, or East Pier, breaks in the mouth of the Kowie River in Port Alfred. Nahoon Reef is named after the suburb, Nahoon, in East London. Battery Beach in Durban is the spot at the beach of the same name in front of the Natal Command military base. African Beach was a blacks-only beach during apartheid. It is now ironically called Country Club. The prestigious Durban Country Club is nearby. Tally ho, old sport.

The rocky shores of Treasure Beach, a few hundreds metres south of Cave Rock, is considered by the scientific community to be a treasure trove of coastal and marine life. Maybe the wave is one of the treasures.

Some South African spots are part of the global surfing lexicon, drawing a descriptive title from the way the wave breaks, often due to the bathymetric contour below. Common are Boneyards, Impossibles, Supertubes, Black Rock, Surfers, Sunset, Sunrise, Off the Wall and Long Beach. Namesakes appear in California, Hawaii, Australia and Portugal.

When describing a wave, the verb can be the noun and vice versa. Does the wave wedge or is it a wedge? Does it ledge or break on a ledge? Does it tube or is it a tube? You get Wedge, Ledge and Tubes. The Wedge is a universal surfing word because it best describes the shape of waves that, well, wedge upwards in an upturned V-shape, also referred to as an A-frame after the triangular design used in building.

There is a Wedge in Port Elizabeth, Durban, Cape Town and Plettenberg Bay (and all over the world). The Ledge normally denotes a wave that breaks on a rocky slab, like the outside of the Inner Kom that lies on the inside at Outer Kom. Does that make it outer Inner Kom or inner Outer Kom? For a tubing wave, Supertubes (nicknamed Supers) is without peer. Like Inuit words for snow, surfers have many names to describe the tubing action of a wave. Others are Pipe, Tubes, Magna Tubes and Dairy Bowl. A Pipe is found in Port Elizabeth, Scottburgh and at the Strand, near Cape Town. You also get Melkbos Tubewave on the West Coast.

Words that conjure a dark sense of dread have been assigned to some hard-breaking spots. Former *Surfer* editor Steve Barilotti says 'Cape Town breaks have forbidding Wagnerian names that imply doom'. Maybe this should include Paranoia, Dungeons, Gas Chambers, Cemetery and Danger Reef.

Legend has it that Dungeons was named when one of the pioneering duo who surfed it, Pierre de Villiers and Peter Button, was sucked 20 feet into the blackness, where he ended up in a swirling basement of kelp and dark terror for a two-wave hold-down – a torture more horrifying than two hours of thumbscrews and body stretches on the medieval rack.

While not Wagnerian per se, a place like The Toilet is descriptive enough. This scary, lurching left-hander near Hermanus is near municipal toilets, but locals say it refers more to what it does to your insides when you watch a 10-foot monster offload its innards all over the reef. Enough to induce involuntary sphincter twitches in the bravest soul.

Other events or verbal throw-away lines find themselves entrenched in surfing lore.

According to a veteran Stilbaai local, nearby Kakgat is precisely that: shit hole.

'There is an old holding tank for sewage where the wave terminates. The municipality has a hole on top of the tank out of which they pump the sewage to a disposal lorry every week. In the seventies, Rob Louw, the rugby player, and a few mates went for a paddle. Rob needed a dump. The manhole cover was off, so he did it directly into the tank. Local authorities still call it Kakgat.'

North Beach, Durban

NAMAQUALAND

Heading south from the Orange River mouth (Namibian border) to Strandfontein, you pass the Diamond Coast, a desolate part of the Richtersveld. Access to the *sperregebiet* (forbidden zone), which ends just south of the Buffels River near Kleinsee, is strictly controlled by De Beers Diamond Company. Namaqualand is swept by strong south winds in summer and dense fog in winter. But when you score, it's like you discovered the diamonds.

ORANGE RIVER TO STRANDFONTEIN

Access to the *sperregebiet* is restricted to diamond workers. Guided groups of tourists have limited access, one group at a time. Most known surf spots occur around Kleinsee. The word 'known' is relative in this forlorn wilderness. Few surfers have explored it. However, there are a few locals who have, mostly diamond divers from Port Nolloth, the regional headquarters of De Beers and the largest town in the area. Sporadic groups of surfers, mostly from Cape Town, have journeyed here since the 1960s. You need a unique resilience to survive here. Physically, you must endure the frigid water and raw-ocean poundings on slabs of rocky reef. Mentally, you must endure endless days of blown-out surf and thick mist that choke your mind, threatening to derail the best of friendships.

Make sure you're stocked with provisions and spares for your four-wheel drive. For the prepared and the patient, these lonely, scraggly beaches and capes can yield day after day of glassy overhead surf, with only jackals, seals and carrion birds to keep you company.

Richtersveld

The coast south of Alexander Bay towards Port Nolloth, the only thing approaching a town in the prohibited diamond coast, is part of the arid Richtersveld region, a semi-desert famous for succulents and reptiles. Needless to say, the unexplored Richtersveld coast is wind-blown and barren. With places called Wreck Point and Jackals Pit, you get the picture. It is characterised by dark-sand beach breaks and points going left and right. Several rocky spits jut from the land, with waves that peel for hundreds of metres. There is awesome potential, and murmurings of perfection from diamond divers. One spot, allegedly called Bakgat, is allegedly better than Elands Bay. Lots of other secrets. Sssh.

Cape fur seal

Here Be Diamonds

A hardy group of surfers dig for liquid gems on the desolate Diamond Coast. By Ross Frylinck

Cape Town surfers have been enchanted by rumours of perfect, uncrowded waves in the Namaqualand diamond reserves for decades. Discovered by diamond divers, these are supposedly some of the finest waves in a country known for an almost embarrassing wealth of world-class surf. Over the years, a trickle of surfers has made the pilgrimage – their whispered testimony slowly seeping into our collective surfing consciousness.

Namaqualand is a windswept semi-desert stretching up the Atlantic coast for more than 1000 kilometres. Known for a fleeting wild-flower riot in spring, it is dirt poor and sparsely populated. Towns have disturbing names like Pofadder (puffadder). But under the shifting, sunburned sands and restless waves sleeps a dragon's hoard like no other. The Namaqualand reserves are the richest source of alluvial diamonds on earth. Here be diamonds: 'tears of the gods' (ancient Greece); 'splinters of fallen stars' (ancient Rome). Forged in a flaming furnace billions of years ago and borne by blazing lava flows and relentless river action, diamonds tinkled towards the sea, resting at last in coastal sands and shallow reefs, patiently weathering the eons.

Diamond conglomerate De Beers has relentlessly mined this area and become one of the most successful cartels in modern commerce. Their skill? To invent a big-money myth that turned tiny crystals of carbon into glittering tokens of wealth, power and romance. The diamond as the standard symbol of marriage did not exist until De Beers came along in 1888. Within 70 years, the diamond engagement ring was de rigueur and the diamond was 'forever' (even though it could be shattered, discoloured or incinerated to ash). Fuelled by shrewd marketing to perpetuate the illusion of scarcity, and a monopolistic business ethic that took no prisoners, the diamond became the most sought-after precious stone on earth.

Now that they've all been collected from the beach, De Beers tentatively allows tourists to trample around their empty treasure chest. Limited permits are available if you pass stringent security checks. Not that there is much demand. Visitors are sparse: sporadic four-wheel drive nomads hitting the Namaqualand trail, occasional botanists fawning over rare flora and sometimes surfers seeking solitude and waves.

The surf is infuriatingly capricious. Prevailing cross-shore southerly winds blow for months, scouring the best swells. Looming coastal fog shadows the coast for weeks, leaching warmth from the land and driving the hardest miners to despair. The frigid sea is a breeding ground for great whites. Then there are the waves: great wind-blasted lumps that randomly strike the jagged reefs like cannon fire, tormenting the most deserving surfers, who gibber in anguish as they wait for better days.

But when warm land breezes blow from the desert – burning off the fog, caressing the sea and composing the swell – these waves become the choicest gifts from old Neptune's sea chest. And there are no crowds – ever. Only one group of surfers gets access at a time. To get a permit you must know someone. Then you need a guide, a four-wheel drive with a winch, GPS co-ordinates and a secret handshake. Bizarrely, you must hire a diamond detective to trail you incognito (well that's what we are told).

We are three Cape Town surfers. Lance, a professional surf photographer, is our reluctant, bearded guru. Having explored this strip over 10 years he has clocked up trips with legendary surf journalists and surfers. Without Lance's insider knowledge, we would be lost. Ray's 'a-friend-to-all-the-world' from way back who has dreamed about this trip for years. Lovely people Ray and Lance: easy-going, indulgent, funny and lazy to a fault. Perfect companions really.

MINING TOOLS: Your equipment for waves.

My naïve exploration here in 2000 was forgettable. The notorious fog warped spring into darkest winter. Visibility and temperature plummeted to the other side of nothing. Taking turns to clutch our gas cooker for warmth, one day bled into another until the dreaded west coast flu took us, one by sorry one. In our hasty retreat, I wrecked my car's suspension. It was a wretched limp back to Cape Town. Our boards didn't even leave the safety of the car roof.

It is with trepidation that I return, chasing the dream of uncrowded waves with friends. Our plan is simple but sketchy: surf, take photographs, play boulles and master the one-egg omelette.

After a long day's drive on hideously gutted dust roads, we arrive at a gulag-style border post with matching watchtower, barbed wire and armed guards. A sign bearing the De Beers logo 'a diamond is forever' is crowned by a crow, impervious to the icy gale that mercilessly subjugates the forlorn coastline. An apologetic winter sun briefly illuminates a bleak wasteland, then skulks behind a mountainous mine dump.

Driving slowly to our base camp, we see disturbing rows of flower-strewn crosses lining the dead-straight road – mementoes of fatal car crashes. In the falling light, we see springbok grazing. Later an ostrich breaks cover and flashes in front of us, narrowly avoiding collision.

We recover with a beer and watch the sun set over the Atlantic. Far away, rows of tiny white ribbons unfurl in the sea, offering a tempting glimpse of what we have come to find.

On the way in, our shelter had looked like a rogue military compound commissioned by Mad Max. The rough-hewn straggle of small cottages are open-plan clumps of asbestos, stone, rope and concrete. But there are endearing touches: a massive whale pelvis is a bench, a large stone fireplace warms the lounge, and mobiles (shells, glass and fragile bird bones) hang from the ceiling.

A massive generator powers the compound from 7 pm to 10.30 pm, even though we are the only guests. The water is undrinkable. It's so hard it hurts to shower. Soap stubbornly

FACE OFF: Desert desolation inspires thought forgery.

The roaring sea taunts us. We are close yet so far - lost beggars on a beach of diamonds.

refuses to lather. Come 10.30 pm and we are unprepared, scratching in the dark for candles. Lying in a wobbly old army bed, I hear the surf hammering the beach and the wind whistling through cracks in the thin walls, trying to remember lines to Arnold's haunting poem about a beach – something about being true to your love, ignorant armies clashing at night, naked shingles and long melancholy roars. My iPod relieves me and I drift off to sleep to a BBC podcast about the impending water wars that will engulf our world soon. Apparently.

We wake to the wonderful sound loved by surfers – long-period surf breaking with metronomic regularity. But the dreaded fog has cloaked us in a veil of gloom. Water, water everywhere, and not a drop to see. The days are spent playing blind-man's golf in the veld until we lose our balls. By the third day, we are fighting amongst ourselves. We stand on the rocky shore, peering into the grey – but it's hopeless. Brandy and Coco Pops for breakfast was a threshold we should never have strayed across. Time has collapsed. We must surf.

Finding the sea is a testy business. There are no signs or roads. Sandy rat tracks snake across the veld like spaghetti dropped from the colander of the gods. There are lots of gates. Matching rusted lock to rusted key is a puzzle Confucius would commend. There are no landmarks. There are no maps. We get lost. We get stuck. Hours later we are unstuck. We quickly get stuck again. A sandy trench ends at a gate we have no key for. Massive heaps of mangled metal litter the path and dunes. Gigantic scars in the land are the dirty work of a dragline excavation that can fling 70 tons of earth with each immoral scoop.

A long list of rules has ironically told us to stay on the path lest we accidentally stand on an ancient fossil. The roaring sea taunts us. We are close yet so far – lost beggars on a beach of diamonds. We are at the source, the hidden haunt of diamonds, the secret root of the Oppenheimer billions where Bizarre and Surreal hold hands and scream while Irony does a mad jig.

Humbled and shattered, lost in a maze, we finally find what we are looking for. A break in the clouds reveals a reeling right-point break and light-offshores – the perfect barrel.

The waves are powerful and unforgiving. Ray and Lance strangely decide to longboard, dropping gracefully into massive pits, reaping rewards and paying dues by turn. I'm riding a retro seven-two single-fin Shaun Tomson replica. It's a work of art and, despite my concern, she takes me into the biggest barrel I have ever known – a frozen moment stripped to the bare: a glittering shard of time.

Paddling back to the line-up I get caught by a close-out set. I stupidly choose to swim for safety. I feel my leash snap. Suddenly my beautiful board is gone. In this heavy swell, I expect to find her shattered on the rocks. She hardly has a scratch. In the time it takes to paddle out again the fog is back, the winds have swung onshore and Ray and Lance are getting dressed. The shoreline is lost in the mist. The dark waves loom ominously as crows drift in and out of the fog. Not all surf trips are coconuts and dolphins.

Back on the beach Lance has finally mastered his one-egg omelette (flour makes up the difference), which we enjoy with a cup of coffee. We laugh wryly at the many ironies crowded around us: that this traumatised stretch of forlorn coastline is the birthplace of possibly the most prestigious industry on the planet. That because of this, the area has remained hidden, and therefore we can enjoy surfing all on our own. That De Beers has the audacity to tell us to tread lightly when they have pulverised this place for over 70 years. But there you go. Everyone knows that life is complicated. Thank God you can't build fences in the sea.

UNPOLISHED STONE: Scratching the surface of the quarry wall.

BOREDOM BOULLES: Waiting for the swell to arrive.

LUNAR LANDING: Preparing to dodge a few bombs in the desert.

Pretty scary because it sucks over a solid rock slab.

Klip Baai (Blou Balle) ✪ ✪ ✪ ✪
Thick barrelling right-hander just north of Port Nolloth. Best in light east to northeast winds or desert berg winds. Likes long-period west swell and, according to locals, only surfable on the high tide, unless you like playing chicken with the shallow reef. Early morning before the wind comes up is the best time, if there is no mist. You mostly surf in freezing upwelled water, hence the nickname *blou balle* (blue balls).

Port Nolloth Reef ✪ ✪ ✪
A right-hand reef off the harbour beyond the fishing boats. Needs a pulsing six- to 10-foot west swell and no wind or a light offshore, usually in the morning. You have to scramble over inner reefs to get to the outside where the waves break. Slightly soft in smaller conditions, but gets good on those thick groundswell days and light winds.

Paradise ✪ ✪ ✪ ✪
In the Kleinsee region, inside a restricted diamond reserve where access is strictly controlled, lies this right-hand point break that works on a small to medium west to southwest swell. Runs along rocks on the inside. A reform wedges over a rocky ledge.

Samson's Bak ✪ ✪ ✪ ✪ ✪
Powerful right-hand point break in the prohibited area that delivers some epic waves when conditions are right: a solid six- to eight-foot groundswell, light offshore and pushing tide. Kelpy and cold.

Trailer Bay ✪ ✪ ✪ ✪
Also in the restricted area, Trailer Bay is similar to Elands Bay, without the crowds. It walls up to give a freight train ride. Pretty scary because it sucks over a solid rock slab, then refracts into a small bay.

Groenriviersmond ✪ ✪ ✪
Kelpy spot at the mouth of the Groen River. Surfed mostly by diamond divers, and a few others.

WEST COAST

Between Strandfontein and Melkbos on the outer fringes of Cape Town, lies the West Coast. Apart from the rocky Strandfontein-to-Doornbaai coast, and contorted Cape Columbine in the south, it is marked by long sandy beaches interrupted by shrub-covered headlands fringed with rocks. The big headlands block the dominant southwest swells, and smaller surf breaks on their northern sides. Strong southeast trade winds in summer keep the upwelled water a frigid 10° to 15°C.

STRANDFONTEIN TO MELKBOSSTRAND

Most of the good surf on the West Coast comes in the form of left-hand point breaks. Breaks such as Elands Bay line the northern rim of a large headland, in this case Baboon Point. Because the common swell direction is southwest, the underwater topography of the headland forces the waves to refract around the headland, resulting in significantly smaller but clean lines of swells reaching the spot. The big, messy stuff is left behind on the exposed southern side – the wild side. Between Stompneusbaai and Saldanha, the coastline concertinas into a contorted confusion of reefs and sandbars tucked between narrow bays and inlets. Spots face all sorts of directions, which demands a variety of swell and wind conditions. Generally, a south to southwest swell direction will yield lean pickings, unless it's a deep energy groundswell of six- to eight-foot-plus. A much higher yield comes from deep-energy west swell and light land-breeze northeasterlies.

Strandfontein ✪✪
Fun but fickle right-hand beach break. Sandbanks shift a lot. Rippy. Best in light northeast winds and small to medium swell on an incoming tide.

Doring Bay ✪✪✪
Left reef break. There is an inside section that runs along rocks. Needs a light southeast or east wind. Best on a clean four- to six-foot groundswell.

Donkin Bay ✪✪✪
Left point break. Needs a solid 10-foot-plus storm swell. A reef on the outside blocks much of the force. Like Elands, copes with southwest winds. Works on low tide. Worth checking if Elands is out of control. There is a quality big-wave reef off the headland not visible from the inside point that not many people have ridden.

Yo-yos ✪✪✪
In front of the river mouth at Lamberts Bay, near the caravan park, are fun sandbank peaks at low tide. At its best in calm conditions or light northeast winds and medium-sized swell.

Garbage dumps ✪✪✪
There are two waves: garbage dump right and garbage dump left. The right is a fun point break in a west swell. The left is a point break, best at low tide. The ride ends in front of a rocky shelf. East winds are offshore. Needs a six-foot-plus swell to work. Lots of kelp.

SPRING CARPET: West Coast flowers come alive in September.

FENCED IN: Some breaks occur on private land. Some owners are lenient, others not.

Bit scary-looking, ridden at

SUNSET SURGE: Wave-sailer Piet Streicher tackles huge Elands Bay.

but has been solid 6 to 10 foot

Farmer Burgers ✪✪✪✪

A rocky shelf south of Lamberts Bay produces a fun, sometimes classic, two- to five-foot wave in glassy or light northeast berg winds. The land belongs to farmer Gerrit Burger, famous for his arty parties, but anyone can surf here. There are lots more quality reef breaks in the area, with varying swell and wind needs – seek and you shall find.

Elands Bay ✪✪✪✪✪

The J-Bay of the West Coast. This wave cranks, but is congested these days. Can be overrun with kiters and windsurfers, to add mayhem to the mix. A rocky, kelp-covered point break that ends at a small river mouth. When big, the swell peaks off an outside reef and refracts down the point, producing a fast cylindrical wall that runs for maybe 200 metres. Needs open ocean west swell of six foot to wrap in at three- to four-foot. If general swell is southwest six foot, it might only be two foot. Handles moderate south wind. Dominant wind is southeast, which pumps in summer. Best in light east to southeast winds and solid long-period west swell.

Stompneus ✪✪✪

Rare-breaking left-hand point in Stompneus Bay, which lies tucked away in the western end of St Helena Bay. Like Pastures, it needs a gigantic west swell to wrap all the way around Shelley Point to reach the inside bowl, which faces southeast – that means a straight west swell has to turn 225 degrees to reach this spot. The offshore wind is southwest and it needs a mid to high tide. Best in

huge winter groundswells (west at 30 to 50 feet). There is an outside reef that prefers a low tide and solid swell, but it is more exposed.

Pastures ✪✪✪

This left-hand point on the northern side of Shelley Point, a double-pointed headland north of Cape Columbine, gets good a few times a year. It needs a giant west swell to wrap 180 degrees around the headland to reach the inside bowl, which faces east. Best during those massive winter groundswells of 20-foot-plus. On an average day, the lulls are long, with sets every five minutes. On rare occasions, it cranks.

Hell ✪✪✪

Heading around from Pastures towards Heaven, this wild and rocky spot faces north. It gets good in southwest to south winds and huge westerly groundswell and a high tide. The swell must be spaced-out and clean. Bit scary-looking, but has been ridden at solid 6- to 10-foot.

Heaven ✪✪✪✪✪

This 'secret' spot is like a busy carnival when the surf is running. When a raging 15- to 20-foot storm swell is pummelling the Cape Peninsula just before or after a cold front has passed, the ous say 'Let's go to Heaven'. This small rock-bottomed reef-point will be from six- to eight-foot. A kelpy foamy cauldron of Atlantic juice, Heaven throws up a thick-lipped wall for about 80 metres, with a stomach-churning bowl section halfway down. Not for the faint-hearted. Heaven is best in light north to east wind. Heaven can't handle any wind direction with south in it unless very light.

Cape St Martin ✪ ✪ ✪
Fun little left-hander on a kelpy reef. Works on south or southeast winds. Picks up more swell than Heaven or Pastures, and is often an option when the southeast starts to mess with Heaven. Requires similar swell size to Elands Bay.

Ascensions ✪ ✪ ✪ ✪
Rocky reef point a short distance south of Cape St Martin. Works from mid-tide in deep west swell and mild winds. Gets good. Hard to find.

Paternoster ✪ ✪ ✪
Quality left reef break at the northern end of this small West Coast town. Works in medium west swell and light east winds. There are beach breaks to the north, scattered along a flat coastline stretching towards Steenbrasbaai. Lots of exploration potential.

Trekoskraal ✪ ✪ ✪
There is a right point just north of Trekoskraal. They call it Supertubes. It allegedly fires in giant swell, sheltered from northwest winds by a big headland. A small right-hander called Corollas rolls into a small, deep bay near a fun camping spot. Needs west groundswell and light easterly or berg winds. Not very consistent. Excellent crayfish diving though.

Vredenberg Point ✪ ✪ ✪ ✪
A good-quality left-hand point break. Needs high tides, a clean four- to eight-foot swell and light winds. Deep water off the rocks make it slightly scary, but it gets classic. Some distance north of Saldanha Bay. The wedge focuses and pitches steeply, similar to the Outer Kom. You have to paddle hard to make the drop, taking off in front of a boulder. Usually out of control when the swell is more than five foot. Good in small swell and glassy berg wind. Faster and more powerful than Elands, but more fickle.

Swartriet ✪ ✪ ✪
You need to pay a small toll to enter the beach area. A peaking, fun beach break that works in two- to four-foot swell and light southeast to northeast breezes or glassy conditions. Very popular wave-sailing spot.

Jacobsbaai ✪ ✪
Left-hand reefs just south of this small development. The usual west swell and light NE winds apply.

Heaviside's Dolphin

This sprightly but small West Coast dolphin, growing to just under two metres long, was supposed to be named after a mariner called Captain Haviside. According to Wikipedia, Haviside took one to the United Kingdom early in the 19th century. At some point, the dolphin's name was confused with prominent surgeon Captain Heaviside (who collected cetacean species). Heaviside stuck. Heaviside's dolphins have a similar mass to a medium-sized human: 70-75 kg. Not to be confused with porpoises, their blunt head is even more pronounced. They have a stocky, solid look to them. The head is dark charcoal in colour, contrasted with much lighter greys over the upper front half of the body and flanks. The fluke, dorsal fin and back half are darker. The underbelly and flanks below the dorsal fin are white. The shades of dark grey, light grey and white are clearly contrasted. Heavisides are found off Namibia and the West Coast of South Africa as far as Cape Agulhas.

OUT TO PASTURE: Somewhere near Heaven.

Churchhaven ✪✪✪
There is no surf at Churchhaven, which is on the Langebaan Lagoon, but on the coastal side a new road extension takes you to a quality beach break on Sestienmylstrand that breaks in conditions similar to Schaapeiland.

Yzerfontein Harbour ✪
Fickle left reef point break inside the harbour blocked from most swell, but allegedly gets Indo-quality once in a blue-green moon.

Schaapeiland ✪✪✪✪
A crunchy wedge on a rock slab that links with sandbars, and a freight train close out. Gets insanely hollow. Needs a light northwest to northeast wind and a three- to five-foot west swell. Hectic when big. Tow ous get slingshot into thick stand-up barrels. Fun sandbar peaks further down.

Ganzekraal ✪✪
A left point – just south of the small resort of Ganzekraal – apparently fires when the swell is massive and the wind is east to northeast.

Bokpunt ✪✪
Fickle and relatively slow-moving right-hand point break off a sharp headland north of Silwerstroom,

marking the western side of Bokbaai. Best in any north breeze and a deep-energy four- to eight-foot west swell. In the bay a left-hand sandbar wedge is also protected by the headland from north winds.

Farmer Duckitt's ✪✪✪
On the Cape Town side of Bokpunt on the eastern end of Sandsteenbaai, lies a fast-breaking right-hander that needs big swell and clean winds. Be sharp. It's testing.

Silwerstroom ✪✪✪
Good waves along the beach towards the holiday resort end. Light winds and clean west swell are needed.

Gas Chambers ✪✪✪✪
This break at Silwerstroom is best when the swell is tiny in Cape Town. The boom gate is closed to cars and you have to walk for 10 minutes. Holds six foot if the swell is clean and spaced out. Light northeast winds or glassy seas are best.

Matroosbaai ✪✪
Just south of the boom gate at Silwerstroom (access to cars is blocked) are sandbar point set-ups from the pumphouse to the southern corner. Works in small to medium swell and light northeast winds.

TABLE BAY

As you head south along the West Coast road (R27) towards Cape Town, the first sign of the city – apart from the view of Table Mountain in the distance – is the Koeberg Nuclear Power Station. Next is Melkbos, the furthest northern suburb of Cape Town on the coast. For our purposes, it marks the end of the West Coast, and the beginning of Table Bay, which ends at the harbour in the southern corner of the bay.

MELKBOSSTRAND TO MOUILLE POINT

Van Riebeeckstrand ✪ ✪
Fickle beach break in Melkbos (north of Ou Skip caravan park). Mushy but can be good fun. Best in light northeast winds and small swell.

Tubewave ✪ ✪ ✪ ✪
Also called Beach Road, this is a good right-hand sandbar point break in Melkbos. It is protected by an outer reef. Works in light southwest or southeast winds and big groundswell. The outside is best at low tide. The inside cooks on the high tide.

Shark Bay ✪ ✪
Sometimes called Captains. Fickle reef/sand set-up in Melkbos area. Best in light southeast or northeast with right sandbars. Best in clean two- to four-foot groundswell. Gets out of control easily.

Holbaai ✪ ✪ ✪
Between Haakgat and Melkbos along a dust road near some small dunes you will find fun sandbar peaks when light easterly winds are blowing and a small groundswell is running.

Haakgat ✪ ✪ ✪
Parallel to the beach about 30 metres out is a sectiony left point, inconsistent and exposed with a boiling reef section that works strictly at high tide only. Check out the A-frame rights across a line of rocks that end at Haakgat. Difficult to ride, but powerful. A proper wave.

Kreefte Reef ✪ ✪ ✪ ✪
Bowling right-hander that breaks on the outside when big. Medium west swell and low tide. The inside left-hander works on smaller swell.

Derde Steen ✪ ✪ ✪ ✪
Good-quality beach break near Blouberg. Needs glassy to light northeast and two- to five-foot west swell. Gets super-hollow and superlative.

Tweede Steen ✪ ✪
Derde Steen's poor cousin, twice removed. Fickle and lacking the same quality, but gets fun.

Eerste Steen ✪ ✪ ✪
Hollow peaking beach break on the coast road between Melkbos and Blouberg. Same old. West swell, light northeast.

TABLEVIEW: Some suburbs have literal meanings.

Cape Town

The splendour of Cape Point hit Sir Francis Drake like a cannonball when he rounded it in the 16th century. Now we know why jealous Gautengers call Cape Town 'Slaapstad' (sleep town) in Afrikaans. Drake must have been struck by that cannonball, and Capetonians have inherited the numbness he felt. Compared to fast-paced Johannesburg, Kaapstad (Cape Town) is dozy. Nestling in a triangulated valley between Table Mountain, Lion's Head and Devil's Peak, some say magnetic ley lines have woven an almost narcotic web of lethargy around the city. Cape Town lies on the northern slopes of Table Mountain, overlooking Table Bay. Beyond the City Bowl lies a vast urban sprawl populated by more than three million people. The Cape Town metro area stretches up the west coast to Melkbos, and across the Cape Flats towards Sir Lowry's Pass. The modern world and the old world form a kaleidoscope of cultures: from the Bokaap of the Muslim community; past the plush suburbs of Bantry Bay, Clifton, Constantia and Bishopscourt; out to the sprawling townships of Gugulethu, Khayelitsha and Langa. Table Mountain is not just the landmark you see hunched over the city. It is the northern face of a wide mountain slab that separates the Southern Suburbs from the Western Seaboard, tapering into a twisting, rocky spine that culminates in Cape Point, separating False Bay from the open ocean. There are 75 ocean breaks within a 45-minute drive around the Cape Peninsula, from bone-crunching reefs and hollow beach breaks to mellow sloping sandbanks. For the purposes of this guide, we have divided the coast of the greater Cape Town area into Table Bay, the Western Seaboard of the Cape Peninsula, the western side of the South Peninsula, and the False Bay coast, all the way from Cape Point to Cape Hangklip, the eastern sentinel that guards the protected waters of the bay.

Horse Trails ✪✪✪✪

A nearby estate belonging to racehorse trainer Terence Millard used to have its own traffic light for grooms to take horses across the road. Hollow A-frames break on sand in small swell up to five foot.

Kamer van Sewentien ✪✪✪

Left, sandy point on the other side of the rocks at the end of Big Bay. Sectiony. Works in moderate southeast or calm day. Best at low tide in a medium swell.

Big Bay ✪✪

Windy beach break popular with sailboarders. Big A-frames break on the outside, then reform before hitting the shore break. Can be good banks here, but gets crowded. Best in light berg winds. Can be disorganised and messy. One of few west-facing spots that can handle a northwest, but not more than 15 knots.

Little Bay ✪

Marginal beach break. Breeding ground for (human) rats. Soft sand peaks.

Tableview ✪✪

Deep outer sandbars break in bigger swell, while the shore break sandbanks break on the reform or can be a stand-alone wave when smaller. Must be glassy or light northeast. Crowded, but lots of peaks, varying in quality and length of ride. Difficult to catch due to an irregular reform that sometimes waits for the shore break before it breaks.

Sunset Beach ✪✪✪

Scattered beach breaks at a relatively new suburb called Sunset. Mostly fickle, but can get good in light northeast and solid eight-foot ocean groundswell, which means shifty four- to five-foot peaks here. At best, a long walling right. Needs northeast berg winds.

Milnerton ✪✪✪

The closer to the city you go, the smaller the swell as the Cape Peninsula closes out the swell window. Milnerton is famous for its market, not its waves. Long stretch of empty beach best in a huge groundswell in glassy or light to moderate easterlies.

CLEAN GREEN: Even a two-foot wave is fun at Big Bay, Bloubergstrand.

Madiba's Left

This world-class left-hand reef on the ocean side of Robben Island honours Nelson Mandela, who spent 27 years on the island. Only a handful have surfed it because the island is a restricted area. Needs a long-period six- to eight-foot southwest swell to start breaking, and holds up to 15 foot. Needs light northeast winds on any tides. Long rides when the swell is big.

Dumps ✪✪
Fickle wave that gets good on occasion at the mouth of the Milnerton lagoon. Best at high tide and big, clean west swell and light berg or southeast winds. Not the kind of wave that is actively sought out.

The Wedge ✪✪✪
Tucked in the corner at the foot of the harbour breakwater, The Wedge is hard to access. You used to be able to park in the harbour and clamber over the concrete dolose but the US Government terrorism strategy resulted in closure of the harbour to recreational users. You have to walk in, and you're still likely to be ejected by overzealous security. Swells bounce off the wall and travel sideways to join other swells in a sharp triangular peak that can be super-hollow. The take-off is often the best part of the wave, with a soft shoulder beyond. Best in mild east wind. Needs a huge general swell to filter into the corner.

CAPE PENINSULA WEST

From the Cape Town harbour breakwater that
juts northeast from Granger Bay, the coast heads in a westerly
direction towards Mouille Point before heading southwest along
busy Sea Point. As the coast turns south at Lion's Head, moving
past the upmarket suburbs of Clifton, Camps Bay and Bakoven,
it becomes more exposed to the dominant southwest ocean swell,
although Sandy Bay, a nudist beach at the end of this section,
is sheltered by the Karbonkelberg.

MOUILLE POINT TO SANDY BAY

Thermopylae ✪ ✪ ✪ ✪
A rare point break in Cape Town, this north-facing left-hander needs a huge southwest or west swell. Can be long lulls, unless a really big west swell is running. You take off over the sunken remains of the *Thermopylae* that wrecked off Mouille Point in 1899. The wave bends around a rock shelf, and ends in front of the luxury Radisson Hotel. The take-off can be hairy, depending on swell size and tide. There have been E-coli issues in the past, due to nearby sewerage outlets.

Off The Wall ✪ ✪ ✪ ✪
The take-off zone of this urban reef break is the size of a mini. Surfers sit on top of each other waiting for a short, sharp take-off and a barrelling green wall that often closes out. Breaking off the promenade wall of Mouille Point, adjacent to Sea Point, has similarities with its counterpart in Hawaii. Insanely hollow and hard-breaking at times.

Rocklands ✪ ✪ ✪
A gnarly left reef on the Sea Point side of Off the Wall, best in glassy seas or southeast winds, a large southwest swell and a pushing high tide. Breaks when other Sea Point spots are too small. The waves wrap around the rocks and freight train onto a rocky ledge, where it stands up and says, 'Smack me or die'.

Milton Pool Left ✪ ✪ ✪
Hectic, fast-breaking left that needs big west swell and clean, glassy seas. It zips along, top-to-bottom, without tapering. Gets epic in the right swell. Usually not a wave.

Solly's ✪ ✪ ✪ ✪
Short reef breaks left and right, depending on swell. Likes clean four- to six-foot west swell and light to moderate southeast to east winds. Fresh southeast winds elsewhere can be totally absent in Sea Point. The spot is near The Pavilion. The outer reef (Solly's Outer) works on big swell. Can be good.

Mutant wave

Llandudno sunset

Off The Wall

Big and mushy and
take-offs and crun

CAPE RIVIERA: All four beaches at Clifton.

fun, with free-fall ching close-outs

Boat Bay ✪✪
When the swell is too small for Off the Wall, this fun right-hander is worth a look. Runs along a rock spit next to the wall of the public swimming pool at The Pavilion. Clean two- to four-foot west swell and light southeast to east winds.

Queens ✪✪✪
This knobbly left-hand reef in front of the President Hotel is the last wave in Sea Point going south. Scattered outside reefs cause the swell to focus unevenly on to a shallow slab, resulting in a big, fat, hairy take-off before it runs into a wide-swinging shoulder. Big and mushy and fun, with free-fall take-offs and crunching close-outs. Likes solid four- to eight-foot southwest swell, high tide and glassy seas. Does not like too much wind or swell – picks up more swell than other Sea Point breaks. Beware the rocks at the end.

Gasworks ✪✪✪
Heavy bombora reef in the middle of Bantry Bay. When the swell is huge, clean and westerly, you need a rhino chaser to snag this top-to-bottom barrel. Breaks in deep, dark water and grinds towards a large exposed rock. Gasworks looks like a right-hand point break in huge swell. Not for wussies.

Moses Beach ✪
Beneath the cliffs on the Sea Point side of Clifton, this fickle spot last worked in 1652 when Jan van Riebeek pulled into a few barrels.

Clifton First Beach ✪✪
There are waves at three of the four major Clifton beaches, but sandbars are fickle. First Beach can get a right-hand sand point with rare days of perfection. You need late winter storms to excavate the sand. In summer, the southeast and longitudinal drift resets the beach to its default setting: evenly distributed sand and shore break closeouts.

Cherry Rock ✪✪
This small, round rock off Second Beach gets good at times, but not often.

Clifton Third Beach ✪
Fickle sandbar between Second and Third Beach. In past years, surfed regularly, but sporadic. Fourth Beach never has waves. Watch out for the greater blinged kugel, a preening sea bird species with sharp claws.

Glen Beach ✪✪✪✪
Hollow right-hander along a sandbar off rocks tucked in the corner of Camps Bay. Many of Cape Town's best surfers were, or are, locals here. A short ride, but yields superlative form in right conditions. Best in three- to five-foot west swell. Quite sheltered from the southeast gales howling down from the Twelve Apostles. Handles mild northwest wind.

Camps Bay ✪✪
Like Clifton, needs a rare confluence of sand, wind and swell to create good waves. Best in front of Blues Restaurant to the right of the rocks.

SWELL LINES: A good day at Llandudno.

MAGIC CARPET RIDE: Sacha Specker streaks skyward.

WIND WARBLE: The late-afternoon sun glints through another pearler.

Barley Bay ✪ ✪
Right-hander that needs solid 10 foot, and very west swell. Imposing big-wave spot surfed by a few die-hards. Closes out from 15 foot.

Bakoven ✪ ✪
Very rarely, on a super-high tide and big west swell, you can ride the outside reef.

The Bluff Left ✪ ✪
As you leave Bakoven towards Oudekraal, at the end of a line of milkwood trees, there is a short, sharp left-hander off the corner of a reef where a fishing boat – the *Bluff* – sank. Not popular but can break with great form in clean west swell. Sheltered from the southeast.

Cannonball Reef ✪ ✪
At the end of the straight where hawkers sell curios lies a clump of round white boulders like cannonballs. A fickle right-hander breaks along the rocks. Mostly used as an indicator when you're on a surf mission to the south. Sheltered from the southeaster, the barrel looks airbrushed it breaks so perfectly – a harbinger of good waves ahead.

> When it fires, the barrel spit realises the ballistic metaphor.

Llandudno ✪ ✪ ✪ ✪
This wave is superlative … or crap. The Gat (English slang for gun) is a sucking right-hand wedge near big granite boulders. When it fires, the barrel spit realises the ballistic metaphor. A sandbar closer to the middle yields hollow rights and occasional lefts. Gets crowded. The water in summer goes down to 10 °C after heavy upwelling from prolonged southeast gales pulls deep water to the surface. Kiff to thaw in the hot sun! Gets epic between spring and autumn. In winter, storms tend to dig big trenches in the sand.

Sections ✪ ✪
A small right-hander that peels past a granite boulder into a small bay. Sometimes called Mac's Spot. Ironically, two unrelated Macs live near it. The older Mac has a house above the younger Mac. Two reasons to call it Mac's Spot.

Sandy Bay ✪ ✪ ✪
When Llandudno is closing out (at eight-foot-plus) and the wind is fresh southeast, Sandy Bay can be a good call. This nudist colony in the next bay is a short wave, often little more than a tubing shore break although perfect sandbanks can develop further out. It handles the southeaster, and copes with light to moderate south. Popular with bodyboarders.

CAPE PENINSULA SOUTH

The jagged spire of the Sentinel, Hout Bay, marks the start of the southern Cape Peninsula. From Dungeons – at the foot of the Sentinel – the next stop is Noordhoek, followed by the villages of Kommetjie and Scarborough and the marine reserve down to Cape Point. Tourism authorities say the South Peninsula includes False Bay, but for our purposes, False Bay is a separate section.

SANDY BAY TO CAPE POINT

We end the boundary of the southern peninsula at Cape Point (despite a chunk from this coast and the False Bay coast occurring in the official municipality) because of differences in water temperature, swell angles and wind requirements.

Dungeons ✪ ✪ ✪ ✪

Made famous by Red Bull Big Wave Africa, this big right-hander is seldom ridden by paddle surfers outside the event, but tow surfers ride it frequently. Just off the Sentinel off Hout Bay, Dungeons starts breaking from eight to ten foot. Best in light winds and a thumping 20-foot west swell. Best on the low tide, otherwise it gets too thick (too much water). Beyond 20 foot, the tide is less significant. One session on 30 July 2006 saw tow surfers tackle monstrous 60-foot faces – the biggest waves ridden in Africa at the time.

Hout Bay ✪ ✪ ✪

Off the harbour wall and on the beach in huge southwest swell there are some waves. On a huge day in northwest winds, the harbour wall gets quite good.

The Hoek ✪ ✪ ✪ ✪

An archetypal Cape Town A-frame peak that barrels over a shallow sandbar in crisp, clean water and a majestic setting. An offshore reef focuses the swell into the corner of a small boulder-strewn bay at the base of the cliffs below Chapman's Peak. At best, a world-class tube – short, round and perfect. The lip sucks top to bottom; throws fast and hard. Protected, slightly, from the offshore southeaster, the Hoek works on a low tide and copes best with a medium-energy four- to six-foot west swell.

Noordhoek Beach ✪ ✪ ✪

This sandy bay, between Chapman's Peak and Kommetjie, is punctuated by peaks of various lengths, shapes and sizes. Some get close to perfect, depending on sand movement and swell quality. Light to moderate southeast and high tide is best.

Dunes ✪ ✪ ✪ ✪ ✪

Long-period southwest to west swell focuses on a submerged reef – the 'mound' – 300 metres offshore. This produces a wedge-shaped kink that continues until it hits low-tide sandbars that can transform into world-class tubes. On a solid six- to eight-foot day, Dunes needs a spittoon it barrels

SUCKER PUNCH: Dungeons offloads with brute force.

WALLING UP: John Whittle goes abseiling.

Several world-class spots lie within spitting distance of each other

AZURE DREAM: A tow surfer's wake streaks the shoulder of a Sunset beast.

WAVE WALK: Surfers look for surf in the Long Beach area.

DUNE PERFECTION: A superlative tube curls over a Noordhoek sandbar.

DOUBLE WHAMMY: A lurching right-hander near Kommetjie.

so much. The tubes might look perfect, but they break on compacted sand like concrete. A wipeout can snap your board and smash you around. There have been shark incidents here, one fatal. Also entails a mega-walk along the beach.

Kakapo ✪ ✪ ✪

Towards Long Beach lies an old wreck in the sand. Only the boiler of the *Kakapo* sticks out. Sometimes the strong southeaster drives the sand away to reveal the ribbed remains of the hull. Rarely ridden shore break nearby.

Sunset ✪ ✪ ✪ ✪ ✪

Out to sea lies a deep-water bombora reef like its namesake in Hawaii. A huge right peak with jaw-dropping take-offs. Backdoor it and a cathedral dome arches on high as your tiny earthly shape passes through sun-glinted Pearly Gates. Wipe out and the heavenly light recedes as you somersault into the roiling madness of Hades. A giant tapered shoulder expends itself on the ledge, then fades into a deep channel. On the other side of the peak, a sharp drop-off in bathymetric contour nullifies the left. The local crew surf here on fun 15- to 20-

foot days, and in 'small' 10- to 12-foot conditions. While it doesn't offer the top-to-bottom, sectioning castle walls of Dungeons, the immense power of this pea-green A-frame has its own romantic attraction. Tow surfing is popular at Sunset.

Krans ✪ ✪

A shore break at Long Beach popular among bodyboarders due to the sucking barrel. Fast and hollow. Often dumps a long close-out section on to a boiling sandbar.

Long Beach ✪ ✪ ✪ ✪

Facing Chapman's Peak on a promontory at the south end of Noordhoek Beach, an established learning ground teeming with surf rats. Because this spot faces almost due north, the southwest wind is offshore here, making it one of the few spots that can handle this wind. The downside is that the swell has to bend from the exposed west side of the coast, almost doing a U-turn to reach this north-facing break. The refraction focuses clean lines towards the beach that result in left-breaking peaks that run for at least 40-60 metres before ending in a shore break close-out.

Boneyards ✪✪✪✪

A long walling right-hander over kelp beds on an outer reef off Kommetjie. Best in west swell and light northeast winds, but works in light south winds. Entails a long paddle. Gets good. Needs high tide, otherwise can be hectic.

Baby Pipe ✪✪

Hard-breaking right-hander off a rock slab into the channel where you paddle to the Outer Kom. On a huge day, this channel is deceptively dangerous. Big wide-swingers turn it into one giant close-out.

Inner Kom ✪✪

On the inside at Outer Kom lies a mini-point. You have to sit virtually in the kelp to catch the waves that bend from the Outer, travel through the kelp and reform near the rocks. Soft, fun walling lefts up to about three foot. Popular grom and longboard spot.

The Ledge ✪✪✪

The inside ledge between the Outer and the Inner. Fun at high tide in glassy seas on a three- to five-foot west swell.

DODGING BULLETS: Photographers avoid a wide-swinger at Dungeons, during the Red Bull Big Wave Africa.

DISTANT ROAR: The regal reef break, Sunset, in full cry.

Kommetjie lighthouse

not bigger, otherwise interlocking reefs merge, and the wave becomes a bone-crunching closeout.

365 ✪✪✪✪

Kelpy reef best in a clean four- to ten-foot west swell and light north to northwest winds. When big, the kelp on the inside ledge can be a nightmare, especially when you get hammered by a 10-wave set. Smaller swell skips the outside reef, but rears into a heart-stopping double-up on a super shallow inside ledge. They say 365 is named after the barrel, which is so round it is 360 degrees plus five.

364 ✪✪✪

The gnarly left that breaks towards 365 on the other side of the channel is called 364. Popular with bodyboarders, it breaks on a focused ledge that can cause problems if you've just kicked out of a long wave at 365.

I&J's ✪✪

A reform wave on an inside reef in the Soetwater Reserve. Looks fun in glassy conditions and clean west swell.

Mysto Freight Trains ✪✪✪

On a six- to twelve-foot swell, an epic line-up can be seen from above Soetwater. Big grinding waves reel off from the back of a series of kelp-covered slabs. Then one will close out across an evil-looking slab. Some have surfed it. Most haven't.

Conveyor Belts ✪✪✪✪

What? Where? Some guys paddle out here when The Factory is crowded. But it's rarely surfed. This wave has similarities with Gericke's Right on the Garden Route – a chunky ledge with shifty right peaks. Needs high tide and clean west swell that wraps from the right, which makes it peel more, enabling life-saving gaps between sets. Some say it's better than the factory.

Crayfish Factory ✪✪✪✪✪

Scary big-wave right-hander that pitches on to an outside reef, then sucks for 100 metres across an inside ledge, before bending into a channel. The factory is one of Cape Town's heaviest, but most

Outer Kom ✪✪✪✪✪

Left-hand point. Thick peaks break on an outer reef, before running onto the inside ledge. On a big day, getting caught inside can set you back a good 15 minutes as you get pummelled in the impact zone. Best in clean six-to ten-foot west swell and any light east wind.

The Boiler ✪✪✪✪

Towards the lighthouse, a juicy right-hander works on glassy four- to six-foot days when the swell is a bit intermittent at the Kom. Sometimes hard to paddle into but once you catch one, a freight train speed line across a long wall that often closes out at the end.

Battery ✪✪✪

Just to the left of the lighthouse, another hollow, grinding right-hander. Like the Boiler, needs a clean west swell of around five to seven feet, but

FALSE ALLURE: Hollow waves at Witsands look good, but rarely deliver.

CONVEYOR LEDGE: A local surfs a small swell at Crayfish Factory.

exhilarating waves. During big west swell, the Kom can be eight foot, but the Factory flat. During a 10- to 15-foot southwest to south swell, this regal right-hander is a walling, sucking, spitting glass monster that heaves tons of liquidised innards onto a jagged, boiling ledge. Most surfers have a tale of terror and anguish here: bone dislocation, bust boards, gashes and star-spangled visions of speckled death by drowning. If you get pounded on take-off, you can get pegged down deep in a dark, roiling tomb, the distant roar of 12-foot monsters overhead. When you surface, spat into the channel like a foul piece of human detritus coughed up by a sea monster, expect to be floating without a board, dazed and confused. But don't dally. Shift back into survival mode. Swim towards the inside like a mutant salmon up a waterfall. You don't want the rip to suck you towards Misty Cliffs.

Witsands ○

This spot is everything Crayfish Factory is not, even though it's only a few hundred metres away. Featuring boring and shifty sand-bottomed peaks, with rips and channels, Witsands is the last resort. A sandbar appears from time to time called Barclays Bank.

Misty Cliffs ○○

Further down lies a fickle spot that only works when the swell is clean, usually when other spots are too small. Sandbar-dependent.

Grumpy local

Scarborough ○○○

The ledge in front of the car park is best in three- to five-foot west swell on clean, glassy days. Gets good when right-handers hit the rock, and reel across the sandbar. A peak in the middle of the beach breaks in two to four foot, and sometimes connects with the shore break. The most consistent wave is the small right-hander in the far corner at the base of the point. Reforming lefts become rights as they bend down the point and swing wide, hitting a sandbar and breaking into a channel that runs up the point. The rip keeps the sand on the sandbar. Waves have perfect form here. Best at two to four foot, not much bigger.

Scarborough Point ○○○○

Left-hander that gets good in specific conditions. A thumping, evenly spaced west swell is the first requirement. A light southeast to northeast wind is the second. A pushing tide is the third. These don't converge often. When they do, it's a proper point break, a rarity in Cape Town.

Underwater Point ○○○○

This right-hander works off a rocky reef. Watch out for the rocks about halfway down that shorten the ride, otherwise it would carry on for another 30 metres or so. Best in glassy seas and smooth, deep west six- to eight-foot groundswell.

Extensions ○○○

A rocketing right-hander that's a bit mushy in everyday conditions. Waves reform from big outside reefs, then zip down a rock shelf sandbank, before refracting around a corner into an outgoing rip. When good, you can take off further around the corner, extracting more juice from a barrelling take-off zone. Best in east winds, or light northerly.

Paranoia ○○○

Needs a super-high spring tide and clean west groundswell of six to 10 foot. The swells expend a lot of energy on the outside, then reform and refract into a small bay, chunky sectioning waves rolling rapidly along shallow rocks. Not for the faint-hearted.

EMPTY PROMISE: Dias Beach perfection. No-one out.

SECRET SLAB: Locals proving their point.

Olifantsbos ✪ ✪ ✪ ✪

Rocky right reef best on southeast wind and large west swell. Best on the incoming to high tide. Very kelpy. Gets super-hollow. Watch out for vicious baboons, especially the ones with surfboards on the roof.

Platboom ✪ ✪ ✪ ✪

Breaks in the kelp, but gets good. This left-hander screams down a rocky ledge. Best in light northerlies and clean six- to eight-foot west swell. Dangerously shallow and sharky. Psychotic locals live in the bush – the result of a special inbreeding program to lessen the impact of foreign visitors by terrifying them with their bloodcurdling screeching. Popular windsurfing spot because the southeast and northwest winds blow cross-shore.

Dias Beach ✪ ✪ ✪

Bodyboarders speak in awe of the day Mike Stewart blew the place apart. It was mostly regarded as a non-spot until the late nineties. Just around the corner from the sheer cliffs of Cape Point, it's an imposing venue. Entails a steep walk up and down. There's not much beach, mostly rock, cliffs and a crunchy right-hander that closes out a lot. Best suited for bodyboarders, but ridden by stand-ups too.

Southwest Reef ✪ ✪ ✪ ✪

Giant walling wedge-shaped A-frame that absorbs the sheer might of Atlantic deep-ocean swells. Breaks off Cape Point several hundred metres out. Has never been ridden at its potential, which is allegedly 40 to 60 feet and perfect.

FALSE BAY

Cape Point is the western sentinel guarding the calmer waters of False Bay, which runs in a giant U shape around to the eastern sentinel, Cape Hanglip. The bay faces south to southeast, and is mostly protected from the raw might of deep Atlantic ocean swells, which must work a lot harder to bend around the craggy cliffs of Cape Point.

CAPE POINT TO CAPE HANGKLIP

Most of the west swell runs past Cape Point, missing the bay, unless a really giant southwest swell wraps around Cape Point into False Bay. The western side of False Bay is the eastern seaboard of the Cape Peninsula. In summer, the water temperatures here can reach more than 22°C so you can surf in baggies and sunscreen.

Buffels Bay ✪ ✪ ✪ ✪
This secret right-hand point break can sport 300 people in the car park when a humungous south to southeast swell breeches the swell window that shields False Bay from the open ocean. On 27 August 2005, a 30-foot south swell translated to a 10- to 15-foot swell here. When firing, hordes of grizzled veterans venture from the woodwork. A difficult wave to master, it holds off in deep water, then suddenly jacks and barrels along a shallow reef for 200 metres. Gets heavy.

Black Rocks ✪ ✪ ✪ ✪
Nearby right-hand reef more consistent than Buffels, but also needs a huge swell between Cape Point and Hangklip. Gets radically overcrowded.

A small take-off zone in thick kelp doesn't help. A classic wedge set-up that handles up to eight- to ten-foot in ideal conditions (southwest winds and an open ocean 15-foot-plus southwest to south swell). Long lulls.

Glencairn ✪ ✪ ✪
Left-hander that breaks off rocks near the Red Hill turnoff between Simon's Town and Fish Hoek. Again, like all the breaks on the western rim of False Bay, needs huge swell.

Fish Hoek ✪
Surfing with a zimmer frame. This large retirement home is mostly asleep. The waves that break along its pretty beach are this way too. In the left-hand corner – Clovelly Corner – fun waves are ridden (but not really) by ballies. When a giant south or southeast swell is running, you will find mostly grommets in the water.

Clovelly ✪ ✪
A short, hollow left reef at this small suburb between Kalk Bay and Fish Hoek. The reef likes glassy conditions or light northwest or northeast breezes, while a clean three- to four-foot groundswell in False Bay needs to be running. Low tide wave. Bodyboard-friendly.

RAY OF LIGHT: Kalk Bay Reef in a small swell.

BIG DAY: The epic swell of 27 August, 2005.

When good,
hollow left rese

BACKDOOR MAT: A local sets up the barrel.

this insanely
mbles Pipeline

Kalk Bay Reef ✪✪✪✪
World-class but intensely localised left-hand reef. Not that the locals are to blame. The take-off zone is the size of a pizza. When good, this insanely hollow left resembles Pipeline. Many a hottie has cut his barrel-riding teeth here. A curious quirk is that the southeast onshore is channelled offshore by mountains behind the break.

Kalk Bay Backdoor ✪✪✪
Hollow right-hander that breaks fast and hard on the other side of the Kalk Bay Reef.

Danger Reef ✪✪✪
A left and right peak on a rocky ledge. A deceptively powerful wave that breaks off a shallow rock shelf. Best on a southeast swell and a light northwest wind. Gets intense, with a thick lip that sucks over a tight, bodyboard-friendly tube.

St James ✪✪✪
Right-hand ledging right reef break off the tidal pool near the colourful bathing boxes. Can be quite a heavy three- to four-foot wave that seems like it will close out, but holds for a few lip bashes before it hits almost dry rock.

Bailey's Reef ✪✪
This is usually a short, hollow right-hand reef in front of Bailey's Cottage. Best in a northwest wind, clean four- to five-foot groundswell and spring-high tide.

Surfers' Corner ✪✪✪
Old-school surf spot in Muizenberg where woodies used to fill the car park and the 10- to 12-foot elephant guns were unsheathed. Today, it's the hub of the Cape Town surf scene. Not a powerful break by the unrelenting standards of the reefs on the western side of the peninsula, but a great hotdog wave. There are lots of peaks, if you can call them that, particularly in front of the car park. It's offshore in northeast to northwest. On a three- to four-foot south groundswell, the outside breaks, and the wave reforms again on the inside. Malibu boards are just right here because they give you enough momentum to make it all the way through. Alternatively, you can pump your six-foot-two board up and down like a jack-in-the-box. When big, entails an arduous paddle through acres of white water to reach the backline.

Rivermouth ✪✪✪
Soft sandbar peaks like Corner. When they release the water from the river, it can be sharky.

Sunrise ✪✪✪
Soft beach break near Sunrise Circle along the coast road to Khayelitsha. Gets a little bigger than Surfers' Corner.

Cemetery ✪✪✪
Another beach break like Corner, with more juice. Best in light northwest winds. There are a few

peaks to choose from: lefts and rights. Expect the swell to be at least one to two foot bigger and slightly hollower than Muizenberg Corner.

Nine Miles Reef ✪ ✪ ✪

Further along the coast road is Nine Miles Reef. Fun lefts and rights.

Monwabisi ✪ ✪

Lots of sandbanks with lots of potential and a few secret spots. Few take the trouble to explore.

Pipe ✪ ✪ ✪

One of several sand- and rock-bottomed breaks in the Strand area, notably the Pipe, which gets good in light northwest to southwest winds and clean south swell.

Bikini Beach ✪ ✪ ✪

During a massive storm swell, a left-hander off Gordon's Bay Harbour wall breaks, ending at Bikini Beach. In a huge southeast to south groundswell and light northerlies this wave is epic, but extremely rare. Usually, when the swell is right, conditions are stormy and wild.

Caves (Koeël Bay) ✪ ✪ ✪

Also called Kogel Bay, Koeël Bay is a beach break in front of low sandstone cliffs around the corner from Gordon's Bay. A fairly fickle sandbar that usually closes out, especially during your common or garden swell. However, on a low tide and proper sand arrangement (especially in summer), some classic wedging three- to five-foot barrels are there for the taking.

SECRET SPOT: Shh ... don't tell anyone.

Koeël Bay Beach ✪ ✪

Usually better on the high tide, the beach break gets quite good, although the rips can be prominent, creating up-turned V-shaped sandbars with channels between them. Not as sheltered from the southeast wind as Caves.

Paranoia ✪ ✪ ✪

At the end of Koeël Bay, Paranoia is as the name suggests. Even without the side-effects from substance abuse, paranoid will be the way you feel surfing it in a six- to eight-foot swell perilously close to sharp, nasty looking rocks. A left-hand point reef, it breaks almost on the rocks. Needs glassy, clean, evenly spaced lines to work. Beginners, stay away.

Off the Mountain ✪ ✪ ✪

A lot of people claim they discovered this spot. This includes sporadic posses of guys who came across it in the nineties, and even in 2006 after a huge swell coincided with Easter traffic. Everyone has a name for it, including Secrets, Virgins, Off the Wall and Ledges. However, we'll give Steven 'Rio' Middleton the benefit of the doubt. Cape Town charger Micky Duffus says Rio was already surfing it in the early 1980s. Near Rooiels on the way from Koeël Bay, it only works in a ginormous swell, running along rocks at the foot of cliffs and visible from the road above. Big-wave boards only. Hard to catch and not as good as it looks in photos.

Pringle Bay ✪ ✪ ✪

Tucked around the corner near Hangklip, this beach rarely breaks. However, the left-hand point on the east side of the beach breaks in huge swell, and can go off at times. Likes a huge southwest to south swell and an east or southeast wind.

Moonlight Bay ✪ ✪ ✪

The traditional name is Bokbaai or Moonshine Bay. It's next to Cape Hangklip on the western side. A short, sharp right-hander breaks off rocks in this small, jagged bay. Similar to Pringle Bay. Southeast to east winds are offshore. Works when you least expect it. Hairy.

OVERBERG

We begin at the end of False Bay – Cape Hangklip –
and end at Cape Infanta in the east. The Overberg marks
the transition from the Atlantic to the Indian Ocean, and includes
the southernmost tip of Africa, Agulhas. The biggest surf
occurs in winter, while summer is often flat and
the winds onshore.

CAPE HANGKLIP TO CAPE INFANTA

The Overberg is wet and stormy in winter, but dry and windy in summer. The best times of year are autumn and spring. Mild weather and lighter winds, with plenty of wave action, are the norm rather than the exception.

Kokkerot ✪ ✪ ✪
Short, sharp right-hand reef break on the end of a spiny rock spit tucked away in the fynbos somewhere in the vicinity of Holbaai. Popular with bodyboarders and skilled stand-ups. Hard to find. Sucking humping squat-shaped wave with a fat lip that lurches over a shallow rock shelf.

Yellowsand ✪ ✪
Sand-bottomed break as you head into Betty's Bay. Handles a bigger swell than Crystal Road. Not surfed that often. Needs a clean six- to eight-foot general swell to bend around outer reefs.

Crystal Road ✪ ✪ ✪
A fun right-hand beach break created from bigger swells that refract around a kelpy outcrop of rocksand reform on a sandbar at about three to four feet. It sometimes looks better than it is, but it gets pretty good if you don't mind weekend crowds. The bigger waves seem to miss the sandbar, and close out across the bay. However, some of the bigger waves hold up just enough to provide a really hollow inside section ending in a long shore-break barrel.

Betty's Bay Beach ✪ ✪ ✪
Still known as HF Verwoed Beach, can you believe. Series of sandbars that get good depending on sand and swell direction. A lot of shore-break dumpers and close-outs, but sometimes smoking left and right peaks.

Kleinmond ✪ ✪
A left breaks towards the car park at Kleinmond in Sandown Bay, but it's fickle and the rip can make paddling out tough, especially if the swell is oversized. The outgoing rip between the rocks and the wave is created by a deep channel, a favourite area for fishermen. The rip kicks when the swell gets to about five or six foot. A light northwest or north wind is best.

Hawston ✪ ✪ ✪
There are two waves that are surfable: the beach break and a left point off a slipway where the boats are launched. Quite a roff area. A lot of cars have been vandalised and people mugged here.

BOMB BAY: Another mission to Bayview finds the target.

Baby J ✪✪✪✪

Big-wave spot between Hawston and Onrus. In 2006, it was surfed at more than 20 feet, breaking top to bottom. The shock wave from the lip has broken windows in the holiday houses across the road. A consistent big-wave spot similar to Crayfish Factory, with a series of kelpy ledges causing a shifting take-off and plenty of clean-up sets. Do not get suckered into paddling for the insiders. You will get spat on to a nasty inside rock. When paddling in or out, you have to negotiate rocks sharper than broken glass. Booties essential. Don't paddle out on your short board no matter how small it looks. Bring big brass balls.

Haardebaai ✪✪✪✪

A big-wave right-hand reef break. It likes a large southwest swell and light northeast winds. A very kelpy wave that needs just the right tide. Generally very fickle, but gets excellent. However, it's unforgiving, and will not be treated lightly. Be warned. A spearo disappeared here in 2006. He was never found. Only his car and clothes were found near the paddle-in spot. Serious.

Onrus ✪✪✪

Best known for the left-hander that breaks in the corner near the car park. When the lagoon – fed by the Onrus River – breaks its banks, this left can get good: hollow and dredging. It works even during a galeforce northwest. Occasionally a right-hander forms on the other side of the beach, but this happens rarely more than once a year for a short period.

Sandbaai ✪✪✪✪

Right-hander that works off a combination of reef and sand. Gets good. Best in light summer (southeast) trades, light northerlies and glassy groundswell. There is a resident great white here. His name is Cedric the Sand Sub. Be careful of the strong rip that sucks you into the deep water behind the take-off rock. Once the rip has taken you past, it is very hard to get back. When you start paddling too hard and sending those panic signals, keep an eye out for Cedric.

Voelklip ✪✪✪

This picturesque beach in Hermanus offers a proper wave with bowling rights. Has a soft tolerant feel but quite hard to catch. Just paddle out on

Kelp and seaweed

There are more than 800 species of seaweed in our waters, making South Africa one of the richest marine flora environments in the world. Vast forests of kelp are rich in nutrients, supply oxygen to the water and host a plethora of sea creatures in the shelter of their wavy fronds. Kelp can be a bit of a nuisance when you're trying to paddle out to a sublime spot at low tide, especially when a surge maroons you on a clump of kelp, where you flail like a horny tortoise. Occasionally, people knock their surfboard fins out because they collide with clumps of kelp while bottom-turning on a wave.

Hermanus

This bustling town – considered the best land-based whale-watching venue in the world – nestles between fynbos-covered mountains and the sea along the shores of Walker Bay. The jagged coastline alternates between small sandy beaches, coves and sheltered bays. *Roridula gorgonias* (vlieëbos in Afrikaans) is the largest carnivorous plant in the world and can be found in the richly endowed Fernkloof Nature Reserve that lies on the slopes of the mountain behind the town. A good spot to use as a base to explore the coast.

A grinding, spittin roil slams into a

the inside of the rock where a lovely rip will pull you out. Don't stay in it for too long. You'll end up mixed in with the bird shit on the front of the rock. Works only on a small swell but can have a fun wave when a big swell reforms on the inside of the rock. The wave and set-up change all the time. Can also be a hollow wedging left that runs into the corner called knerses – a cartoon wolf on SABC a long time ago. Holds clean four- to six-foot swell. Needs any north wind.

Bayview ✪✪✪✪

Big-wave right-hander in the middle of Hermanus. Set in a small rock-fringed bay, a grinding, spitting beast of a rock roil slams into a big slab of granite, then surges against short sharp cliffs, the sucking backwash surging back out to sea. Tourists can watch you wash along the rocks, stranded with no exit point as 10-foot groundswells pummel your pip. Bayview has many problems. One of them is the small colony of seals that cluster where you kick out (if you make it that far). It's like a yummy takeaway stopover for you know who. A second problem is that after a big set surges into the cramped bay, the water vents back into the ocean in one place. If you are caught in this rush of water, only the NSRI will get you back. In 2006, a great white splashed two local surfers as it breached four metres into the air, swallowing a baby seal whole. No bullshit. And then you still have to contend with the wave. There are four reefs. Each one tries to outdo the other in psychotic attempts to mutate the wave. Yet you can

have the wave of your life. The sound in the second reef barrel is like a B52 flying through a tunnel.

De Kelders ✪

At the far end of Walker Bay, in the corner near a large Strandloper midden and interesting caves, is a fun but fickle little beach break that hardly anyone surfs – mostly for good reason. It rarely breaks properly. Other options on the way from Hermanus along the beach.

The Computer ✪✪✪

A long, hollow left fading into a bay. Has been tow-surfed a few times and prefers a big 10-foot-plus groundswell. Needs lots of well-directed swell, and is offshore on the summer trades. One teeny weeny snag. A fleet of shark cage-diving boats are constantly driving back and forth to shark alley around the back of the line-up. Not everything that breaches is a whale.

The Toilet ✪✪✪✪

A sucking triple-double-up ledging left-hand barrel-thing that would scare the living daylights out of the most hardened surfer. This spot lies somewhere between Gansbaai and Pearly Beach and becomes unsurfable over six foot. The locals call it ChowPoo. But that's not why it got its name. Okay, so there are some public toilets nearby, but upon sight of it, your bowels will loosen involuntarily – intestines squirming in unbridled terror. Keep an extra bog roll handy.

g beast of a rock
big slab of granite

Uilenkraalsmond ✪ ✪ ✪
River mouth sandbar set-up in sharky area (there was a non-fatal attack here in 2005). Some fun waves, depending on sand build-up. Dangerous rips on the outgoing tide. Shady milkwood forest and caravan park on western bank of the river mouth. Nice lagoon.

Pearly Beach ✪ ✪ ✪
Occasionally, good waves break here. A right-hand reef break. Best in a northeast-northwest breeze and clean groundswell. Some waves along the beach. Rip currents can be a problem.

Struisbaai ✪ ✪
Just east of the southernmost tip of Africa, Cape Agulhas, you get a tiny bay called Skulpiesbaai (Little Shells Bay), and then Struisbaai. There are two main breaks. A symmetrical outside reef and a right-hand point called Maclears. The reef breaks to the left and right. Very sharky area. Like many of the bays in this area, the point faces northeast, and needs a huge southwest swell before there is enough juice to wrap the swell in. Otherwise, a southeast to east swell does the trick.

Arniston (Waenhuiskrans) ✪ ✪ ✪
A beautiful white-washed fishing village is located hunched around one of several rocky bays on the inside of Struispunt, at the eastern end of Struisbaai. The transport ship HMS *Arniston* ran aground here in 1815. Six out of 378 survived.

Gansbaai

The British war ship HMS *Birkenhead* sank off Danger Point, the aptly named finger of land that juts far into the sea at Gansbaai. There are a few reef breaks in the area. Best conditions are light southeast-northeast and a clean groundswell in the six- to eight-foot range and bigger. Mostly reefs. Lots of kelp. Lots of sharks – after all, it is the centre of South Africa's shark cage-diving industry. The construction of the harbour wall at Gansbaai apparently ruined the best surf spot in the area.

Many houses have beams from the ship. Bays and rocky outcrops have names like Otterbaai, Fennebakbaai, Waenhuiskrans (Wagon House Cliff), Preekstoel (Preaching Stool or Pulpit) and Spuitgate (Blow Holes). There are a few spots in the area, some near the town, such as the main beach which gets fun. Others are in the De Hoop Nature Reserve heading east. If you can find a local, ask him to show you. He will pause from gutting his kob with his bare hands, stare stonily at you and shake his head super slowly – a signal that means, 'If I tell you, I kill you.' Actually, not really. Best in light southwest to northwest winds and clean south swell.

GARDEN ROUTE

The scenic Garden Route, starting at Cape Infanta and ending at the forest-lined Tsitsikamma River, is cool and wet in the winter and warm and dry in the summer. Mountains form a spine that sweeps towards the Eastern Cape. The surf is best in mild north or northwest winds and a clean groundswell, particularly in autumn and spring. In winter, the surf can be often wild, especially when big cold fronts blast through.

CAPE INFANTA TO THE TSITSIKAMMA RIVER

The coastal terrain of the Garden Route is rugged, with steep cliffs and thickly wooded ravines that snake up into the mountains. There is an abundance of wildlife in the many nature reserves of the area, including leopards in the more remote kloofs, baboons, lynx, porcupines, buck, tortoises, rock rabbits, mongooses, honey badgers and even elephants, although the once prolific herd of Knysna forest elephants – once numbering thousands – can now be counted on one hand. During winter, countless rivers and streams cascade towards the sea, filling up lakes and lagoons. The river water is rich in minerals, and runs the colour of cola – a translucent rust-red over the shallows, but black where the water runs deep. This creates interesting colours at many river-mouth surf breaks.

Cape Infanta ✪

Right point on the east side of Cape Infanta. Generally lacks form and needs solid, deep-energy rollers with a long interval coming through from the south and light west to northwest winds.

St Sebastian Bay ✪ ✪

The Breede River widens into a beautiful estuary as it flows into the sea at the western end of St Sebastian Bay. On the southern flank of the Breede is Infanta, and to the north, a vast sandy beach called Witsand (White Sand). The beach break gets good in summer during a small to moderate south to southeast swell. Doesn't like big swell. Needs light west to northwest breezes.

Jongensfontein ✪ ✪ ✪

When you're headed to Stilbaai in the mistaken belief that it will be firing, Jongens might appease you. Jongens prefers a two- to five-foot southwest to south swell, and breaks off a reef running right. The northwest to west wind is offshore, but it needs to be light.

Kakgat ✪ ✪ ✪

Triangular-shaped reef with right-handers peeling off the top of the reef, sometimes running up to a shore-break close-out. Prefers light west to northwest wind and clean three- to five-foot groundswell. Careful when pulling off the floater at the end. You might get a sand enema you won't

WHITE-CAPPED: Looking from Plettenberg Bay towards Keurbooms.

DAY OF DAYS: You don't get more perfect than this.

forget. On the scatological theme, Kakgat was named in the 1980s when former Springbok rugby player Rob Louw took a dump into an underground municipal sewage tank at the break.

Ramyatoolies ✪ ✪ ✪

A fast, powerful left-hander off some rocks further down the beach. It was first surfed in 1984 but the locals did not have a name for it. Then someone told a derogatory joke: 'What do you call a gay man from the Himalayan region? Ramyatool Upmabut.' The name Ramyatoolies or 'Toolies' stuck. That's the story anyway.

Dolfines Point ✪ ✪ ✪ ✪

A gnarly, ledging right-hand point reef with some seriously hollow sections deep in wild fynbos. Needs a solid 10-foot-plus south swell before the swell wraps into the bay, or southeast swell of course. Needs light northwest to northeast wind. Only good surfers need apply.

Skulpiesbaai ✪ ✪ ✪

In the middle of the bay across from Dolfines Point lies a small triangular reef with good right-handers in clean groundswell and light winds. On the eastern side of the bay, which is in effect the reverse side of Stilbaai Point, some good lefts break off the rocks. Best when a powerful five- to eight-foot southeast swell is running.

Stilbaai ✪ ✪ ✪ ✪

Another grinding right-hand point break with a classic mid-break section, and sometimes a deep, thick outside section for the stout of heart. When big, a strong rip pushes you down the rocks. Like many points along the east coast, Stilbaai likes a lined-up south to southeast swell. A huge west or southwest swell bends around the outside point and reforms a lot smaller on the inside, with much of its energy broken up. As the swell angle moves to southeast, the swell comes in straighter, avoiding the outside reform. Best in glassy seas or light westerlies on a pushing mid tide in clean four- to eight-foot swell.

Gouritsmond ✪ ✪ ✪

A right-hand point break running into the mouth of the Gourits River. A seldom-surfed spot that breaks on sand built up over the rocks. It works in large southwest groundswells and moderate west winds. Hard to find.

Kanon ✪ ✪ ✪ ✪

Tucked away around a point, this rock-shelf right-hander is the Cave Rock of the Garden Route. It's an awesome barrel, but only breaks when a solid southeast swell pushes around the corner in similar fashion to Vlees. Keep a look out for great whites. You don't really want to surf here. Named after three cannons mounted at one of the houses salvaged from the French man o' war *La Fortune*, wrecked in 1763.

Mossel Bay

Like many east coast towns, including Plettenberg Bay, Jeffreys Bay and Port Elizabeth, Mossel Bay lines the southern rim of a large, sweeping bay, tucked in the lee of a protruding point – Cape St Blaize. On the open-ocean side of the cape, jagged cliffs loom above thundering surf. The rock strata have been laid bare. Massive caverns have been ground out by the relentless force of the elements. The massive Mossgas oil-from-gas project – offshore rigs mine gas which is then converted to petroleum – as well as a property boom, saw the town grow rapidly in the 1990s and 2000s. Like most coastal towns, gets frantic in the holiday season. Bartholomeu Dias, the Portuguese explorer who 'discovered' South Africa, landed for the first time at Munro's Bay, a calm little cove three kilometres around the corner from Cape St Blaize. There are numerous historic houses, including about 200 stone houses built by Cornish stonemasons in the early 1900s. In the distance, the jagged blue line of the Outeniqua Mountains keeps an eternal watch over the coast. The surf spots lie near the town itself, starting near the caravan park around the corner from Cape St Blaize.

Vleesbaai ✪ ✪ ✪ ✪ ✪

Protected point that breaks like Bruce's Beauties in Cape St Francis, but needs as much east in the swell as possible. It turns on when a big east to southeast swell or huge south swell pushes in, aided by an incoming tide and sometimes southeast winds. This break is not a great option. Firstly, it is fickle, and breaks rarely. Secondly, it is hard to find, and entails a sweaty walk fighting off alien wattle trees oozing poisonous sap and riddled with boomslang. If that doesn't get you, the horny razor-toothed tortoise could. This hectic herbivore hates humans. Thirdly, a large colony of great white sharks breeds just off the take-off zone.

Inner Pool ✪ ✪ ✪

Somewhat overrated, the Inner Pool is a small inlet where the waves break right off rocks to the right of the better break, Outer Pool. Tends to be a bit slow-moving and mushy, but popular. Walls up nicely sometimes, often when Outer Pool is flat.

Outer Pool ✪ ✪ ✪ ✪

The main wave at Mossel Bay. 'The Outer' gets big and hairy, and sharky. Often entails a tough paddle against a rip that surges along the point and big walling waves that trick you into paddling too far on the inside. In a clean orderly south swell and light west winds, it fires.

Santos Reef ✪ ✪ ✪

In front of a caravan park, Santos is a reef peak tucked into the south end of the bay. Needs giant southwest to south swell to register sporadic two- to four-foot sets. On a south to southeast swell, gets consistent and quite good in a fun, hotdog kind of way. Lacks raw power. Likes light west to southwest breezes.

Ding Dangs ✪ ✪ ✪

A fun wave on the inside rim of Mossel Bay that needs a huge groundswell to wrap around the headland at Cape St Blaize, bending down past the town and eventually reaching Ding Dangs. Best in southwest to west winds and four- to six-foot general east swell. Needs a low tide. Otherwise, a little soft.

Dias Beach ✪ ✪

A fickle beach break that depends on the sandbanks. Needs light offshore winds and a moderate swell.

Hartenbos ✪

Weak, poorly formed sandbars can rearrange into semi-decent beach-break peaks. Light northwest to west wind and clean southeast to east swell.

Klein Brak River ✪ ✪ ✪

As Mossel Bay sweeps eastwards and away from the shelter of Cape St Blaize, the surf gets bigger. The sandy rim of the bay stretches far into the distance, for more than 10 km, past Klein Brak and Groot Brak. Mostly beach breaks along this stretch, with the odd sand-covered rock reef. Quite fickle and a bit sharky. Can't cope with big swell, when dredging rips come into play. Best in light north to northwest wind and a clean, nicely spaced four- to seven-foot southwest groundswell. A few secret spots deliver the goods for surfers in holiday houses along the top of a long dune parallel to the beach.

Herolds Bay ✪ ✪ ✪

When the sea is flat everywhere else, Herolds is likely to be a clean two- to three-foot if not four-foot. One of the most consistent breaks in South Africa, but only surfable in small to medium swell. Best in a clean three- to five-foot groundswell with a slight east to southeast angle to it. Breaks on a mixture of reef and sand. Classic shore break. When sand is properly arranged, you can get so slotted. Needs light north to northwest berg winds. Picks up lank swell.

Victoria Bay ✪ ✪ ✪ ✪

Vic Bay is a classic set-up on a small scale. This bay between steep tree-covered hills is probably only 200 metres wide. The west side of the bay, an established holiday getaway for the fortunate few who have a house at the water's edge, produces perfect point break walls. You take off near a rock that sticks out the water. The wave walls away from you and down a shallow line of rocks. The bigger waves angle further away from the rocks and into

Wilderness

Heading from George and Vic Bay, you drive through the Kaaimans River Pass, which cuts through a forested gorge. Crossing the river, the road meanders back up and turns a corner at the edge of a mountain that overlooks many kilometres of beach and verdant wetland. There are beach breaks as far as the eye can see. You coast down to sea level into the aptly named town of Wilderness around the southern rim of the Touw River Lagoon, the first of a series of mostly interlocking lakes that continue all the way to Knysna. The wetland is bird-watching paradise. A long dune, like a sandy rib, separates the wetlands and the sea – a popular paragliding spot due to the gentle onshore breezes that create good ridge lift along the edge, keeping the paragliders drifting back and forth for hours. Inland lies a vast closed-canopy afromontane forest on the slopes of mountains that roughly follow the coast.

the middle of the beach. Best in a four- to six-foot south to southwest swell and glassy or offshore (northwest to southwest wind) conditions. Handles light south to southeast winds.

Wilderness ✪ ✪ ✪
A long beach with sandbar set-ups interspersed with occasional clumps of rock and reef. Picks up a lot of swell, and is not surfed often, although there are good waves at times. Needs deep, spaced groundswell when bigger, otherwise it gets wild and woolly. Settled, smooth seas and light winds essential.

Gerickes ✪ ✪ ✪
On the way to Sedgefield lies a shale headland to the right of the Swartvlei car park that becomes almost an island on high tide. You need to walk for 20 minutes along the beach to reach the tiny

left-hand point break on the other side, preferably at low tide unless you want to rock climb or wade through the shorebreak. Picks up lank swell. One of the few spots that works in – actually needs – a northeast onshore wind. It gets out of control easily. Best at two- to four-foot. Provides zippy waves that reel for about 30-40 metres along a volcanic rock shelf. Short, sharp and sweet. On the other side of the channel, a right-hander breaks over a jagged reef. Picks up more swell, but can be tricky with interspersed rock slabs and protruding rocks. Sharky.

Swartvlei ✪ ✪
Beach break in front of the car park at Swartvlei. Depends on sandbanks but gets quite good. Best in light northwest to northeast winds.

Goukamma ✪ ✪ ✪ ✪
A long beach runs along the Goukamma Nature Reserve, with beach breaks galore. However, perhaps the best wave breaks at the Goukamma River Mouth. Can get epic when the sand is in the right place. The river runs from the majestic Outeniqua Mountains, passing through verdant forests. Humic acids leached from the organic leafy mulch of the forest floor make the river run a dark red, almost black. In light north winds, this spot fires on all cylinders.

Fish Boma ✪ ✪ ✪
In the corner further down off a rocky outcrop is a low-tide peak that breaks along a rip. Best in a clean three- to five-foot swell and light north to northeast wind. Gets good here, but a shark attack in 2000 slowed the interest. As local Charles Smith said: 'I never thought our sharks would do this to us. It was quite a shock.'

Buffalo Bay wild side ✪ ✪ ✪
The exposed south side of Buffalo Bay gets messy easily and can't handle too much swell because the open ocean swell comes directly on to the beach here, often breaking on outside banks and closing out. However, on small, glassy days or light northwest to north winds, a clean and powerful left-hander breaks off a sandbank in the middle

SECRETS: Somewhere near Sedgefield.

of the beach. Gets rippy though. Occasionally, a wedge breaks in the corner on the right of the beach. Locals say that its epic days have been over for years, although there seems to be no reason why they shouldn't come back again.

Buffalo Bay ☯☯☯

On the inside of Walker Point lies a series of overlapping reefs offering a consistent but generally slow-breaking right-hander that needs an easterly tinge to the swell for it to run properly. Swell from the southwest hits the outside point and has to work hard to wrap around and into the bay before reforming and breaking on the inner point. This is a common malaise afflicting South African points, making them B-grade set-ups. However, when the swell runs out of the southeast or east, they instantly become A-grade spots. Examples include Coffee Bay, Seal Point and Stilbaai. Buffalo Bay needs a west wind and four- to eight-foot southeast to east swell.

Murphys ☯☯☯

A fun left and right peak can be found down the beach from the point at Buffalo Bay. A rip current tends to pull you towards the left, a churned up and reef-based sandbank. However, fun and hollow inside waves, as well as the occasional solid left on the outside, can make this spot worthwhile. Best in a low to pushing tide and light west winds.

The Knysna Heads ☯☯

There is actually a surf spot just inside the Knysna Heads. The locals ride it now and then. On a low tide when big swell runs outside the cliffs, the sandbars gladly accept fun and hollow three- to four-foot waves. The fun is tempered with the knowledge that you have to paddle across the channel to the other side, often when the tide is pushing through the heads. Incidentally, the Knysna Heads is one of only two places in the world that Lloyds shipping agents will not insure.

Noetzie ☯

Small bay with varying quality sandbars off a deep shelving beach where a dark red river meets the sea. Noetzie means 'black', referring to the almost black water coloured by humic acids leached from the carpet of leaves on the forest floor.

Robberg ☯☯

The break along the northern shoreline of the Robberg headland faces into the calmer waters of Plettenberg Bay. Because the headland pushes into the sea in an easterly direction, its southern shores absorb the dominant southwest to south swell. It takes a huge southeast swell or medium to big east swell to inject some life into this spot, a combination of rocks and sand. Inconsistent, but gets good occasionally.

The Wreck ☯☯☯

Not to be confused with the Wedge, the Wreck is also a wedge-shaped wave. However, it has a lot more going for it, when it breaks, that is. Not as consistent, but offers a longer ride and better form. Needs a monster swell to wrap into the bay around Robberg, or a lot of east in the swell. Waves bounce off the peninsula and peak off the wreck, forming wicked A-frame barrels.

LIQUID PROPULSION: John Henry tow-surfs an outer reef near Plett.

Knysna

On the eastern shore of the glistening Knysna lagoon sprawls this former logging town surrounded by large tracts of closed-canopy indigenous forest. A tiny outpost once, Knysna lay in the midst of a breathtaking paradise, but unrelenting development is slowly eroding it. In the waters of the lagoon, you might see the endangered Knysna seahorse. Off the foaming seas at the base of the mighty heads – two cliffs that guard the entrance to the lagoon – dolphins and whales are a common sight. Scattered on the beaches is a treasure chest of shells, including the pansy, while deep in the forest, lurk birds like the Knysna loerie, and the remnants of South Africa's only forest elephants. The stately Outeniqua yellowwood – dripping with lichen or 'old man's beard' – is the king of the trees. The town hosts flea markets, craft shops and cosy cafés that ooze a rustic, small-town charm. The locals are mellow and hospitable, with a high proportion of crafts people and artists. In outlying forests, communes of hippies chill out in cosmic union, a little like Nimbin, near Byron Bay in Australia. Knysna has access to a range of surf spots, and is within easy striking distance of the rich surfing area of Cape St Francis and Jeffreys Bay, two hours' drive to the east.

The Wedge ✪ ✪ ✪

In sight of the Beacon Isle Hotel built on an outcrop of rocks in Plettenberg Bay, the Wedge breaks on sand off the next rocky outcrop north of the hotel. It gets insanely hollow and powerful for its size. Swells bounce off the rocks and head parallel to the beach where they merge with oncoming swells, creating the wedge. Not all the waves wedge up in this way. However, if they don't, it usually means a close-out because the wave breaks too close to shore. A short but zippy little barrel that provides lots of fun in the right conditions: low tide and a clean three- to four-foot swell.

Lookout Beach ✪ ✪ ✪

The main beach break at Plett is traditionally a fickle break due to erratic sand movement. However, in August 2006, unprecedented flooding disgorged tons of sand and debris into the sea, creating some of the best surf locals had ever seen off the rocks at the southern end. Big-wave tow-in riders had a field day off the rocks at the western end, which became a super bank. It handled up to a solid 12-foot on some days. Then, in March 2007, a gigantic southeast swell and a big storm wiped out the beach, but there are still waves and the sand is slowly returning. There is also surf further down the beach near the river mouth, often just a small channel between the lagoon and the sea. Usually though, Lookout is not the most alluring of temptations. There are many other, better spots nearby to choose from.

Plettenberg Bay

This large bay is framed by the huge sandstone Robberg Peninsula in the south and the deep blue-green estuaries of the Bitou and Keurbooms rivers in the north. The over-sized holiday town that nestles in the southern half used to be an unspoilt village with acres of pristine coastal bush and endless beaches. The beaches are still there, but they are framed by acres and acres of concrete. Even the beaches have taken a knock, although not by humans (directly anyway). In March 2007, a huge storm annihilated Lookout Beach, ripping the sand out and bringing the sea almost to the car park. The sand slowly began to return later in 2007. Plett is the spiritual home of many holidaymakers who still make the pilgrimage from inland cities and other coastal towns, but the burgeoning shopping malls and other trappings of urbanisation have merely created a home away from home. There are a few surf spots in the bay, but they don't pick up a lot of swell. Robberg acts as a buffer zone to the open ocean. A large southwest swell or south to east swell bends into the bay to produce the surf.

Tsitsikamma National Coastal Park

This verdant stretch of rugged coast runs for 75 km from Nature's Valley in the west to Oubosstrand in the east. Coincidently, two rivers with the same name, Grootrivier, mark the park's coastal boundaries. You will need permits to explore the park, which is pockmarked by steep cliffs, small rocky coves and river mouths. It's a wild, untrammelled coastline that is inaccessible by road, except for the roads leading from the N2 highway to Storms River Mouth, which splits the park into two halves. The popular hiking route, the Otter Trail – from Storms River heading west to Nature's Valley – yields several surf spots, but lugging a surfboard on a five-day hike will not be pleasant.

Keurbooms ✪ ✪ ✪ ✪

This glassy beach break, inhabited by a group of friendly bottlenosed dolphins, is a gem. However, you've got to polish it first. Patience pays off at Keurbooms, on the way out of Plett and heading towards J-Bay. It's sensitive to wind, offshore or onshore. Best time is in glassy seas on a mid-tide pushing, with a clean three- to four-foot groundswell, or on the high tide itself. Can be a bit rippy between tides, with the surge pulling you on to sandbanks on the right, away from the left-hander. The left works on a lowish tide and the right needs a high tide. Keurbooms has similarities with KwaZulu-Natal beach breaks. When good, it has glassy tubes, water as clear as liquid glass and playful dolphins. It is quite fickle though, and has a slight shark reputation.

Nature's Valley ✪ ✪ ✪ ✪

A small residential area in the Tsitsikamma National Coastal Park, the scenery around this beautiful beach and lagoon is stunning. Offers a classic sand-bottomed right and left peak sensitive to currents, wind and swell. Needs a smooth and well-spaced two- to five-foot southwest to south groundswell and no wind, or light northeast to northwest breezes. Gets super-hollow and crunchy. Dangerous undertows when the swell is big. Very sharky.

Storms River Mouth ✪ ✪ ✪

As the name suggests, the sea is often wild, with uneven wave action and strong rip currents make it a lottery. However, you get really good waves here on small to medium days and light north to northwest breezes.

SUNSHINE COAST

Between the Tsitsikamma River and Cintsa, just past East London, lies the warmer waters of an aloe-strewn coastline dominated by two huge bays – St Francis Bay and Algoa Bay. Falling within the Eastern Cape, the Sunshine Coast is flanked by mountains to the northwest and the Indian Ocean to the southeast. Good surf breaks all year round at a varied mixture of point, reef and beach breaks.

TSITSIKAMMA RIVER TO CINTSA

The Sunshine Coast marks a steady but slow transition from the fynbos of the Western Cape to the increasingly sub-tropical flora of the Wild Coast. At the end of Algoa Bay, which is lined by the city of Port Elizabeth, the coast heads northeast, rather than travelling due east, making it harder for the dominant southwest swells to make landfall. The landscape between the mountain spine running parallel to the coast towards the Drakensberg and the shoreline is mostly flat and, in summer, dry. Vegetation is characterised by aloes, fleshy sour figs (good for jellyfish stings), fynbos and shrubland. Distant views of steely blue crags and vast, sweeping bays make for beautiful landscapes. A glassy afternoon at Jeffreys Bay can be a divine experience, especially when the dolphins appear, shadow-surfing the wave beneath you, showing us how to share.

Seal Point wild side ✪ ✪ ✪ ✪
This rugged stretch of exposed coast includes Slangbaai, Oyster Bay and Thysbaai. Surfed in summer in small swell and northeast winds (offshore here). Mostly rock slabs offering short, powerful waves with sketchy access. Locals know.

Boulders ✪ ✪ ✪
Fickle reef point running into a small rocky bay in front of the car park above Oyster Row. Requires huge swell similar to Bruce's Beauties, but Boulders is a left-breaking wave. To get it good, buy a local lots of beer.

Seal Point ✪ ✪ ✪ ✪ ✪
Seals, with its landmark lighthouse, is a rocky point break divided into two sections by a fullstop rock that marks the take-off zone for the mid break. The outside gets classic, especially on a medium to big south to southeast swell. Prevailing southwest swell must refract around the outside point and reform at Seals. You can ride waves all the way past the fullstop rock down the point – about a 150-metre ride. Beware the fullstop. It can take you from hero to zero in a millisecond as you pull in to the barrel, then pull in to a rock. Also, mind the urchins.

Seals beach ✪ ✪ ✪ ✪
Depending on banks and tides, pick your spot from the caravan park to the bottom of the point. Consistent wave in the corner. The beach at Seals gets plenty of swell. It is a good summer spot. However, the sand banks tend to close out during big winter swell. Needs west winds.

ALOE GOLD: The aloe ferox is to J-Bay what the Eiffel Tower is to Paris.

Ducks ✪✪✪
Sandbar and reef combination on the other side of the bay. Sheltered from the northeast by the northern rim of the bay. Again, usually a summer spot. Gets good. Sharky.

Killers ✪✪✪
Around Cape St Francis and into St Francis Bay at the top lies Killers, a sketchy spot that breaks viciously hard along evil-looking rocks. Needs east swell and west winds.

Bruce's ✪✪✪✪✪
A clean, green jewel. Forget the gentle tubing hotdog waves you saw in *Endless Summer*. When the east swell is grinding, this wave churns down the point at Cape St Francis like a runaway steam train, growling and spitting. The drop at big Bruce's is a stomach churner. And slotting into the gaping barrel is to dice with a juddering lip cracking along a jagged line of rocks. The reef lies at the same depth and angle to the swell, creating a perfect curling consistency. To feast your eyes on these grinding green room tubes is to see one of the surfing wonders of the world, even though the sand does not cover the point like it used to. Best two hours on either side of low tide, unless dik.

Huletts Left ✪✪✪✪
Same as Bruce's. Needs huge south swell or big east swell and a low to mid tide. Nice beefy left with a mellow take-off that improves down the line. Easy access through slipway.

Huletts Right ✪✪
Right-hand reef point that also suffered from sand redistribution. Not as good as before. Mellow wave, ideal for longboarders. Incoming to high tide. Good protection from strong westerlies.

Main Beach ✪✪✪
Bad development has ruined it like Anne's. Sand is gone, no beach at high tide. Suffers from back wash. Occasionally gets good if sand builds up. Needs west winds.

Anne Avenue ✪✪✪
Used to have excellent sandbars, but poor development has killed the beach and ruined this spot. Gets good sometimes, but not as consistent.

Soweto's ✪✪✪
Also called Rushmere's, the quality of this sand and reef combination depends on sand distribution. Breaks left and right. Wind must blow from the west.

SAND PITS: The point break that gave South Africa a good name.

FRANK ROAD

J-Bay

J-Bay is a giant surf shop. Named after a store owner who provided victuals to seafarers in 1849, Jeffreys Bay was a quiet, undiscovered fishing village for many years. In the 1960s, Afrikaner farmers used it as a rustic holiday spot. Then a small band of surfers found tubular nirvana at the Point, a few stops down from Supertubes, which was too fast to surf.

During the 1970s and 1980s, the surfing scene grew in tandem with places like Torquay in Oz. Both were hippie hangouts from whence came surf dynasties like Rip Curl, Billabong and Country Feeling.

SUPER TUBE: What more do you want?

Apart from surfing, J-Bay subsists on chokka (squid) fishing, property development and tourism. A strong Afrikaner core brings a conservative element to society here. In the off-season, there isn't much to do. Some might even consider it boring. However, the locals wouldn't have it any other way. When swell arrives out of season, the locals get their reward. Like nearby St Francis, J-Bay is a holiday town riddled with caravan parks, campsites, chalets, hotels and backpackers. During summer, it bursts with holidaymakers. In winter, hordes of surfers descend, giving estate agents and property owners an all-round boom in occupancy.

Visitors will notice how surfing and tourism are in a perpetual state of conflict. The mood oscillates between warm South African hospitality and hostile surf localism. Residents who surf and work in tourism struggle to reconcile the two. On land it's all warm smiles. In the water, it can be unbridled aggro.

A sad consequence of the housing boom and the selfishness of property owners are the crude buildings that have mushroomed everywhere – block after block of ugly concrete and brick. The Supers car park has shrunk. The famous aloes that lined the pristine bush along the point have been herded into an artificial plantation as part of a dune reclamation project. Yet hordes of foreign surfers, clutching strong currency, descend on J-Bay to enjoy cheap surf holidays. They don't care. They often stay for months on end, getting into the stoke of surfing one of the best waves on our planet.

Please treat the wave and other surfers with respect, otherwise you will come off second best. Moving on from all the human nonsense, there is a side to Jeffreys that makes it special, apart from the perfect cylinders of swell that sweep in from the south. Dolphins are regulars. So are whales and seals. When the sun rises, casting its golden hue over the sea and lighting up the misty Elandsberg in the distance, schools of dolphins stop by on their feeding route. They turn on an exhibition of free surfing, like no human could ever hope to emulate. Streaking beneath and above the waves, these grey torpedoes are an exhilarating combination of grace and power. Good wave selection too. If you are lucky to be sitting in the line-up at dawn when the waves are a perfect four to six foot, a light offshore is blowing and the dolphins are on song, you experience one of nature's most exquisite moments. Bear it in mind when screaming blue murder at the guy who ruined your perfect wall during the weekend bun fight.

MESSAGE IN A BOTTLE: The Kelly
Slater of marine mammals.

The exit is an oval fleck of light at the end of a long blue cave

Clapton's Coils ✪ ✪ ✪ ✪ ✪

Long, tubing, left-hand reef point. Best in a light northwest wind and big east swell. The quality of this wave is inversely proportional to the depths locals will go to protect their last outpost. To get there, leopard crawl through the fynbos at night with board and suit, catch and ride four waves as fast as you can as the dawn is breaking. Then make sure your getaway is a hired perlemoen poacher who snatches you from the surf in a super-fast speedboat before the locals get a chance to identify you. Otherwise, live in Jeffreys Bay for about 10 years. Living in J-Bay means sacrifice. To score, you have to live there as well.

Kitchen Windows ✪ ✪ ✪

As you enter Jeffreys Bay, there are spots that are surfed mostly by locals and rarely by anyone else. Unless you spend a fair amount of time in J-Bay, Kitchen Windows won't be on your itinerary. You'll probably spend most of your time salivating over the prospect of surfing Supertubes. In fact, you will surf mushy, two-foot slop at Supers, oblivious to cooking two- to four-foot waves here. Not as powerful as other spots.

Magna Tubes ✪ ✪ ✪ ✪

The reef slightly around the corner from Supers in front of the Beach Hotel. Fast and hard-breaking off an exposed reef, left and right. Closes out often, but best when the swell is small. Picks up more swell than Supers.

Boneyards ✪ ✪ ✪ ✪ ✪

Occy in his former heyday ruled this spot for extended periods of the surf season. To go right is to negotiate a hectically fast wall that barrels in varying sections towards the main take-off zone at Supertubes. To make it through these sections, especially backhand, is a noble feat. It's even possible to take off outside Boneyards, fly through some heartstopping barrels and exit right at Supertubes, then scream obscenities at the numerous jealous surfers trying to drop in on you. Boneyards works differently at different sizes. When it's generally flat, and there's hardly a ripple at Supers, Boneyards can be three foot. In these, and slightly bigger conditions, you can go left and right.

Supertubes ✪ ✪ ✪ ✪ ✪

One of the top right-hand points on earth. When on, Supers is superlative. Best in moderate westerlies and medium big south swell between four and eight feet but handles up to 12 feet on clean swells. On epic days you can ride all the way down if you pick a 'sidewinder' that wraps wide of Supers, the bulk of its energy bunching towards the reef further out. Even then, you still have to draw a fast speed line through the barrel section at Impossibles. Some guys raise both arms and point down the point – a signal that they are going for it. The idea is to draw speed lines near the top of the feathering wall, and when it looks like the entire section is about to close, you drop wide and deep and carve the longest bottom turn possible, then trim back up the face and wind it again before trimming the rail and pulling in. Deep in the pit, the sunlight recedes. The exit is an oval fleck of light at the end of a long blue cave. The pendulum swings back. The hole draws nearer. It hovers once or twice, flirting, before unfolding as it arches over your head and you bust back into the sunlight. The swell at Supers can come up within hours. On small two- to three-foot days, most waves break too fast, and it becomes sectiony.

Supertubes is best in a southwest or west wind. The northwest, usually offshore for the east coast, is cross-shore here. Locals call it the devil's wind because it creates sideways chop up the face of the wave.

Salad Bowls ✪ ✪ ✪ ✪ ✪

At the end of Impossibles lies a short barrel section called Salad Bowls. Not really an official spot, but some people refer to it as such. If you're freaked out by the 150 people scratching for occasional waves chaotically up at Supers, you can surf down here by yourself.

Tubes ✪ ✪ ✪ ✪ ✪

Fast-breaking section on the other side of Salad Bowls and Impossibles. A classic wave that's slightly more forgiving than Supers. Shows the same superlative form as Supers, but is not quite as fast.

Point ✪ ✪ ✪ ✪ ✪

The Point lies about two thirds down from Supertubes – a mellow mirror of Supers, with fairly fast walls and a couple of short barrel sections. Laaities and longboarders love this spot. The atmosphere is more congenial than Supers.

Albatross ✪ ✪ ✪ ✪

The last spot before you run out of ocean. If you have ridden all the way from Supers, you've surfed for 1 200 metres. A smaller and mellower version of the Point.

Maitlands ✪ ✪ ✪

Beach break around the Maitland River Mouth. Best in small swell. Gets heavy, with hectic rips in bigger swell. Likes any north wind. Winds are onshore from west to southeast and offshore from northwest to northeast. Sharky.

Beachview ✪ ✪ ✪ ✪

Sandbar in front of tidal pool. Gets really good depending on banks. Prefers low tide. Any wind from the north.

Sardinia Bay ✪ ✪ ✪ ✪

Beach break that can be epic, or just a close-out, depending on the banks. Sharky. Needs any wind with a hint of northerly.

Noordhoek ✪ ✪ ✪

Right-hand reef point. A fickle break that needs a clean southwest to south swell, an incoming tide, and mild north to northwest winds. Handles light west wind. The southwest must not be stronger than about 10 knots.

Rockies ✪ ✪

On the other side of the bay from Noordhoek. A sketchy left-hander that breaks on a low to mid tide in light westerlies.

Main Rights ✪ ✪ ✪ ✪

Right-hand reef point. Prefers mid tide and west wind. Easy paddle out in the gully in front of the break. Holds a decent-sized swell.

Algoa Bay wild side

The coast west of Cape Recife, the southern promontory of Algoa Bay, where Port Elizabeth is situated, is exposed to the southern weather systems that bash up the coast. It picks up all the prevailing southwest swell, but spots are exposed and sensitive to any south wind and big swell. This coast prefers north winds or light westerlies, which makes it an ideal locale in summer, when northeast winds blow and the swell is small. Best conditions are light northeast to northwest winds and clean three- to six-foot groundswell. Some breaks get epic when the rest of the coast is blown out in mangling northeast winds. Some spots angle more to the east or northeast, and you revert to the traditional 'west wind is offshore' permutation. Many of the waves are located in the Maitland Mines Nature Reserve, Island Forest Reserve, Seaview Game Park or Cape Recife Nature Reserve.

RULER LINES: The underwater topography at J-Bay filters the swell.

Loch Ness ✪✪

Right reef running into a small bay. Nice take-off but fades quickly. Short ride. West winds. Low to incoming tide.

Secrets ✪✪✪

Nudist beach with sandbar peaks. Likes the summer northeast. Works in all tides depending on banks. Surf naked.

Boilers ✪✪✪✪

A beach break that entails a bit of a walk. Can be good. Depends on sandbanks. Works in all tides.

Noncom ✪✪✪✪

Sometimes called Padi. Good left and right sand peaks break into a gully in front of the Cape Recife Nature Reserve car park. Northeast winds are best. All tides.

Virgin Bay ✪✪✪✪

A 10-minute walk left of the Cape Recife Nature Reserve car park. Right sandbar, can be epic, but fickle. Very dependent on sand. Doesn't like too much swell. Light west or northeast. All tides depending on banks, normally low to incoming.

Cobbles ✪✪✪

Mellow right reef point ideal for longboarding. Cobbles is just on the bay side of Cape Recife and gets a wave when the bay is flat. Handles size if you can handle the paddle. Pushing tide best. Can be surfed on the low, but entails a long walk over dry reef. West winds.

Rincon ✪✪✪✪

Moving towards PE from Cape Recife, you will come across this good-quality right-hand point, but it gets sectiony. Best on pushing tide. Prefers southwest to west wind. Needs decent swell.

Blackbottoms ✪✪✪✪

Right reef that gets good, but depends on sand. Must have west winds.

Pipe ✪✪✪

There is usually something to ride at the Pipe, which is the reason why it is infested with groms. Fun beach break that varies from good to crap, depending on how much sand there is and where it has been deposited. Picks up the most swell. Apartment blocks protect it from strong westerlies. Better on pushing or high tide.

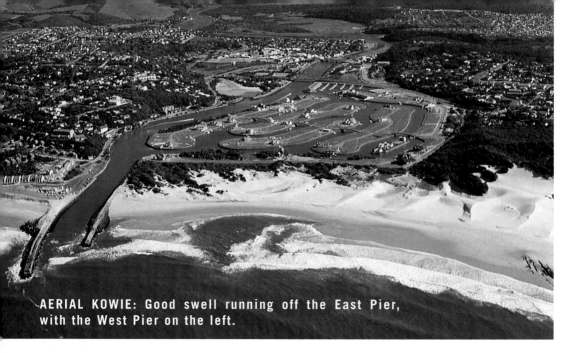

AERIAL KOWIE: Good swell running off the East Pier, with the West Pier on the left.

Clubhouse ✪✪✪✪

Right reef. Only breaks over six feet. Goes off in solid storm swell. Any southwest or west wind.

Avalanche ✪✪✪✪

Right-hander breaks on a sandbank behind a rocky outcrop and runs into a small bay. Can get a weird bump on it from sidewash off the rock, which makes for interesting sections. Quality

Port Elizabeth

This sprawling city lines the southern rim of the vast Algoa Bay. As you head around from the southern tip of the bay, Cape Recife, the coastline becomes more built up after Cape Recife Nature Reserve. Like Robberg in Plett and many point breaks in South Africa, Cape Recife acts as a natural breakwater to the dominant southwest swells emanating from the roaring forties. South swell must also work hard to get into the bay. Unlike the wild side, most of the surf spots in PE like southerly winds, but are manky in northerlies. Even the northwest berg wind causes a ruffled 'morning sickness' in the bay.

wave if sand is right. Low tides are best, although rideable through the high if the swell is big.

Millers ✪✪✪

Long right-hand point. Breaks over rock shelf, but mellow. Picks up less swell than breaks closer to Cape Recife. Likes high tide. Holds big swell, but rips kick in and the paddle is challenging. Best in south or southwest winds.

Shark Rock Pier ✪✪✪✪

Sandbar next to pier. Can be excellent depending on sand. Usually better after the summer easterlies have pushed the sand in. Low tide only. Backwash issues. One of the few places in Algoa Bay that likes east swell. Wants southwest or south winds.

Baked Beans ✪✪

Right reef between Shark Rock and Humewood. Depends on sand covering. Rarely surfed, usually only by bodyboarders on bigger swells.

Humewood ✪✪✪✪✪

Right sandbar next to the old pier. Gets excellent – one of the best waves in PE. You can hook insane barrels here. Handles east swell well. Handles south wind but likes southwest, with some protection from strong southwest.

Port Alfred

The Kowie River runs through the sleepy coastal town of Port Alfred (*pictured left*). The Royal Alfred Marina has slightly tainted the old-world charm of the town, but it remains quiet in the off-season. Students from Rhodes University in nearby Grahamstown bunk lectures to come surfing here. It only takes 45 minutes to drive down to 'Kowie'.

Denvils ☺☺

Sandbar off a rock at public pool. Depends on banks. Usually small. Closes out a lot. Many of the surf schools hang out here. Best on pushing tide and west winds.

Fence ☺☺☺

Sand-bottomed left in a land of rights. Fence wedges off the harbour wall. Gets good on its day, but the sandbanks have been off for years. The ballies say that it was much better years ago, and that there is too much sand now. Likes east swell in west to southwest winds. Needs incoming to high tide.

Brighton Pier ☺

Sand-bottomed right off the pier. Gets good (if you don't mind getting robbed, carjacked and infected with waterborne diseases). Dodgy area.

Bluewater Bay mouth ☺☺☺

Only spot in PE that handles the northwest berg wind, which is straight offshore here while the rest of the bay has morning sickness. Picks up a lot of swell. Excellent rights and lefts sometimes break off a sandbank into a river mouth. Beware currents and sharks.

Hougham Park ☺☺

Beach breaks along this beach pick up more swell as you leave the swell shadow caused by Cape Recife. Likes northwest, but sketchy and sharky. Not surfed often.

Kelly's Beach ☺☺

Port Alfred surf rats cut their teeth here, gearing for their first session at East Pier. A reform low on juice, but high on fun- and sun-filled summer days. A jagged rock spit juts from the sand. A right peaks to the left. Further down are little left-hand peaks. Best when the overall swell is four to six feet, which is about two to three feet on the inside at Kelly's. Sensitive to the wind, Kelly's prefers light northwest or west winds.

West Pier ☺☺☺

The solid concrete West Pier protects the entrance to the Kowie River Mouth. A left-hander breaks off the West Pier, wedging into a barrelling peak when swells bounce off the side of the pier. When bigger than four feet it is challenging, with vertical drops and gaping tubes. The five-metre-high pier shields it from north to northeast winds, making it one of few breaks that work in an onshore.

East Pier ☺☺☺☺☺

If you want to wrap your grubby paws around this Eastern Cape jewel, be patient. This right-hander, which breaks on the east side of the Kowie River off the shorter of two piers that channel the river out to sea, is fickle. Kowie has many faces: rugged and uncompromising, oily and smooth, or pure barrelling filth. Best on a pushing low tide and a four- to seven-foot south swell. The swell wraps around the West Pier and breaks on a sandbar in the mouth. This peak gets so square, Pythagoras would be stoked. The top-to-bottom wedge then elongates into a long winding wall that runs across the East Pier sandbank before hitting a long freight-train section at the end. When the banks are aligned, the barrel sections merge and some waves tube a long way. During a small to medium east swell, or when the tide is high, the waves break off the east Pier. Ragged tooth sharks feed off the West Pier, but they're not really into humans (much).

Riet River ☺☺☺

Heading from Port Alfred towards East London, Riet River is a point with a good bowl section on the outside. However, it tends to back off down the point and can be frustrating. West winds and a clean six-foot south swell are optimum. Strong rips can pull you into the middle of the beach where you get the unpleasant feeling of being shark bait.

Kleinemonde ☻☻☻

A sectiony right-hand point break with a mediocre beach break. Gets good occasionally during clean southeast groundswell and light berg winds. During predominant south to southwest swell, rips are strong and the waves are all over place.

Mtati ☻☻

In sight of Mpekweni Casino, privately owned Mtati is tucked away on the east side of a vast beach. Some fun peaks heading from the hotel, especially near Mtati River mouth at the end – a two-kilometre walk.

Hamburg ☻☻☻

A series of reef slabs and a wide rock spit on the southern end. Looks like a great longboarder wave, with slow-moving chunks running over the reef. Potential in east swell. Light northwest to west wind and a medium southeast groundswell.

Kidd's Beach ☻☻☻

A beach break just south of East London that occasionally has barrelling lefts when the sandbanks are lined up. A small holiday town where families come to unwind from their hectic lives in the metropolis of East London.

Igoda ☻☻☻☻

There have been some shark bites, bumps and scary moments here. But epic barrels too. The best wave breaks near the rocks. Picks up a lot of swell. Everyone heads here when East London is tiny or flat. Best in north winds, from northwest to northeast, and a medium south to east swell.

Eastern Beach ☻☻☻

Fickle spot in East London along the promenade near the Holiday Inn. However, if the sandbanks build up properly off the boulders and pebbles along the shore, this wave gets epic. Easterns, as it is affectionately called, is best in clean three- to five-foot south swell and mild westerlies.

East London

This busy little port is the last major city on the east coast before Durban. East London lies on perhaps the most consistent surfing coast in South Africa. In winter, swell comes from local cold fronts and distant storms in the westerly windbelt. In summer, swell pushes in from easterly trade winds and big groundswell marches in from cyclones off Madagascar. The temperate coastal climate is dominated by warm currents flowing down the coast, driven by the Agulhas Current. Summers are hot and humid, but winters are mild and sunny, interspersed with cold snaps when storms sweep up the coast. Water temperatures are cool in winter – between 14 ° and 18 °C – and warm in summer, between 18 ° and 22°C although fresh northeast onshores upwell the deep, colder water. The best surf time is late summer to early winter, mid-March to early June, when it is still warm and sunny, and the onshores are easing. Days are calm, winds light variable. Swell is beginning to push from southern storms and cyclone east swells are still common up to mid April. As we move into June, winter exerts its prominence. There are more cold snaps. But the occasional storm – cold fronts that bring fierce southwest busters and scudding rain squalls – also brings big grinding groundswell. Between fronts, days are calm and warm.

GONUBIE REEF: One of many great spots near East London.

Nahoon Reef ✪✪✪✪✪

World-class right-hand reef that delivers all kinds of conditions. Has two sections. When glassy and six to eight feet, an outside bowl links with the middle slab and hits an inside reef, with three distinct sections. The type of ride you have depends on the angle the swell hits the reef. At its best, a spaced out south swell of six to eight feet is running, the wind is light west or glassy, and the tide is low, starting to push. Many people surf here, despite a few shark incidents. Too good to waste.

Corner ✪✪✪✪

A beach break at the end of Nahoon Reef that works when the outside is out of control. Protected from the elements, Corner is popular when Reef is blown-out southwest. In a big southeast swell you can ride from Reef to Corner.

Bonza Bay ✪

Mediocre beach break in front of the Quinera River Mouth.

Black Rock ✪✪

In Gonubie, an average wave that breaks over flat rocks fairly far out to sea. The lefts are usually better and longer than the rights. Works best on a two- to four-foot east swell in light northerlies. Can handle fresh northeast winds.

The Point ✪✪✪✪✪

Hit it on the low tide and you will be hooked for life. A short point break on the western side of Gonubie that wedges into an A-frame peak that you can backdoor and get the barrel of your life. Works on a small to medium southeast swell. Handles strong west winds.

Rock Wave ✪✪✪

Fun right-hander that runs along a mini-point and ends in front of a tidal pool along the Gonubie beachfront. It's easy to ride but gets nasty when the swell is large and the tide is high.

Gonubie River mouth ✪✪✪

Works on any swell and wind direction. Best on a low tide. Offers long rights and easy-to-ride lefts. Strong rips can make it difficult to find the right take-off spot.

Gonubie Reef ✪✪✪✪

Works on a medium to big west to southwest swell and mild westerlies. Classic walling left that offers one of the longest rides around.

Rainbow Valley ✪✪✪

Good wave for beginners and longboarders. A soft shoulder runs along a mellow point. A left-hander on the opposite side of the bay has major potential.

Kwelera Point (Yellowsands) ✪✪✪✪✪

This exposed point runs out just south of the Kwelera River mouth. The beach break is more consistent, with hollow lefts and rights, depending on sand around the mouth. The beach also handles strong southwest winds. The point needs solid, long-period south or southeast groundswell, pushing high tide and glassy or light northwest winds, otherwise it can be fickle, and you end up chasing shadows. On a good day, wedgy take-offs and long tubing sections along the rocks. Getting caught on the inside is tricky.

Glen Garriff ✪✪✪✪

Right-hand point break on the west side of the bay offers a long ride, when swell is big and wind light northeast or west.

Glen Eden ✪✪✪✪

Charging right-hander. One of few spots that work in northeast, a persistent summer onshore. Best in small to medium swell.

Queensberry Bay ✪✪✪✪✪

Queensberry Bay is the 'berries' – one of the juiciest waves around. The relatively short ride is made up by its quality. The wave walls up along a shallow rock shelf, then bends around into deeper water and fades. In glassy conditions, it can be classic. The bigger the swell, the deeper you take off and the longer the ride. A south to southeast swell of six to eight feet in light land breezes is best. Sensitive to wind. There is an inside left on the far side of the bay that gets good in east swell. There is a caravan park, camping sites and bungalows. Quiet during the week.

WILD COAST

A large chunk of this coastline between Cintsa in the south and the Mtamvuna River in the north (just south of Port Edward in KwaZulu-Natal) was part of an apartheid-era homeland called Transkei (over the Kei River). When apartheid fell, the homelands were reattached to their respective provinces, in this case the Eastern Cape. The Kei is a special place – untrammelled, wild and beautiful – with superlative point breaks.

CINTSA TO THE MTAMVUNA RIVER

When you head to the land that gave birth to Nelson Mandela, you step into another world, rustic and laid-back. Beware Pondoland Fever – a soporific holiday vibe bordering on extreme inertia brought on by warm weather, pastoral living, relaxed locals and illegal crops.

In summer, the weather is humid and hot. Rivers are swollen by rain and the ocean can be dirty around river mouths. The detritus that washes out attracts sharks. However, the Sardine Run in mid-winter (June or July) also brings predators inshore.

The best surf occurs in winter, when the Wild Coast is mostly dry and warm, with consistently light variable winds. Best time to visit is late summer to early winter when groundswell arrives, cold fronts are rare, and cyclonic east swell is still common. Infrastructure along the coast is rudimentary, but there are well-run hotels, resorts and backpackers at Mazeppa Bay, Coffee Bay, Hole-in-the-Wall, Qolora, the Haven, Mngazi, Mngazana and Port St Johns.

Cintsa West ✪ ✪ ✪
Intimidating point break with steep take-off and short, intense tube. Needs a fairly solid southwest swell and westerlies. Surf at high tide only.

Cintsa East ✪ ✪
Below-par beach break. Sparks occasionally. Best in clean winter swells and light west winds.

Haga-Haga ✪ ✪ ✪
Quaint and friendly resort right on the beach. Close to East London, with good surf in the general area. There is a left-hand point in front of the hotel. Bit rippy. Not great. There is also a kiff reef point just around the corner. Seek and you might find.

Double Mouth ✪ ✪ ✪
Right-hand reef south of Morgan's Bay that breaks into a channel. Best on moderate south swell and light northwest. Good camping. Check it from the top of the hill.

Morgan's Bay ✪ ✪
Rustic resort that comes alive in season. The Eastern Cape is peppered with small towns that

DAWN PATROL: Dolphins leap from the back of another Mdumbe bomb.

DISTANT HOLLOW: The former Transkei is riddled with world-class waves.

Good food. Friendly
One problem. Few

SURF AND TURF: The Wild Coast big five comprises the cow, sheep, goat, pig and donkey.

staff. Cold beer. waves.

Kei Mouth

The town of Kei Mouth comprises many holiday shacks and a small hotel. The Kei River marks the old border between South Africa and the former apartheid homeland of Transkei. Along the beach there are left- and right-breaking peaks, best in an east swell and northwest winds. Not the best surf, but a fun place to chill. During the holidays in December and January, it is packed with school-leavers and university students.

are dead in the off-season, but cook when townies from around South Africa arrive for summer holidays. An exposed beach break that works in small swell and light offshores. Average.

Barbel Point ✪ ✪ ✪
Another right-hand point. Offers more juice than spots to the north. A more defined line-up, although the sections only connect when the swell is right. Needs large, clean south swell and light west. Best when light berg winds blow.

Wacky Point ✪ ✪ ✪ ✪
Right-hand point break and beach. Fickle wave at times, but can get world class. Two full-on barrel sections – round, powerful and fast. Accessible from Kei Mouth, but the road is bad.

Whispering Waves ✪ ✪
Marginal right-hand point break west of Kei Mouth. Tends to be a bit 'pap', lacking in power. Best on small swells and light to moderate southwest.

Periwinkles ✪ ✪ ✪ ✪
Close to Weymouth, Periwinkles is a hollow peak that breaks on a shallow rock shelf close to shore. Works on east or southeast swell but needs light northwest wind and low tide, otherwise it becomes a rocky shore break. Sublime when good, according to some locals.

Qolora Mouth ✪ ✪
Range of beach breaks and reefs along a 1.5 km beach. The Qolora River flows into a large lagoon open to the sea at high tide. Nice spot. Waves are sensitive to wind, and the sea needs to be clean and lined up. Can be fickle: very dependent on sand movement. Home to Trennerys Hotel.

Mazeppa Bay ✪ ✪ ✪
Another laid-back Wild Coast resort. Friendly staff. Good food. Cold beer. One problem. Not many waves. There is a short right-hander near the island and a left that breaks into a rip on the east side. Lots of exploration potential by four-wheel drive.

Qora Mouth ✪ ✪ ✪
One of many river mouths along the Wild Coast. Series of scattered sandbanks flanked by rocky coast on each side. Some potential, but summer is rainy season and the sea is often brown and muddy.

Jujura River ✪ ✪ ✪

Beautiful river cuts through hills to form steep bushy cliffs. There are sandbars around the mouth, while on the eastern side, a long rock point juts out from the left side of the mouth. Sandbars all around. Hard to get to.

Shixini Estuary ✪ ✪ ✪

Series of waterways leading into the ocean. Out-of-the-way spot. Exploration potential.

Mbashe River ✪ ✪ ✪

Large river surges into sea, with interlocking sandbars and large expanse of white sand. Exploration potential.

The Haven ✪ ✪ ✪

Classic old-style Wild Coast hotel – The Haven Hotel – sandwiched between two nature reserves and two rivers. Dwesa nature reserve lies in the west and Cwebe in the east, while the Mbashe River lies in the west and Mbanyana River in the east. Surfers go to nearby Breezy (20 minutes by four-wheel drive) for cooking point break waves,

or to Holmes Gully near the hotel, which can be fun. Long beaches. Sandbar potential.

Ntlonyane (Breezy Point) ✪ ✪ ✪ ✪ ✪

Shark risks aside, this is a regional classic: a long, tubing right-hand point break similar to J-Bay. Best when the swell is from the south and wind from the west or southwest. Sharky when rivers are in flood during summer or Sardine Run is happening in mid winter.

Mpame ✪ ✪

Not great. A right-hander off the point into a deep channel. Best on a south swell and light northwest.

Sharpleys Reef ✪ ✪ ✪

Rocky point break with sectiony rights. Best swell is south. The waves wrap on to the sandbank.

Mncwasa Point ✪ ✪ ✪

Further north from Sharpleys Reef. Point break with potential on a big southeast groundswell, but that is conjecture at this point.

Hole-in-the-Wall ◒◒

The Wild Coast's most famous landmark – a freestanding sandstone cliff with a truck-sized hole in the middle: open ocean outside, calm lagoon inside. At the main beach 500 metres before the hole is a fun beach break that breaks off rocks on the right. At the Hole, you can ride waves that rumble through the hole, refracting weakly into a shallow lagoon.

Mbomvu ◒◒◒

This small protected bay lies adjacent to Coffee Bay, where the Coffee Shack and Mbomvu Backpackers are situated. Mbomvu is a rare sandbank and boulder set-up, where the waves break into a small river mouth. Hollow and fun. Best at two to four feet with a light westerly. Can be defunct for years, and then suddenly come right for a few months.

Coffee Bay

Legend has it that a ship carrying coffee from southeast Asia to Europe ran aground here. For a while, coffee beans took root and trees grew. No sign of them now. In the sixties and seventies, Coffee Bay used to be a quiet holiday haven for regional businessmen. Now it's a busy little community, with several backpacker hostels, trading stores, two hotels (The Ocean View and the Coffee Bay Hotel) and a campsite in a grove of milkwood and other indigenous trees. The bay, between the Mbomvu and Nenga rivers, is flanked on the left by rocky cliffs, and on the right by a mellow point that runs a few hundred metres out to sea. Coffee Bay is a great spot to spend a week or two. There are fun waves on the beach and the point. It can be used as your adventure base. It is near Mthatha River Mouth, an hour's walk to the northeast, which is great for fishing and exploring. Coffee Bay is a two-hour walk from Hole-in-the-Wall to the southwest. There are world-class points within an hour's drive, and good hikes in the area, with waterfalls, cliffs and patches of forest.

RUGGED HEADLANDS: Mbomvu Bay, with Coffee Bay in the background.

FRESHLY GROUND: Start the day with a mellow surf at Coffee Bay Point.

Coffee Bay Point ✪✪✪

Mellow right-hand point on the south side of Coffee Bay. Take off over a small rock shelf and hotdog down the point. Best in a three- to five-foot east swell in mild westerlies. In normal south swell, most of the energy is expended on an outer point. The broken swell refracts and lines up again on the inside. The ride depends on sand further down, where a small river enters the sea. In a light west or northwest wind, and a lined-up three- to six-foot groundswell, the beach break around the rivermouth gets good. Similar to Yellows.

Mpuzi ✪✪

This right-hander breaks off a rock shelf and grinds across a river mouth, but is not surfed often. Fickle and sharky (they are caught off a headland nearby).

Mthatha Mouth ✪✪

River-mouth beach break. Fickle and sharky, but good peaks sometimes.

Whale Rock ✪✪✪✪

Short, fast and hollow reef where a large sandstone rock sticks out of the water just south of Mdumbe. Best in medium south swell and calm seas.

Mdumbe ✪✪✪✪✪

Another perfect point. Gnarly in big swell. When swell and sand line up, Mdumbe breaks for up to 800 metres, depending on whether you make the never-ending freight train section across vast river-mouth sandbanks. Best at six to ten feet in moderate west or southwest winds. The paddle-out can be daunting. Once you lower yourself into the best entry point, a narrow gully in the rocks, you can't see the waves. You need a wave spotter on the rocks to signal between sets. Mdumbe rivals Jeffreys Bay but gets (more) sharky in summer and during the Sardine Run. Campsite and backpackers nearby.

Lwandile ✪✪✪✪✪

Perfect sand-bottomed point break set-up. World class on a low tide when a clean six- to eight-

Kei the beloved country

The author – a former Transkei resident – waxes lyrical about a surf trip to his old haunt.

Trundling along a winding dust road, testimony to a dry winter, we topped the hill and stopped. The distant line-up had not fully imprinted the message on our brains before we began emitting a caterwauling cacophony of high-pitched hoots. A cow gazed stonily at us. It seemed to say 'Naught bru! These Two-Legs are crazy.'

As the visual information began to register, synapses overheating in a vain bid to stem the flow of adrenaline, the fit of whooping cough began to alternate with robust yells, chortles and snorts.

Line upon line of swell creased the seascape. A distant point, encased in blue, was going off its pip. Shaggy lumps slid along the spear of rock and greenery that thrust out into the sea. Spray spumes arched behind each watery bump. It was as though a procession of slow meteors was converging upon the shore. It was like that first across-the-bay view of J-Bay. You know, when you're on the highway out of PE and you see distant blue bumps running shoreward and a sea laid out like ruffled silk.

We got back on the road, kombi revving, occupants babbling. My companion, Pete, hadn't been in a hurry till then, but now we bounced and yawed at 60 km/h, close to top speed for that cabbie, over dongas, ruts and potholes.

The crew was small – me, head of ichthyology at Rhodes, Pete Britz, and his 12-year-old son Phillip. The walk to the point along a vast beach – split in two by slabs of volcanic rock – took aeons. It was hard not to burst into a full-tilt sprint, legs pumping and arms flailing. But the usual fears (Are cars with boards coming down the road? Anyone else walking to the spot? Is the onshore going to blow?) were totally ill-founded. Any residual urban plaks were subsumed by Pondoland fever, a mental blight that eats away at the brain, throttling it back, placing the conscious mind in idle mode.

EARLY RAYS: Another pearler peels down the point.

There was no need for stress. We were on an empty beach on the Wild Coast. Not a soul in sight. The weather was crisp and clear. The surf was cooking.

A light northwest offshore – warm and dry – was feathering a perfect six to-eight-foot south swell into deep textured lines. It was a swell with meaning. The close-outs on the beach broke with barrelling intent. Each foreground curler was backed by swell grooves stretched taut to the horizon.

I surfed for four hours straight – wave after wave after wave. Ruler-edged walls, top parallel to bottom, rolled through, mind-bending around the peripheries of my vision, bombs blasting on the shallow section on the inside section of the outside section. The smaller, deep ones seemed to creep up more, suddenly sucking into a thick-lipped convulsion across the ledge, a vertical wall then winding down a deeper sandbank 25 metres in front of the metronomic curl.

The springish low tide meant the bigger ones stood up on the outside rim of the basin away from the shelf, reeling along for 400 metres, slowing down and backing off momentarily as each swell encountered a slightly deeper patch – a bathymetric no-man's land between point and beach break. But after the slight pause, the wave would bowl at least three times more as it slid over a series of staggered sandbanks that took you sweeping towards the shore.

On my second wave, I rode as far as I could so that I could count the paddle strokes back, jumping off my board into knee-deep water just about on the shore. My arms stroked back 498 times before I sat back up on my board in the take-off zone.

After about an hour or so, the offshore began to die. The sea slowly became smooth like glass. Still the sea heaved, each set gradually getting a little 'fatter' as the tide filled our idyllic corner of the vast sandy bay.

After four hours, the paddle became burning pain. Spaghetti arms screamed for release. 'Just one more, just like the last,' said the mind, ever selfish in its insatiable quest to fill the video vaults with barrel clips.

Eventually, a building southeast wind and rapidly deepening tide was the mediator, and the decision was wrested from both entities. No-one complained. Both were sut.

Mouths caked numb by a throat-cracking berg wind, we lurched back along the beach, bumbling along the craggy rocks to rest beneath the overhang, surfed out strandlopers looking wild and red-eyed. Stoked.

foot south to southeast groundswell is smoothed by light land breezes. The take-off zone lies off a slab of rock – a tubing entry point, then a long hotdogging wall as the wave moves away from the rocks, and runs over deeper sand, before it bends wide of a rocky outcrop and hits a series of sandbanks. On some waves, you can ride to the beach, a ride of maybe 250 metres. As in many Wild Coast spots, this depends on the time of year and sand movement. Even when the sand is not right, the point is a good wave. When the sand is right ... eish, what a wave. Accommodation can be tricky. There are holiday houses at nearby Presley's Bay – a long walk down the beach. Some people rent them out. You can free-camp on the point (rocky and a bit uncomfortable) or on the banks of the Lwandile River (guard your stuff), but most people drive from Coffee Bay. Between sessions you can cool off under a small overhang looking over the point.

Presley's Bay ✪

Just down from a row of rustic holiday cottages, best during a small swell early in the day in a light land breeze.

Ebalow ✪ ✪ ✪ ✪

Another good point break: a rare left-hander in the Eastern Cape. Needs a fair-sized swell, preferably a cyclonic east swell, or frontal swell from the southeast. Best in light berg winds. Turn off from the Mpande road to the south. You will need a four-wheel drive but the scenery and surf will make it worth your while.

Rame Head ✪ ✪ ✪

Long peninsula with a fast right-hand point two hours' walk from Mpande along the beach. Only works in big swell when other spots are out of control. Rame Head needs winds coming from westerly directions. Relatively protected from the strong southwest busters that bash up the coast.

Sharks Point ✪ ✪ ✪ ✪ ✪

Great waves, but is difficult to get to. In a bay sheltered by cliffs, the point is on the south side. Gets good in a south swell at four to six feet and light to moderate westerlies. About half an hour walk south of Mpande.

Mpande ✪ ✪ ✪

A good left-hander breaks into a channel near the rocks. Needs a two- to four-foot east swell and light west winds. Accessible from the Port St Johns to Mthatha road. There is a campsite near the lagoon.

Dorado in the dwang.

Meyrick Stockigt goes fishing on his surfboard.

I was surfing off the point at Coffee Bay early on the morning of 16 January 2006. The wave was going to be my last. As I kicked out, I noticed something break the surface about 20 metres from me. The water was dirty. I couldn't see what it was. I got on my board and stared at the spot where I had seen the movement, not breathing in anticipation.

The fish reappeared with part of its head and back sticking out of the water. I knew that it wasn't a shark, but some species of game fish. I thought I would try and paddle up to it to see

how close I could get. I couldn't believe that it didn't swim away. I know that game fish are strong and don't give up easily when caught on fishing rods.

I touched it on the back and it slowly moved away, so I grabbed it by the tail. It gave two half-hearted kicks and gave up. I paddled the fish to shore. The people who know say the dorado must have been stunned by the cold water and strong offshore currents. The water had been pretty cold the previous day but had warmed somewhat with the west wind on the day. It weighed 17 kilos. We had it for dinner. It tasted delicious. Adieu Dorado.

Port St Johns

This spectacularly beautiful, former frontier town is a warped blend of Mpondo and colonial culture. The town has a derelict, unkempt look to it. Many of the buildings have cracked walls and peeling facades that hint at a once-thriving port built on the mighty Umzimvubu River and fuelled by trade in ivory and skin. The jungle and rivers teemed with wild animals such as crocodile and hippopotamus. Umzimvubu is Xhosa for 'home of the hippopotamus'. Cliffs tower where the river slices a steep gorge to the sea. Monkeys still chatter in the undergrowth. The three beaches are hemmed in by lush plants, birds and other wildlife, including the hippie ferals who subsist in the bush. You will meet fascinating people in Port St Johns – New Age travellers and former city-slickers who have chilled here semi-permanently. Some settlers enjoy the crops and marry the tribesfolk. There is even a white sangoma fully kitted out in witchdoctor regalia. The surf is not great, and more than a little sharky, but it's a good place to relax for a few days. There is surf at the Umzimvubu River Mouth, but the sandbanks are fickle. Try to muffle the 'Der dum, der dum' refrain in your head. Second Beach is marginally better than Third Beach. Both spots, south of town, have mediocre waves best in light offshore or glassy seas. They don't handle big swell.

FOAM FEATHER: Remote point break does its thing. No-one out.

MBOTYI: Another headland, another perfect point.

Mngazi ✪✪

Beach break peaks in front of the river mouth are best when the sea is glassy or a light northwest breeze is blowing, and the swell is two to five feet. It's signposted from the main road between Port St Johns and Mthatha. Mngazi River Bungalows is a very comfortable family-oriented resort where you can spoil yourself.

Mntafufu ✪✪✪

Beach break with a right-hander that breaks off a reef on the south side. Best in a small swell and westerlies. Unridden and isolated, a typical Wild Coast point break.

Mzimpuni ✪✪✪✪

A large bay with a right-hand point break at its southern end. This place needs a large south swell and land breezes. Some people walk here from Mbotyi – about four kilometres heading south. A four-wheel drive will get you there quicker but be warned that off-road driving is strictly illegal on the coast to protect certain species.

'Sorry boss, it has been raining for weeks. The roads have washed away.'

Mbotyi ✪✪✪✪

A beautiful long beach dotted with A-frame peaks. Best in a small to medium east swell and light westerlies. From Port St Johns, take the Lusikisiki road and follow the Mbotyi signs. As you approach the coast, the road gets steep and can be impassable after heavy rains: 'Sorry boss, it has been raining for weeks. The rivers have flooded. The roads are washed away. We're stuck here indefinitely.' There is a great campsite and very nice hotel.

Mkambati ✪✪✪

This is a nature reserve north of Mbotyi along the coast to the Mtentu River just before the border between the Wild Coast and KwaZulu-Natal. Loads of exploration potential.

SOUTH COAST

This region – between Port Edward and the southern perimeters of Durban's urban sprawl – has always been called the South Coast. It is also called the Hibiscus Coast, which stems from tourism marketing strategies. Whatever you call it, though, one thing remains immutable. It is point break heaven. Some of the best waves in the world lie beyond those wild banana palms, and that is no idle boast.

MTAMVUNA RIVER TO WINKELSPRUIT

The quality of barrels you get on the South Coast is sublime. Many spots are 40 minutes from Durban by car – making it feasible in summer to have a two-hour surf and be back at your desk by 9 am – but happily, many townies don't bother. A furtive mission from Durban in the dark, arriving at 4.30 am as the first sliver of red and orange frames the horizon, can yield sessions that will be indelibly stamped in the video vault reruns of your brain.

Most breaks are uncrowded during the week. The water is warm. The dolphins are friendly. Eish. Paradise. However, northeast onshores can dominate for weeks at a time in summer. Even when the offshore does come through, it can be the infamous southwest buster, which smashes the surf sideways due to the exposed angle of the coast. But a day or two later, be ready for feathering corduroy lines in a classic early morning land breeze. Because most breaks are right-hand point breaks, best swell direction is generally from the south, between southwest and southeast, allowing for refraction around the points, which are geographically quite shallow, unlike the deep bays and long points you get in the Western and Eastern Cape. Many points

start off on rock and finish on sandbars, sometimes in the shore break. The best season for south swell is between autumn and spring when southern storms are more active and land breezes tend to blow, sometimes all day. Even in winter, you get warm balmy days and water temperatures of more than 20 degrees, punctuated by vicious cold snaps as the odd rogue front smacks through. Some mornings, freezing offshores blow down from the Drakensberg Mountains inland – sucked towards the sea by slowly rising warm air off the temperate ocean during the night. You need the full length wettie more for the wind than the water.

TO Strand ✪ ✪ ✪ ✪
Just north of Port Edward, right-handers break off a small grassy headland. Gets super-hollow at low tide. One of the better big-wave breaks on the South Coast. Big gaping tubes.

Glenmore Beach ✪ ✪ ✪
Sandbar peaks just south of Southbroom.

Palm Beach ✪ ✪ ✪
Beach break that runs off rocks on the right of the beach. Can get good in a light northwest wind and clean swell.

BLUE STINGER: Bluebottles washed ashore by easterly onshores. They sting, but are not fatal.

A big-wave right
a deep bombora re

SWELL SWEPT: Sand-bottomed point at Southbroom.

hander breaks off ef on the outside.

Trafalgar ✪✪✪

Famous for nearby marine fossil beds, Trafalgar Beach is a fun beach break, with a big-wave right-hander that breaks off a deep bombora reef on the outside. Long paddle out through pounding sandbars. Holds moderate southwest winds.

Marina Beach ✪✪

River-mouth sandbank peaks. When summer rains fall, the river creates left and right peaks.

Southbroom ✪✪✪✪✪

Good-quality sand-bottomed point that refracts around a grassy hill lined with rocks. As with most South Coast point breaks, likes mild westerlies and a three- to six-foot south groundswell. Someone died once there. Apparently he took off on a wave … and vanished.

Lucien ✪✪✪✪

A good summer spot sheltered from the summer northeast. A left-hand point break best on the high tide. Runs into a grinding shore break. Gets good on an east groundswell and light north to northwest winds. Handles light northeast winds.

Margate ✪✪✪

A long beach with shifty peaks. In front of the point, a small shallow reef provides hollow take-offs. Best up to four to six feet in a light west wind at low tide.

Manaba Beach ✪✪

Mediocre beach-break peaks. However, it can work but this depends on sand movement.

Uvongo ✪✪

Small beach with rocks and sand huddled around a river mouth. The waves are fair to middling. Needs a medium to big south to southwest groundswell to wrap around rock slabs on to the beach. Depends on sand build-up.

St Mikes ✪✪✪✪✪

Grinding right-hander that breaks off a tidal pool in the seaside town of St Michaels-on-Sea. St Mikes is a reef point break and sandbar rolled into one. The swell hits a rocky reef on the corner of a tidal pool and then jacks up into a long wall that freight-trains on to the beach. Gets murky. Popular. Crowded.

Oslo Beach ✪✪

This suburb just south of Port Shepstone is fringed by a scraggy coastline, but some fair waves to the left off the rocks onto sandbars.

Mbango Beach ✪✪

Beach-break peaks in Port Shepstone on the beachfront. A number of reefs and sandbar peaks can be found along the coast from Port Shepstone to Sunwich Port, including Umtentweni, Sea Park, Bendigo and Southport. Explore.

Sunwich Port ✪ ✪ ✪

About five minutes' drive south of Banana Beach, this fickle right needs solid swell. Breaks super-hollow over shallow reef to create sucky foam-filled sandbarrels. Best on an outgoing tide in a three- to six-foot southwest swell.

Banana Beach ✪ ✪ ✪ ✪

The next spot – just south of Umzumbe – is a right sand-bottomed point break that runs off an outcrop of rocks. On good days, gets ridiculously hollow. Closes out from six to eight feet. Needs light westerlies. Home of the wild banana (*Strelitzia nicolai*) that grows to eight metres high.

Umzumbe ✪ ✪

South of Hibberdene, Umzumbe is a right sand-bottomed point break with two distinct sections. When they link up on lined-up southwest swells with proper long intervals, they can produce long rides. Holds moderate southwest winds.

Hibberdene ✪ ✪

Fickle, rock-strewn stretch with a number of sand- and rock-bottomed peaks that break okay … kinda sorta.

Mfazazana (The Spot) ✪ ✪ ✪ ✪ ✪

Show respect to this rural Zulu community when you surf here. Be friendly, pay your way and you'll get good waves. Don't leave valuables in the car. There are no nets, so it can be a tad sharky. Great walls and a barrelling inside section. A good left breaks on the wild side of The Spot sometimes. Likes light west and deep south to southwest groundswell. A proper point break that sticks out to sea more than most shallowly positioned South Coast points. Typical South Coast point set-up, with a river at the bottom, and sand along the point.

DTs (Don't Tell) ✪ ✪ ✪ ✪

Another typical South Coast point that breaks off rock and runs on sand. Rich in Zulu folklore. Not bad, but watch out for wild white feral natives who have gone mad from too much home brew.

Betty's ✪ ✪ ✪

Named after Auntie Betty who owned land nearby, this is a fickle reef slab with hollow lefts. Waves abound in the area. So do boomslang, rabid monkeys and crazy locals.

Pennington ✪ ✪ ✪

Plenty of sand and reefs in the area. Best in autumn and winter.

Happy Wanderers ✪ ✪ ✪ ✪ ✪

A right-hander near Kelso that runs off a short reef point before linking up with shifting sandbars and bending wide towards the beach. When the banks are lined up, you can get long walls with insane tube sections. Breaks at three to eight feet. Locals are protective but friendly. Like many breaks on the South Coast, gets epic when conditions are right, but when flat or onshore, go back to your day job.

Bluebottles

Looking rather like tiny, translucent blue plastic bags tided together with long tentacles, bluebottles (pictured on page 229) are often washed ashore when the east wind blows. They cause painful stings but are not fatal. Bluebottle tentacles contain millions of stinging cells. If you touch them, tiny filaments shoot into your skin, releasing a toxin that causes a burning pain. On the scene, wash the area with sea water to remove the filaments. Rinse the area with vinegar or brandy. If you don't have either, urinate on the wound. The uric acid helps to neutralise the toxin, serious. Try rubbing fleshy sour figs (vygies) – common in the Cape – on the sting. If you can get to a chemist, take an antihistamine tablet and spread cortisone cream on the sting.

THE SPOT: One of several points on tribal land in the deep south.

Park Rynie ✪✪
Stretches of beach with peaks here and there. Not commonly regarded as much of a surf spot.

Scottburgh ✪✪✪✪
The wave off the swimming pool at Scottburgh is a typical KZN South Coast, sand-bottomed, right-hand point break that is epic when good, but horrible when bad. In summer, when the river comes down in flood, it cuts deep holes through the banks. The sandbars go awry and the wave virtually disappears. Scotties handles a strong southwest wind and a south swell up to 10 feet. There is fierce localism around though, so make sure you show some respect. Some excellent reef breaks on the wild side in this area. Sssh.

Green Point ✪✪✪✪✪
Another point break set-up. Long-period south swell hits a short rocky point at Clansthal and bends wide, running along sand and linking up with another sand-covered reef before hitting more sandbars down the beach.

Widenham ✪✪✪
Some reef and beach breaks in the area.

Umkomaas ✪✪✪✪
The known break here – High Rocks – was not the best spot until the March 2007 storm rearranged the sand and exposed a hollow reef. Time will tell whether it will remain a good spot. Umkomaas River Mouth is the launching pad for trips to the popular Aliwal Shoal, a protected offshore reef with a profusion of tropical marine life.

Umgababa ✪✪✪
Sandbank peaks around the river mouth.

Baggies ✪✪✪
Warner Beach, the beginning of the build-up towards the high-density urban sprawl of Durban, is home of the South Coast surf underground. On any given day at Warner Beach there is an army of good surfers shredding the waves with trademark aggression. High-tide shore breaks ease the summer doldrums. The beach break at Baggies handles light to moderate onshore winds.

Pulpit ✪✪✪✪
To the north of Baggies is Pulpit, a semi-point break that needs a fair bit of swell before it starts to work, but can fire on a honking groundswell and light west wind.

Amanzimtoti ✪✪✪
The concrete jungle mixes with real jungle here. A straight strip of coastline offers rideable waves all the way along, as well as the occasional reef. Inyoni Rocks and Toti Pipe are both popular. Best early in the morning, during light offshore winds and moderate swells.

Winkelspruit ✪✪✪
Just for the record, the Inyoni Rocks to Winkelspruit stretch once had the unfortunate distinction of having the most recorded shark attacks in the world. However, the majority of these occurred before shark nets were put in place in 1962. This is an extension of the long straight coastline of Toti heading towards Durban.

DURBAN

Bursting with surf shops, shapers, factory stores and brand HQs, Durban is the surfing capital of South Africa. The weather is warm. The waves are consistent. There is a huge variety of spots – soft sandbars, grinding reefs, dredging beach breaks and, not far away, long tubing point breaks. Surf City mostly lies between the Bluff, a large headland to the south, and the Mgeni River to the north.

WINKELSPRUIT TO THE MGENI RIVER MOUTH

The harbour breakwater is an artificial extension of the Bluff. Oceanside spots on the Bluff get a lot of swell. However, the Durban beachfront – in the lee of the Bluff – picks up less. On a southwest swell, the Bluff can be six feet and cranking, but New Pier is only two feet, and Addington is flat. South swells have to bend around the Bluff to reach the beachfront. As you head north away from the swell shadow caused by the Bluff, the surf gets bigger. However, when an east swell runs, most of the beachfront turns on. The cool thing about Durban is that wherever you live or work, you can be surfing in minutes. The beachfront is in the centre, with the suburbs extending outwards in an arc. The Bluff is around the corner. Otherwise, entry points to highways heading north or south are a short drive away. In an east swell and light land breezes, head for the empty reef/sandbar set-ups of the North Coast on the M4 north. For point break tubes in a south swell and light to moderate west wind, drive south. There is almost always a wave in or near Durban. In summer, endless northeast trades are onshore but keep the windswell coming. Between December and April, cyclones push in a big east swell. In winter, more offshores blow and a south swell kicks in. Barring sporadic cold fronts, Durban is warm – a big incentive even when the waves are sloppy or small. During the rare times when flat or badly onshore, there is lank stuff to do. For good food and buzzing nightlife, visit Florida Road. Get Mexican chow at Taco Zulu, started by local charger Richie Sills who has opened one at New Pier. Sample Italian bistro Spiga do Oro and eateries Butcher Boys and Tribeca. If you want to hit the jorl, try Casablanca and Del la Sol, or a sundowner at Joe Cools on North Beach.

Isipingo Beach ✪
Mediocre beach breaks in an industrialised area south of Durban International Airport.

Reunion ✪
A legacy of apartheid, this predominantly Indian region lies on the way to Isipingo. The Bluff protects this beach from the northeast. Best in a light northwest wind and small to medium swell. Not surfed often.

Treasure Beach ✪ ✪ ✪
Study area on the Bluff for oceanographic and other marine studies in a former coloured township called Wentworth. A stretch of super-hollow peaks

WITHOUT PEER: A surfer takes off below New Pier looking towards the Bay of Plenty.

BARREL ENVY: Davey Weare locks into a sublime tube at Cave Rock.

FORWARD SLASH: Dylan Stone sets up the unmistakeable tube of Cave Rock.

on shallow sandbars and rock slabs. Best at low to mid tides. Short and intense with heavy take-offs. Epic waves at times. Breaks are two to six feet.

Pigs' Hut ✪✪✪
Below the police station on the hill, hence 'Pigs' Hut'. Classic deep-water reef point on the Bluff that works in land breezes and a solid groundswell. Handles size. Not as sensitive to swell direction and tide as the Rock.

Brighton ✪✪✪
On a medium, deep-energy east swell, cooking lefts break along interlocking reefs off the Cave Rock tidal pool. Hectically hollow rock slabs. The middle peak is popular, with plenty of barrels. Waves are best in a light northwest wind at four to seven feet. Closes out from about eight feet.

Cave Rock ✪✪✪✪✪
This spot consists of two waves that, legend has it, used to link up. According to locals, the one you see in the photos is Tidal Pool and the proper Cave Rock (the end of the original wave) is in front of the sandstone rock where there is a series of razor sharp rock slabs. Fewer people surf here after the road washed away in the March 2007 storms. You walk from Ansteys, or down a steep path from the Bluff. The reassuring sandbar is gone: you have to take off Indo-style over exposed reef.

Ironically (since fewer people were surfing it) the storm also marked an increase in localism. On a wall at the tidal pool is the graffiti cliché: 'If you don't live here, don't surf here'.

The Rock is an insane, top-to-bottom tube. Holds a 10-foot swell if spaced evenly and cleanly. Stay away if you don't have brass balls.

Main Cave ✪✪✪✪✪
Hollow peaks between Ansteys and the tidal pool on sand-covered reef. Needs a three- to six-foot groundswell and light northwest wind.

Ranch ✪✪✪
The Ranch is part of the Ansteys section of the Bluff. A fickle left-hander breaks on sandbars in front of the Green Dolphin restaurant. Funny deep banks that shift around. A light northwest wind and clean four- to six-foot south swell is good.

Ansteys ✪✪✪✪✪

For townies, the attraction of the Bluff is that it handles the northeast, staying smooth for several hours longer than town. However, as any local will attest, the Bluff is best when the townies are stuck in their urban groove. Best in a light northwest wind and clean four- to six-foot groundswell. Ansteys Corner is the utility wave – a zippy right-hander over a nicely tapered sand-covered reef spit, best in a clean southeast to south groundswell. Handles size and has been ridden at bigger than 12 feet from further back. Gets epic.

Garveys ✪✪✪

If you walk north from Ansteys for 20 minutes along Sloane Road, you will come across a concrete pipe that sticks out of the sand. Sometimes good sandbar peaks, but plenty of local aggression evident in vitriolic graffiti, such as 'Surf here and die'. No shark nets – the locals are more dangerous.

Old Cave Rock ✪✪✪✪

Did you know that the original Cave Rock was blown up by the Allies during WWII? The remnants of this reef lie in a military reserve heading towards the breakwater. You have to wade around a fence that goes into the water. Nearby right-hand reef breaks get superlative but are guarded by heavy

localism, vicious Zambezi sharks and trigger-happy ghost snipers. Shrouded in myth. There are other spots on the northern end of the Bluff but access is restricted by the military. Not surfed often. For a core group of locals only.

Vetch's Reef ✪✪✪✪

Moving around the Bluff into Durban, Vetch's is a failed breakwater created by Captain James Vetch of the Royal Engineers in the early 1900s. He built it from his London office without even visiting Durban! Built as the main breakwater, the rocks lie submerged, curving out to sea for 500 metres. This provides the perfect trajectory for long but dangerous waves that grind like a mutant point break in a big northeast groundswell from cyclones in the Mozambique Channel. Vetchies is the longest wave in Durban. There are two sections: the outside Block and the inside Urchins reef. They link up when the swell is right, but it sucks over the reef deceptively dangerously. High-tide entry only. Beware the stonefish.

Vetch's Beach ✪✪

Soft peaks along the beach at the bottom of Vetch's. Mostly a learner wave. Only works when Addington is closing out. Needs a massive swell to break. Otherwise, like Muizenberg on a soft day.

SMOOTH SEA: Fun peaks at the Wedge in front of Ushaka Marine World.

Good old bad days

Columnist Ben Trovato ponders our evolution

Surfing has changed more than any other local sport in the past 50 years. Soccer and cricket are much the same. Tennis racquets may have gone from wood to carbon fibre but surfing is virtually unrecognisable. When my mother was a surf groupie on the Durban beachfront, her heroes were Max Wetteland and Ant van den Heuvel. It took two people to carry their 18-foot barges to the water and South Beach was where it all happened. Turning one of these brutes was almost impossible. Now 12-year-olds are tearing up waves at warp speed and pulling off 360-degree backhand aerials at breaks that didn't exist when their folks were young.

But it's not just the equipment that has changed. Surfers themselves have, some would say evolved, but I'm not so sure. When I was a skinny little grom sitting wide at Wedge and praying for the big dudes to wipe out so that I could snare the shoulder, my heroes were Gerry Lopez, Rabbit Bartholomew, Rory Russell and Barry Kanaiaupuni. My first local hero was Mike Esposito because one day he paddled in, went to his car at the aquarium, fetched a baseball bat, ran down the wooden pier and laid into fishermen deliberately casting sinkers at the surfers. I also used to watch in awe as JJ chased paddleskiers along the beach in front of Dantes, hitting them with their own paddles.

JJ lived in a Wendy house on my parents' property for a few months, which was interesting, to say the least. He sold his board halfway through one of the Gunston 500s in the 1970s and had to borrow mine for his heat. I remember him almost making it to the final on that board. The sponsors must have had a word with the judges. 'What if he wins? Can you imagine his acceptance speech?' JJ once gave me half a cake baked by a girlfriend of his. I have never again experienced such a thought-provoking bout of food poisoning.

On the rare occasion that a surf movie came to Durban, it was screened at the YMCA, a peculiar venue given that many serious surfers back then were hardly the clean-cut, hard-working, health conscious people they are today. The sight of Gavin Rudolph going over the falls on a 20-foot monster on his way to winning the 1971 Smirnoff in Hawaii was enough to get the suede-booted, velvet-jacketed, seriously stoned soul surfers up on their chairs hooting and screaming.

Today's generation of surfers is far more restrained. They wear designer gear and have jobs. They work out at the gym and watch what they eat. They never get arrested, and they drive fancy cars. Their hair is bleached from the bottle, not from the sun.

I had girlfriends who warned me against telling their parents that I surfed. Today, parents are quite happy to have their daughter dating a surfer. He is, after all, an athlete, not the long-haired womanising drug fiend he was. We used to be anarchists and social misfits – not corporate ladder climbers and tie-wearing clowns.

Back then, we never needed eight hours sleep. One or two was enough. Often we wouldn't even leave the beach. When the sun came up, we opened the kombi door to let the smoke and girls out, pull on a pair of baggies, wax up and paddle out.

Now, surfers arrive at the beach well after sunrise, freshly showered and hair neatly brushed. Then they spend half an hour doing warm-up exercises. By the time they get into the water, the onshore has picked up and the swell has dropped. Not once have I stretched before going surfing and the only muscle I have ever pulled is the one between my legs. We stayed fit by having sex and running from cops. You are a surfer, not a gymnast. Stop touching your toes and flailing your arms about. All you are doing is giving surfing a good reputation.

* This and other invaluable advice on staying alive can be found in Ben Trovato's Art of Survival.

101 ✪ ✪
Next to Vetch's is a bathing beach in front of a café called 101. Again, mostly soft sandbar peaks.

Addington ✪ ✪
Opposite Addington Hospital, the beach hasn't starting curving north yet, which makes the southwest wind offshore. Best at low tide. Good waves at times, depending on the sand and solid east swell. Very protected from the south swell and mostly flat in winter. Good for learners.

Tramps ✪ ✪
At the northern end of Addington Hospital are left and right peaks sheltered by the Bluff and usually flat. Hobos hang out on the grass at the trampolines after receiving treatment at the outpatients.

South Beach ✪ ✪ ✪
More consistent than Vetch's and Addington, but still very protected from the south swell when it will be smaller than spots to the north. Handles strong southwest. A huge south swell sees a moderate boost in size. At low tide there are good waves, depending on sand movement. A soft wave good for learners.

Wedge ✪ ✪ ✪
Just in front of the beachfront promenade south of the New Pier is a sandbar that offers respite from the crowds. Best on a broken swell at low tide. In the old days, before longshore drift created by the new piers covered it with sand, the Wedge was a fast, hollow wave that broke on a reef.

Balmoral Bank ✪ ✪ ✪ ✪
Right-hander on the south side of New Pier that breaks towards the pier. Sometimes called Frogs. Good in an east swell and light northwest wind.

New Pier ✪ ✪ ✪ ✪ ✪
This is surf central. New Pier (with North Pier) may have ruined the Bay of Plenty, but it created this spitting right-hander. Although the older guys still shake their heads at how much better Bay used to be, New Pier gets world class. At low tide in a lined up southeast swell with light southwest winds, this wave peels from the back of the pier head and winds all the way down to Dairy. It has been ridden bigger than 10 feet. At best, it is a fast and hollow tube that sucks over sand straight from take-off. Enter by jumping off the end of the pier during lulls. On average days, it's a consistent hot dog wave.

AIRBRUSHED: Early at Balmoral.

BAY OF PLENTY

Once there was a winding, sand-bottomed tube that went on forever. When it was six to eight feet, the barrel was longer than Kirra in Australia, and even longer than G-Land in Indo, Shaun Tomson told Craig Jarvis in an interview for *Men's Health* magazine. Shaun remembers getting 15-second tubes at the Bay of Plenty – the wave he credits with giving him the tube-riding technique that blew minds overseas. The Bay was the home of the Gunston 500, now the Mr Price Pro, which remains the longest-running professional surf event. Sadly, in the late 1980s, this classic break was ruined. Three piers were built – Bay, North and New – supposedly to prevent longitudinal drift eroding the beachfront, a prime tourist venue. The sand changed irrevocably. Surfers began to hang out at Dairy Beach between New Pier and North Pier. At the turn of this century, the hub shifted to New Pier, notably Bruce's Coffee Shop, now a Mexican restaurant called Taco Zulu, opened by local charger Richie Sills. The piers overhauled Durban's surf spots, and from the memory of the sublime waves of the Bay, new spots were born. North Beach and New Pier offer powerful sandbank barrels in big south swells and medium to big cyclone swells. When big east swells arrive, the Dairy Bowl turns on. On rare occasions, the Bay will deliver an epic day that hints at its old self.

New Pier

New Pier

North Beach

North Beach

SUBLIME: North Beach perfection.

Dairy Bowl ✪ ✪ ✪

On the north side of Dairy Beach, heading from New Pier, is the Dairy Bowl, a slow V-shaped peak that works best on a deep tide when it's cross-onshore north to northeast. However, the real diamonds of Dairy are the lefts that break during clean east swells. Sucky sandbar wedge on the right side of North Pier looking out to sea. Mostly a left, a combination of wave refraction, outgoing rip and shallow sandbar creates a hollow left-hand bowl that breaks off the pier. Short, sharp right-handers can be ridden but you head straight for the pier. The lefts tend to be hollower and longer.

North Beach ✪ ✪ ✪ ✪ ✪

An incredibly good wave when it's on. North Beach is more consistent than Bay of Plenty and home to a zillion bodyboarders. A crunching right-hander that barrels its way across a sandbank. Handles up to 10 feet and has been the scene of some epic barrel-riding feats. On the lower tide, stick to the strong-shouldered right that comes off the pier, as these seldom close out or run fat. Anything from one to 10 foot looks good. A pushing tide brings the action closer in with a walling, left-hand bowl that pushes towards the pier. Best conditions are a solid swell and a light westerly breeze. If you're a hard-board surfer, surf only when the blackball is up, and stay away from the bathing area.

Bay of Plenty ✪ ✪ ✪ ✪

The replacement of the solid Patterson groynes with new pylon piers ruined one of the best man-made waves in southern Africa. What remains of this once perfect beach break is still a reasonably consistent wave that peels right on the outside with the occasional left bowl at higher tides. Although not in the same category as North Beach or New Pier, it's the least crowded of the pier waves in Durban. There are only a few days a year when the wave will link right through. Even for those who know the ins and outs of negotiating the Bay, this can get frustrating. When this wave does link up, it becomes superlative.

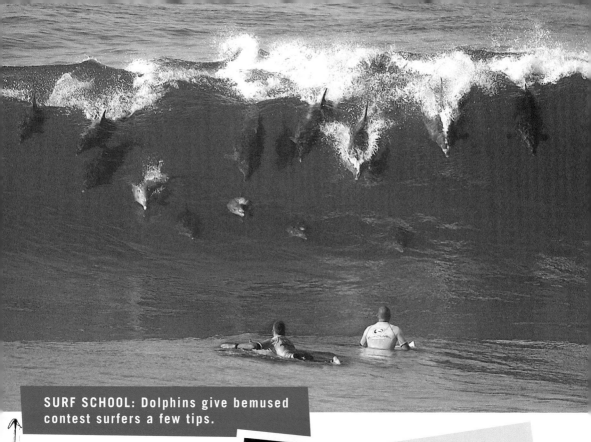

SURF SCHOOL: Dolphins give bemused contest surfers a few tips.

Stonefish

Regarded as the most venomous fish in the world, the stonefish is found in tropical waters, mostly in northern KwaZulu-Natal, but also in Durban too and further south. Adding to the mystery of Vetch's Pier in Durban are the stonefish that lie beneath the surface in the rubble of the old pier's ruins. The dappled colours of the stonefish enables it to blend perfectly with its surroundings, either coral or rocks.

They usually lie in wait for their prey under and against rocks, so encounters with humans are rare. Thank your lucky stars for that. When you step on a stonefish, you are blinded by pain as your foot is skewered by a tough spine. Then you die. Be careful when wading through coral. Hot water and urgent medical attention are the best ways to survive a stonefish sting.

TROPICAL DELIGHT: Ryan Ribbink rips it apart.

Snake Park ✪✪✪

The utility wave at the Durban Snake Park is the midbreak wave that peels off the shotgun pier (double-barrelled pipes). Further down the beach in front of the wire-frame lighthouse is a dual direction peak that gets good. Unfortunately this peak isn't always there: the fickle nature of sand means that the bank regularly builds up and gets washed away. In the old days, Snake Park had a reputation for being a hard-core locals-only spot, with many outbursts of aggression. However, over the years the old crew has dissipated or moved on to other parts of the beachfront. The venom of the original Snake Park crew is now a thing of the past.

Battery Beach ✪✪✪✪

This beach break can be found at the northern end of Durban's beachfront in front of the military base. It gets incredibly powerful at times. When the swell is three to four feet at New Pier, Battery can be a solid six feet. Like all the northern beaches, surf here on low tide for the outer banks, and high tide for the shore breaks.

> Over the years, the old crew has dissipated or moved on

Country Club ✪✪✪

Formally known as African Beach, this beach break used to be a blacks-only beach during the apartheid days. Ironically, it now lies in front of the fancy Durban Country Club. Sensitive to tides, it breaks left and right. Goes off when sandbanks are right. Excellent shore break. A 'shotgun' pier separates Country Club from Battery – so-named because when you look to shore from the line-up, you see the opening of two large pipes that look like shotgun barrels.

Mgeni River Mouth ✪

Right at the end of Country Club, and Durban's northernmost break before you hit the North Coast, lies the Mgeni River, with left- and right-breaking sandbars. Gets bigger than the beachfront, but known as a very sharky spot. These days, you see more jetski riders and kiteboarders.

NORTH COAST

The north coast of KwaZulu-Natal runs from the Mgeni River to the Tugela River. It is a verdant sub-tropical paradise known in marketing parlance as the Dolphin Coast. The surf is mostly characterised by sandbars, reefs or combinations of both. The left-handers turn on in an east swell (mostly in summer), and the rights generally prefer a south swell (mostly in winter).

MGENI RIVER TO THE TUGELA RIVER

All along the North Coast there are numerous breaks that add more options to Durbanites. There are probably more secret spots here than along any other part of the South African coast. Don't be fooled by the lack of named spots in this section. In summer, you get sick sessions in six- to ten-foot Hawaiian-like perfection as big cyclone swells mack through from intense low-pressure systems off Madagascar and Mozambique. Sometimes, endless easterly trade winds blowing off Madagascar are enough to conjure up epic surf. Best surfed in glassy, offshore conditions early or late in the day. Hot and humid in summer, warm and dry in winter, water temperatures rarely drop below 22 °C.

Glenashley ✪ ✪ ✪ ✪
A big-wave sandbank found near the Mgeni River. A deep channel separates it from the coast. Handles big surf.

Umhlanga ✪ ✪ ✪
A thriving, vibrant, upmarket beach resort area. Several surf options, including wedging beach breaks and a few reefs, one of which is a big-wave spot. At the southern end, Cabana Beach is the main spot. It's a left or right peak with the occasional high-tide bowl.

Bronze Beach ✪ ✪ ✪
Slightly further north, a shifty sand-bottomed peak best in a small swell and light land breezes.

Newsel ✪ ✪ ✪ ✪
At the bottom of Umdloti, this powerful, hollow right-hander has been compared to Surfers in Ballito. The barrel is top to bottom. It handles up to six feet. Needs glassy or light offshores. Best at three to four feet.

Umdloti ✪ ✪
Built-up, busy coastline with a series of exposed beaches. Fickle, shifting banks make for a bit of a lucky dip sometimes. The onshore dominates in summer.

La Mercy ✪ ✪ ✪ ✪
Beach-break peaks on sandbar and reef set-up. Holds a big swell. Long wave in right conditions. Likes a long-period south to southeast groundwell and light northerlies.

One Eye ✪ ✪ ✪ ✪ ✪
Called One Eye in reference to the wide open barrel. An exceptionally hard-breaking wave

SO SLOTTED: Another left-hand reef delivers the package.

T-REX

Concrete bathymetry and chlorinated contours at Gateway Mall, inland from Umhlanga. Breaks from three to five feet left or right or both, depending on the setting. Sometimes called Flow Rider. Pay your bucks and pull into an endless barrel inches from the floor on a layer of jet-propelled water. Entertain the crowd as your bruised ass bounces on the bricks and you get klapped off the back and spat down the drain.

URBAN WAVE: Hollow right-hander at Sunrise.

that barrels across sand and reef with Hawaiian quality. Breaks right and left, but it is the left that drenches the synapses with endorphin overload. A big cyclone swell and light land breezes bring the berries. You won't find it.

Tongaat ✪ ✪ ✪ ✪
There are two exposed spots in the area, both with an aversion to wind. The point and beach breaks fire on a clean three- to five-foot groundswell. Produces a running, top-to-bottom barrel with the right conditions.

Bog Bay ✪ ✪ ✪
A fickle spot sensitive to tides, wind and longshore drift. Big south swells scour away the sandbars and ruin this spot, while onshore winds and east swells push the banks back into place. Excellent at times, terrible at others. Low tide only.

Surfers ✪ ✪ ✪ ✪ ✪
Just north of the main lifeguard hut at Ballito, a fast, hollow right-hander breaks off a large rock. Best at low tide in a southwest swell with light offshore winds. Good from two to six feet. Needs the low tide because, like most North Coast spots,

it develops a deep inshore channel at high tide. On a big day, the rip can push you across the bay towards rocks on the other side. Can be a bit hectic. Lots of white water, close-outs and constant paddling.

Sunrise ✪ ✪ ✪ ✪ ✪
At the northern end of Ballito lies this protected beach. A semi-point that enjoys excellent sandbar build-up in front of the rocks. The wave is faster than you expect, so positioning and the subtle art of the weave are the go. Right-handers only, unless you want to dive for crayfish. Fires on a small to medium east swell and gentle offshore winds.

Willards ✪ ✪ ✪
At the northern end of Ballito Bay lies this protected beach break. Needs a small east swell and gentle offshore wind. In summer, best early.

Thompsons Bay ✪ ✪
This is a small, sheltered beach with a streamlet that runs through it. Breaks fast and hard close to shore because of shelving banks. Lefts on an east swell and fast right-handers off the pool on a south swell. Low tide only.

WALLING UP: Sublime Ballito.

Shaka's Rock ✪✪

Named after the fabled Zulu chief, the surf spot is not quite as majestic, or noble. There are a few reefs and beach breaks to choose from, pending sand movement and swell direction. Don't expect adrenaline rushes. Just some fun.

Umhlali Beach ✪✪✪

Some fun but fickle peaks along the main beach at Umhlali during a cyclone swell, leftover wind swell after the northeast wind, or when a large southwest swell pushes through. Best in light westerlies. Depends on sand movement.

Salt Rock ✪✪✪✪

Near Salt Rock town lies this classic sandbank and reef set-up. A glassy left and right peak breaks on rock and sand. It handles a two- to five-foot swell in light offshore winds (northwest). Best time is early, particularly during summer.

Tiffanies ✪✪✪✪

A small reef that breaks mostly left. Doesn't work that often, but has clean and excellent form when it does. Small to medium east swell, glassy conditions only.

Tinley Manor ✪✪✪✪

Reef/sand combination off a rock spit. Breaks clean and fast, sometimes ending in a shore break close-out. Needs a clean and spaced southeast to south swell and light west wind.

Salmon Bay ✪✪✪✪

The northern end of Salmon Bay juts out slightly, so the break lies on a wild side, but it is one of the last spots to get ruined by the onshore northeast wind. The bay is flanked on both sides by left- and right-hand points. The left likes an east swell and the right likes a south swell. The left likes north winds and the right likes west winds.

GOOFY PARADISE: Lots of lefts to choose from.

Lionfish

The lionfish, a fantastical looking striped creature otherwise known as the devil firefish, is found along the East Coast, particularly KwaZulu-Natal. It is beautiful, but deadly to its prey. The lionfish uses its poison-tipped pectoral fins to corral small fish into corners. The aggressive predator consumes its prey whole after a lightning-fast lunge. Lionfish rarely cause death in humans, but their venom causes severe pain and swelling around the wound, as well as nausea, dizziness, weakness, hypotension, headaches and shortness of breath. While lionfish pose no real threat to surfers, unless you grab or somehow fall onto one, it's good to know what they look like. Just in case.

Blythedale ✪ ✪ ✪ ✪
Fickle beach breaks and shifting sandbanks. But, as with many spots in KwaZulu-Natal, it can get classic. Doesn't handle over five feet and needs light west winds. Some excellent secret spots to the south. Wine and dine a local.

The beach is narrow and rocky with good sand and reef options

Zinkwazi ✪ ✪ ✪
South of Tugela lies a small resort near a marshy lagoon fed by the Zinkwazi River about 45 minutes from Durban. The beach is narrow and rocky with good sand and reef options. A consistent right-hander – protected from southwest winds by a headland that juts out in the south – breaks in solid southwest swells. Winter is better, when the sea is cleaner. Summer rains wash muck into the sea.

ZULULAND
AND MAPUTALAND

This tropical coast starts from the Tugela River, the official Zululand border, and ends just north of Kosi Bay at the Mozambique border. As you head away from the busy seaside resorts of Umhlanga and Ballito, the terrain gives way to increasingly bigger pockets of unexplored coast, hills covered with thick sugarcane, cut through by tight meandering rivers camouflaged by thick jungle. Point breaks are rare, with most spots either reef or sand, or combinations of both.

TUGELA RIVER TO KOSI BAY

After the heavily industrialised port of Richards Bay, you enter into a wild wonderland of jungle, pristine wetlands and beautiful tropical country. From the St. Lucia wetlands, a world heritage site, to Sodwana Bay and Kosi Bay, there is a lot of potential that has barely been realised.

This is a mostly unexplored coast largely made up of marine and other reserves. Maputaland is a 100km stretch of coast from Sodwana Bay to Kosi, where big mama turtles lumber up the beach to lay their eggs and – a while later – baby turtles scuttle back to the sea. The water is clear and warm, often around 26°C in summer and marginally colder in winter.

You will be surrounded by lush marsh forest, mangroves, ferns and orchids. Along the gleaming white sands lie a host of secret breaks with good potential at or near landmarks such as Gobey's Point, Hully Point, Island Rock, Black Rock, Dog

Point and Boteler Point. Much of the coastline is protected and isolated. You will need permits and a good guide to find your way around. Because it's illegal to drive on the beach with a 4x4, access to many potentially world-class breaks is limited. But it is a magical place, so surfing should not be the only goal of your mission.

In the far north of this coast, just below the border with Mozambique, coral reefs abound off the shoreline. A typical set-up comprises a long sandy beach split by a river mouth, and an inland estuary running parallel to the beach. In many instances, the beach shelves steeply into the sea, with a calm inshore area protected by outer reefs that break up open-ocean swells that expend their energy in the form of long lines of pounding surf. Many of these outer reefs run parallel to the shore - their flat angle often results in dumping waves that mostly close out. However, there are reef passes – gaps in the coral – where surfable waves break, as well as beaches and the rare point that are directly exposed to the ocean.

TURNING TURTLE: A loggerhead turtle is silhouetted against shafts of sunlight.

WORTH THE WAIT: A goofy-footer flies along the line at Alkantstrand.

TIGHT TUBE: The pristine waters of the north

Best winds are light west or northwest. Swells approach the coast anywhere from a south to northeast direction. Like the North Coast, the more east in the swell, the more the left-handers turn on, while south swell is better for right-breaking spots. In summer, the occasional southwest buster breaks up the continual summer trade winds that blow from the northeast, making for a messy, white-capped ocean that is not too appetising for surf. Apart from brief offshore interludes, when the southwester is often too strong anyway, the onshores sometimes blow themselves out overnight. You get a short window early in the morning before the cycle renews itself.

For the right-handers, the best swell directions – south to southeast – emanate from cold-water low pressure storms passing below the country, mostly in winter. The weather is not as hot or humid in winter, and you get more calm or offshore days, with steady south swells pulsing up the coast. While the surf tends to be more consistent in summer, it's usually mushy and weak from endless onshores emanating from high pressure activity out to sea. From mid-summer, when cyclones form off Madagascar, plenty of big east groundswell starts to grind through. This coast is closest to the cyclones, and bears the brunt of their energy. Tropical cyclones can form quickly and powerfully, sometimes generating seriously big waves on a par with Cape Town, except of course you are wearing boardshorts and nose cream – rather than full steamer and hoodie – as your protection against the elements.

There are rumours of proper big-wave outer reefs discovered by Durban's big-wave crew. Go forth and explore.

Wedging right-handers rebound off the dolosses

Mtunzini ✪✪

This beach resort area is near the Mlalazi River (Place of the Grinding Stone) and Umlalazi Nature Reserve. There are plenty of beach breaks on wide-open beaches that stretch far to the north and south. Surf spots come and go as the fickle sandbanks shift. Explore between Mtunzini and the mouth of the mighty Tugela River, about 60 km to the south. Heavy inland rain means brown muck pours into the sea, which becomes brown near the river mouth. Watch out for sharks here. An exposed point at Siyayi, about 12 km to the south of Mtunzini, holds potential. It works in a moderate swell and light northwest winds.

Richards Bay ✪✪✪✪

Protected from the southwest wind by the piers, a big dredger pumps sands onto the banks creating some really fun waves, but only at certain times. When it works, it's a clean, well-rounded wave, offering barrels along the piers with long down-the-line waves. Needs a long-period south swell.

Alkantstrand ✪✪✪

Sandbanks are held in place by the massive north breakwater, making Alkantstrand the best spot – certainly in terms of consistency – in the Richards Bay area. Wedging right-handers rebound off the dolosses and peel down the beach. As with most KZN spots, it's best in a southwest wind.

When the northeast blows, you might like to check out Inside, a sheltered left-hander that breaks off the other side of the groyne. Amazingly, right on the edge of the shipping lane, inside Richards Bay Harbour, is the rare but excellent Señoritas, a bombora that comes to life in only the biggest cyclone swells.

St Lucia ✪✪✪✪

This spectacular 100-km stretch of coast runs adjacent to a vast inland estuary, Lake St Lucia. The mouth lies to the south, at St Lucia town. Covered in a verdant mantle of jungle, this protected area is a world heritage site. Comprising long beaches and warm water (how's 27 °C?) it is paradise. However, the prevalent northeast onshores make the waves messy. Most coral reefs are too near the shoreline Word has it that there are several world-class beach breaks and one or two reefs that go off in cyclone swells. Befriend a local, or go exploring on the beaches in the area. Otherwise, take a look at the point to the south of St Lucia at Maphalane. Besides Cape Vidal, other landmarks in the reserve are Mission Rocks and Leven Point.

Cape Vidal ✪✪✪✪

There is a good-quality reef/sand combo near a crocodile sanctuary inside the Greater St Lucia Wetland Park. Gets super-hollow. It starts on a slab and barrels across sand. Consistent. Left and right peaks. Needs a clean cyclone swell or long-period south to southeast swell. Clean west winds.

Jesser Point ✪✪✪✪

Good waves can be found at Jesser Point, on the southern end of Sodwana Bay. The prevalent winds are northeast, but land breezes often blow at sunrise and sunset in summer. During winter, some days are glassy and the surf gets classic when the swell comes out of the south or southeast. A cyclone swell in summer turns this coast on.

Sodwana Bay ✪✪✪

This is a tropical diving and angling paradise. Large, lush coastal forests to explore. Stunning coastline. Good waves can be found on the beach in Sodwana Bay itself. Breaks left and right. Fickle banks, but can go off, breaking at up to six feet. Cyclone swell territory.

Kosi Bay ✪✪✪✪

A stone's throw from the border with Mozambique, the Kosi Bay area is an eco-tourism paradise. The protected estuary is a pristine waterway. Crocodiles and hippos lurk in the Sihadhla River. Loggerhead turtles nest at nearby Bhangha Nek, slightly to the south. The surf potential of this wild and beautiful tropical coast has not been realised.

SURFRIKAN

Slang

DON'T TUNE Me !

Chapter 9

When men come to like a sea-life,
they are not fit to live on land.

Samuel Johnson (1709–84)

South African surfers talk funny – mostly because they're surfers, but also because they're South African. Our local slang is a strange mixture of words and phrases from the languages of European settlers, the Cape Malays (who are actually from Indo) and indigenous peoples, notably Xhosa, Zulu, Sotho and Khoi-San. South African surfers use this linguistically disparate melting pot as their base, before bolting onto it the universal surfing lexicon.

We've included some southafricanisms that are used by non-surfers, as well as some surfing terms that are almost universal. Language is dynamic and slang changes particularly fast, so check out page 29 for some of the more out-dated slang that only the old ballies* will remember.

Most of the pronunciation is obvious, but where it isn't we've spelled it out for you in brackets, with the emphasis on the italicised syllable. We haven't used formal phonetic symbols, but what we think will be easiest.

gh   guttural sound in the back of the throat like the 'ch' in the Scottish 'loch', or the German 'ach'.

ô   like the vowel sound in fork or walk, but shorter and sharper, not common in English.

oe   the short vowel sound in book, cook and bull.

u   the short sound in cup or mud, which is not as obvious as it looks.

r-r   rolling the 'r'.

uh   that peculiarly English sound, as in the second syllable of 'batter'.

Also – sometimes we've used Surfrikan words to explain other Surfrikan words, in which case they're marked with *, so you can look them up. **Have fun.**

A

ACE
Alone, solitary. 'I was out there on my ace when someone on the beach shouted "Shark!" '

ACTION
Stupid or mean act. You pull an action when you do something dof* or mean. A goofed action is when you do something stupid because you're goofed*.

AG (U-GH)
This multi-purpose interjection precedes any sentence for an emotive effect, such as 'Ag, no man' (sign of irritation), or the more neutral, 'Ag, I don't know.' It can also be a stand-alone expletive.

AGGRO
Aggressive. If you are aggro, you bring bad karma into the water.

AHOY
Greeting. Lank* younger surfers use this old mariner's greeting. Also aweh, hoesit, howzit, hooit.

AIKONA (eye-kor-na, sometimes hi-kor-na, and eye-kor-na if very emphatic)
Means 'No way', 'Absolutely not' (Xhosa or Zulu).

AITA! (eye-tah)
Greeting that originated amidst the township youth. 'Aita bra*!' Common among politically correct people. Rabid racists in the past have miraculously become PC.

AMPED
Full of energy. Usually induced by adrenalin, feeling wired or high on fear, either before paddling into a huge ocean, or the sheer stoke of being alive afterwards.

ARVIE
Afternoon. The Australian equivalent is arvo. Not to be confused with avo*.

AS WELL (az-well)
Also, me too. If you say, 'Jees, I'm kussed* bru,' you might get this reply, 'Ja, as well.'

AVO
Avocado

AWEH (ah-wear)
Greeting.

AWESOME
Incredible, very nice, top quality. Used when describing the quality and size of a wave. 'That wave at Muizenberg was awesome, bru!'

AXED
1. Crushed, wiped out, whacked. Also, see 'carrots'. 'The lip of that big wave axed me.'
2. Dropped, excluded. 'She was axed from the team.'

B

BABALAS (bub-ba-lus)
Hangover from hell. The Babalas is no mythical beast, especially when you look at yourself in the mirror and see that furry tongue slithering in a mumbling, parched mouth; those puffy eyelids scraping bloodshot eyeballs. From the Zulu word *ibhabhalazi*.

BACKSIDE
Surfing with your back to the wave. Has nothing to do with your posterior. If you are facing the wave, you're surfing frontside. A goofy-foot* surfer rides a left-breaking wave frontside. A natural surfer (left foot forward) rides a left-hander backside.

BACKSTOP
Layer of tobacco and pitjies* at the bottom of a bottleneck* to stop it from burning down to the gerrick*.

BAGGIES
We don't call them board shorts or Bermudas or other naffy names. They are baggies. You wear them when the water is lekker* warm.

BAIL
To jump off your surfboard, usually when the wave is about to close out, or you have taken off too late and are about to wipe out.

BAKKIE (buck-kee)
Pickup truck in the United States, 'ute' in Australia. Many people own bakkies

in SA, particularly in the rural areas. 'My boet* and my ballie* parked* on the back of the bakkie.'

BALLIE (Bul-lee, with the u as in up)
Parents, old people. 'A weird old ballie lives in that cave.' 'My ballies won't let me go to the jorl*.'

BALLISTIC
Excellent waves. With the use of 'firing', 'going off' and 'smoking' it is a natural progression to ballistic terminology. 'I tune* you bru*, the surf was ballistic!' Also cooking, cranking, going off, off its face, pumping, smoking.

BANKIE
Bank packet. The plastic bag issued by banks for coins is a common receptacle for dagga*. Bankies and stoppe* are standard packaging. 'Me and my boet* went with the bergies* in the bakkie* to score* a bankie.'

BARK THE DOG
To vomit, puke. In South Africa, you also kotch, park a tiger, blow chunks or make a technicoloured yawn.

BARREL
Tube. When you get tubed, you ride the barrel. You do this by pulling in* and getting slotted*.

BEACH BREAK
A surf spot where waves break on sand.

BERGIE (bare-ghee)
Homeless person in Cape Town. The word comes from the 'Berg' (Mountain) of Table Mountain, where bergies lived under bushes and in caves. Many stay in the city now. You might see them wrapped in a blanket wrapped around a bottle of booze in a doorway. They are a colourful people, with their own mores and subculture. Bergies are infamous for their use of bastardised Afrikaans obscenities.

BERG WIND (burg)
Wind from the mountain – usually hot and dry – but can be cold in winter.

BETTERS
Good. Another synonym for lekker*, as if that word didn't have enough uses. 'We scored a betters section*.'

BILTONG
Dried raw meat. Originally it was 'bul tong' (bull's tongue). Specially prepared dried raw meat made from beef, venison or ostrich. Specialities are springbok or kudu. Ostrich is tasty. Good biltong is manna to your average full-bodied Surfrikan.

BISCUIT
1. Cookie. In America, a biscuit is a scone. In South Africa, a biscuit is a cookie. Favourites are Marie, Romany Creams, Nuttikrust and Eet Sum Mor.
2. Twit, idiot. Only in South Africa can a word mean a small crunchy cake, or an idiot. 'John, you biscuit!'

BLEAK
Disappointed or sad. 'Since Lorraine axed Rick, the oke's* been lank* bleak.'

BLIND
Bummer, nasty. If you pull a blind action on your bru*, you have done something nasty. 'Bru, that's blind – you scaled* my Britney Spears poster.'

BLOW CHUNKS, see bark the dog

BOATMAN
Paddleskier, also eggbeater, windmill, goatboat.

BOBOTIE (buh-boor-tea)
Traditional Malay dish made with spicy mince, baked in the oven with an egg custard topping, and served with yellow rice and raisins. Delicious.

BODYBOARDER
Surfer who surfs prone on a sponge-like board. Also called booger, doormat, gutslider, shark biscuit, speed-bump and sponge. To their credit, bodyboarders usually rise above these insults.

BOERE (boer-rre)
Farmers, Afrikaners. English-speaking people used to refer to the police as boere. Still in use, but fading away in the new South Africa.

BOEREWORS (boer-re-vors)
Farmers' sausage. Sometimes just wors, or boerie. Spicy sausage made from many secret recipes, and consumed in quantity around South Africa.

BOET, see bru

BOMB
Powerful big wave. 'I scored* a bomb.'

BOOGER, see bodyboarder, doormat

BOTTLENECK
A dagga* pipe made from the broken neck of a bottle.

BOTTOM TURN
The initial turn off the bottom of the wave after you take off.

BRAAI (rhymes with high)
Barbecue. Perhaps the biggest semantic gift given to the world by South Africa? You braai with wood in a metal drum or between bricks. You cook your boerewors*, steak, lamb chops and sosaties* on a grid over the flames. You eat mielie pap*, salads, rolls and other stuff. You drink Castle beer, or maybe a spook and diesel*. Sometimes, if you catch kreef*, you have a crayfish braai.

BRAH, brahdeen, see bru

BRASSE (brah-se)
Posse, group of friends. 'Where's my brasse?'

BREW
Beer. 'Buy me a brew bru*.' (Buy me a beer bro.)

BRICKS
Rocks, reef. First I got klapped* by the lip*, then I moered* into the bricks at Brighton (hard-breaking KwaZulu-Natal surf spot).

BRO, see bru

BROWN EYE
Mooning, exposing your buttocks.

BRU (broo) My bru (may broo)
Brother, friend, mate, china, buddy. Another all-purpose South African word. Variations include brah, brahdeen, boet and bro. From Afrikaans for brother (broer), pronounced broor with a roll of each 'r'. Lazy English speakers say it without the roll. Variations emanate from all over South Africa. Spelt 'bru' by most South Africa surfers. In the Eastern Cape, a semantic hotbed of slang, often pronounced 'brorr', 'bree', 'bra' (same as underwear), 'brah' and 'braaah', with a drawn-out vowel.

BUBBLE BITERS
Blue bottles. Floating, stinging jellyfish-like organisms similar to a Portuguese man o' war.

BUNNY CHOW
Curry in a hollowed out half-loaf of white bread. Surfers from Durban grew up on bunnies. You get the curry in the bread with the removed square chunk, used to dunk back in the curry. Best when the bread is fresh. Some bunnies are served with slap chips*.

BURN
When two surfers are riding a wave, and the one in front 'fades'* the other into the impact zone by cutting him off, the second guy gets burned.

BUSTER
Strong wind. The southwesterly buster accompanies a cold front as it sweeps up the coast.

C
CAPE DOCTOR
Southeast wind or southeaster. This howls across the Cape Peninsula in summer, forming a creamy white cloud over Table Mountain like a table-cloth. Because the wind blows for up to a week or more at a time, often gale-force, pollution is blown away. The air is clean and crisp afterwards, hence 'Cape Doctor'.

CARROTS
Screwed, broken, done over, beaten up. 'Greg wiped out in 15-foot Dungeons. It was carrots for him.' 'If you hit my dog again, I will give you carrots.'

CARVE
When a hottie* uses his surfboard as a carving knife. Another term for high-performance surfing, but with more style than other synonyms, such as rip, tear, shred or lacerate.

CAUGHT INSIDE
Trapped in the white water where the waves are breaking. 'I was caught inside when a 25-wave set* broke.'

CHARF
1. Flirt, court, seduce.
2. Pretend, lie.

CHECK
Look, do you see? 'Check this' (Look at this), 'You check?' (See what I mean? Do you follow? Are you with me?)

CHINA
1. A friend, colleague or acquaintance. 'Mike is my china.'
2. Also a term of address for same, or even a total stranger 'Are you tuning* me china?'

CHOON, see tune

CHOP
Idiot, twit, dolt. 'Yissus* bru*, you pulled a blind* move klapping* Clayton with the Tassies* bottle. You are such a chop!'

CHORB
Pimple.

CHUCK
Depart, leave, go, split, waai*. 'Let's chuck.'

CLASSIC
Excellent, perfect, incredible. 'The waves are classic.' 'That person is classic.' 'I had a classic time.' 'My car is classic.' (Not a vintage car, but it gets me to the surf, and the rust hasn't eaten the floor away yet.)

CLOSE OUT
When a wave stops being rideable because a long section* breaks all at once. 'That wave closed out on my head.'

COME SHORT
Get taken out, get into trouble, die, fail. 'Bru*, if you drop in* on me again, you're going to come short.'

CONNECTION, CONNEKO, KANONI
Friend, buddy. 'Jimmy's my big connection bru*. We surf together every day.'

COOK
Good surf. When the surf cooks, it is going off its face, firing, pumping, cranking, going off its pip, sick, rad, ballistic. Consistent, big, clean, beautifully shaped waves. Someone who cooks is not a chef. He or she is a good surfer.

COOL
Like kiff and lekker, a universal word that refers to things hip, okay, good and nice. 'He is cool because he wears funky shades.' 'That's cool.' 'We had a cool time at J-Bay.'

COVER-UP
A brief tube ride when the lip, or curl, of the wave momentarily passes over your head.

CRANKING, see ballistic

CRASH
Sleep. 'Do you want to crash at my porsie*?'

CRIPPLE
Kneeboarder.

CUT-BACK
A turn on the wave face where you cut back towards the curl of the wave.

CUZ
Cousin, mate, friend. Durban slang for bru.

D
DAGGA (Dugh-ghah)
Marijuana, dope, ganga, cannabis. Originates from the Khoikhoi word *dachab*.

DAWN PATROL
Early-morning surf as the sun is coming up, otherwise called a dawnie.

DEAD BEES
Durban slang for dagga*.

DIAL ME IN
Get me interested. 'My china* dialled me into your website.'

DIK (duhk)
Thick, beefy, big, full (Afrikaans). A person can be dik or you can get dik after a big meal. 'That rugby player is lank* dik.'

DODGY, DODGE
Suspicious. 'That oke is lank* dodgy.' 'His claim that he beat Kelly Slater is a bit dodge'.

DOENING IT
A mutated English variant on the Afrikaans word 'doen' which means 'do'. Another example of our mal* hybrid culture. 'The surf was doening it.'

DOF (dôf)
Dull, stupid (Afrikaans). It can also describe a temporary loss of brain cells. 'Don't be dof.' (Don't be a moron). It can also be used as a noun. 'You doffie.'

DOLOS (dôlôss)
This large H-shaped concrete block – with a mass of up to 20 tons – was invented in East London in the early 1960s and is used in breakwaters and piers around South Africa. Plural dolosses.

DOOBIE
Joint. Originates from the Doobie Brothers.

DOORMAT
Derogatory, but vaguely descriptive term for a bodyboarder. Doormats prefer this word to 'boogie boarder'. Also booger, gutslider, shark biscuit, speed-bump, sponge. In Oz, there are variations, like esky lid (cool box lid) and toilet lid.

DOP (dôp)
1. Booze, drink (Afrikaans). 'Let's go for a dop.' Wine farmers once used the dop system. Labourers were paid in cheap wine. This created a generation of winos.

Partly responsible for the sad existence of the bergie*. 'Dop' may have come from 'doppie' – the cap of a screw-top bottle (one tot).

2. Fail, flunk (Afrikaans). 'I dopped high school because I surfed Glen Beach all the time.'

DORP
Small town (Afrikaans). Don't be confused when you hear, 'Let's go for a dop in that dorp.'

DOSS (dôs)
Sleep. 'In the 70s, I dossed in my Kombi at the Point in J-Bay.*'

DRILLED, see axed, carrots

DROOGIES, DROËBEK (Droe-ghies, droo-er-beck)
Dry mouth (Afrikaans). Normally associated with a cracked, parched mouth and thwollen tongue when you have thmoked too muth doobie*, or drunk too much tassies*.

DROP
When you take off on a wave, you take the drop.

DROP IN
When someone takes off and drops in front of you on a wave and breaks surfing etiquette. At J-Bay, this has led to many fights.

DROP-KNEE
While riding a wave, you kneel on the bodyboard with one knee up. Otherwise known as a DK.

DUCK
Leave, depart. 'As soon as I checked the boere* pull in*, I ducked.'

DUCK DIVE
Technique to duck under oncoming waves. Push your surfboard under the wave, then lever it with your knee or foot as the wave passes overhead. The desired result is to pop out behind the wave, where you can smirk at the guy next to you who has been washed 15 metres back.

DUMP
1. Wipeout. A close out* wave dumps you.

2. Defecate. You go to the toilet to take a dump.

DURBAN POISON. DPS
Choice marijuana vintage. Grown in KwaZulu-Natal, minty, almost peppery, and makes you on*.

DURBS
Durban. Affectionate name for the surf capital of South Africa.

DWAAL
Dazed and confused (Afrikaans). This word describes a vacuous, blank, dreamlike state. 'I am in a dwaal after surfing for 12 hours yesterday.'

E
EGG BEATER, see boatman

EINA (ay-nah)
Ouch (Afrikaans). Widely used. You can shout 'Eina!' in sympathy when a shark chows your buddy's buttocks while surfing in the Kei.

EISH (aysh, or eesh)
Surprise, bewilderment, shock (Khoi). 'Eish. I forgot my leash and it's 10 feet.'

EK SÊ (Eck-sair)
I say (Afrikaans). Used for affirmation or impact. 'Let's hit the jorl, ek sê.'

F
FADE
1. Lose strength. A wave fades when the water gets deeper.
2. Back out. If you back out of something, you fade.
3. Cut off. When two surfers are riding a wave, and the one in front fades the other into the impact zone by cutting him off. The second guy gets burned*.

FIRING, see ballistic
'Hey bru*, Nahoon is firing on all cylinders, ek sê*.'

FLASH
Think, decide, work out. 'I flash that it's cooking* there bru*.'

FLOATER
Surfing manoeuvre that entails gaining speed along the wall of the wave and ramping laterally over the top of the wave as it folds over. Good surfers can cover 10 metres before free-falling over the foam – a move that scores highly in competitive surfing.

FOAMIES
Broken surf. White water washing sedately towards shore. Ideal for toddlers, little children and Vaalies*.

FOLKS
Parents. 'My folks won't let me go to the jorl*.'

FOREST FAMILY
When your pubes get stuck in your wetsuit and painfully pull at your skin but you can't reach in to untangle them.

FRONTSIDE, see backside

FULL-ON
Absolutely, right on, to the limit. Affirmation or agreement, but also refers to an act or person that is extreme in some way. It could be used in this context: 'That was a full-on drop-in*.' 'That oke* is full on.'

FULLY
Affirmation. 'Did you check Occy pull off that insane move at Boneyards?' 'Fully bru*.'

G
GAFFED
Stoned. 'That number* made me so-o-o gaffed.'

GATVOL (ghut-fôl)
Fed up. Literally, 'hole-full' (filled to the brim). 'He was gatvol of the crowds at J-Bay.'

GAUTIES (ghow-teas), see Vaalies.

GERBE (ghair-bear)
Eastern Cape term for a shark.

GERRICK (gher-rick)
Rolled up paper bent into circle to prevent the skitsels* from falling out of a bottleneck*.

GLASSY
When the texture of the ocean is like glass because there is no wind.

GLOBE
To look at intently. 'Don't globe me out, bru*, or I'll moer* you'.

GOATBOAT
Paddle ski. Kind of like a wave canoe that resembles a half-sucked lozenge. Stand-up surfers don't like them because boatmen* paddle faster and catch more waves. In the wrong hands, they wreak havoc in the water.

GOING OFF, see ballistic, cooking, cranking, firing, off its face, pumping, smoking
When the surf is really good, it's 'going off its face!'

GOOFBALL
Dopehead. 'Pete is such a goofball. He's always pulling goofed* actions*.'

GOOFED (goefed)
Stoned. 'That number* made me so goofed.'

GOOFY-FOOT
Stance on a surfboard with right foot forward. The 'natural' stance is with the left foot forward. Similar to being left- or right-handed.

GOT OFF WITH
Get lucky with the opposite sex. 'John got off with Barbara at the jorl* last night.'

GRAFT
Work, or place of work. 'Where do you graft?' 'At my graft, I sit next to a sumo wrestler who sings in the choir.'

GRAZE
Eat. There is a strong agricultural tradition in South Africa. This might explain graze, which means 'to eat' as in 'What are you grazing?' 'What's for graze dad?' Be warned, don't mention sheep. That joke refers to another southern hemisphere country.

GRIEF
Trouble, strife, backchat. 'Are you tuning* me grief china*?'

GROMMET
Usually affectionate term for a young surfer of school-going age. Shortened to Grom.

GUAVA
1. Fruit. 'He slipped on a guava…'
2. Bum. '…and fell on his guava.'

GUN
A longer board with more volume that lets you surf bigger waves.

GUN IT
Gaining speed on a wave to make it through the section*. You have to gun it to keep up with fast-breaking waves like Supertubes in J-Bay.

GUNNED
If you are undergunned, your board is too short for the size and power of the waves. If you are overgunned, your board is too long.

GUTSLIDER, see doormat

H
HAK (huk)
To pester, irritate. 'Stop hakking me'.

HALF-JACK
Half-bottle of spirits. 'Me and my china* klapped* a half-jack of Klippies*.'

HANG THE BROWN BEAR IN THE PORCELAIN CAVE
Defecate in a white enamel toilet

HECTIC
Radical, extreme, over the top. 'Footage of that oke* on the electric chair was hectic bru*.'

HOESIT, see howzit.

HOLLOW
When a wave breaks powerfully on a shallow reef or sandbar, the lip* throws further and the barrel* is deemed to be hollow.

HONE
Stink. 'Your feet hone bru'! 'That ou has serious lung hone.' (That guy has serious halitosis.)

HOSE
Laugh. 'He was hosing himself when he fell in the pool.'

HOTTIE
1. Good surfer
2. Attractive member of the opposite sex.

HOW'S YOUR MIND?
Are you mad?! This question refers to the mental stability of the subject after performing a stupid, idiotic or irritating act.

HOWZIT, HOESIT
Greeting. Short for 'How is it?' Refrain from saying, 'It's fine, thanks'. You will get a funny look. You can say: 'No, fine.' This means 'Yes, I am fine'. 'No' often means 'yes' in South Africa. An Afrikaner might reply: 'Ja, well, no fine', a more emphatic, long-winded version of 'No, fine'.

HUM
1. Busy. 'Surfers' Disco was humming last night.'
2. Stink. 'He hums like a skunk.'

HUNDREDS
Good, excellent, enjoyable. 'Hey bru*, I skeem* the jorl* was kiff*. What do you skeem?' 'Ja, bru, it was hundreds.'

I
IMPACT ZONE
Area where the waves break. When it's a 12-foot day at Crayfish Factory you don't really want to spend time there.

IN THE EYES
Exposed, sticking out like sore thumb, vulnerable. People who smoke too much dope get paranoid. They start worrying about 'being in the eyes'. You would be too if your hair stood up like a fizzed furball and your eyes blazed like blinking red beacons.

INSANE
Absolute, excellent, superlative. Surf doesn't get better than 'insane'.

INSIDE
An area closer to shore where the waves are breaking. At some

breaks, there are a number of reefs or sandbars, some further out than others. In small swell, the waves will break on the inside. In bigger swell, they might break on the outside, but you can get caught on the inside.

IRIE
State of nirvana for Rastafarians. Goofball South Africans in dreads think this is their word. Indicates good vibes, agreement, and positive associations. 'Good surf, bru*. Irie.'

IS IT? (iz-zit?)
Conversational word used widely in response to anything. Derived from the English 'Is it really?' If you don't feel like talking to a dik* ou* at a braai*, but don't wish to appear rude, just say 'is it' at appropriate gaps in his description of how he decapitated a kudu with his bare hands.

J
JACKED, JACKING
1. Rising swell. 'The surf is jacking*.' 'Supers jacked to six foot in an hour.'
2. Organised. 'That oke* is jacked.'

JAGS (yughs)
Horny. 'Checking Pamela Anderson and Tommy Lee on video made me jags.'

J-BAY
Does this need explanation? Jeffreys Bay, the Mecca of surfing in South Africa. The town is similar to Torquay in Australia, home to big-name surf brands near a world-class wave. J-Bay ranks as perhaps the best right-hand point on earth.

JOHNNY
Slightly outdated term for the surfers' nemesis: the shark.

JORL
Party, have fun. The word jorl, like the word kiff* can be used in any context. 'I am going to a jorl (party).' 'I am having a jorl (good time).' 'That spectacular wipeout at Supertubes was a jorl (rush).'

JUST NOW
In a while. It will be done eventually, but maybe never. If someone says 'I will do it just now', be warned. It could be 10 minutes, 10 hours or never. 'I'll clean my room just now, Ma.' If someone says 'now now*', you're making progress. It won't be done immediately, or instantly, but probably in less than 10 minutes, barring distractions that relegate it to 'just now'.

K
KAALGAT (kaal-ghut)
Butt-naked (Afrikaans).

KAK (kuck)
Shit (Afrikaans). This is used in weird and wonderful ways in the same way as 'shit'. 'Don't talk kak.' 'Don't tune* me kak.' 'You're so full of kak.' 'I am having a kak day.' 'He is in the kak.'

KANALA (kuh-nah-la)
Friend, buddy. 'Hey my kanala, haven't checked* you for a while.'

KAP (cup)
Cut, strike, do it. 'Let's kap another dop*.' 'The southwest buster* is going to kap the coast.' 'Kap it bru*.'

KÊFFIE, KUIF (kef-fee, kayf)
Café. Many South Africans deliberately don't pronounce words properly.

KEI (kye)
The Transkei. Usually called the Kei, this former apartheid bantustan is part of the Eastern Cape. It remains rural and beautiful, with rolling green hills that fall into the sea as jagged cliffs along the aptly-named Wild Coast – a famous dagga*-growing area and birthplace of our former president, Nelson Mandela. The Kei is known by surfers for great camping, excellent point breaks and sharks.

KICK OUT
At the end of your ride, you kick out of the wave in a controlled way.

KIFF, KIEF, KEEF
Nice. Like the all-encompassing word 'nice', used by semi-literate English speakers the world over, it can be used in any context, and is a convenient way to express a limited vocabulary. 'This chow is kiff ek sê*.' 'I just had such a kiff wave.' Can be pronounced keef (drawing out the syllable).

KITTES (kuh-tiss)
Clothes, gear, kit. 'You have lank* marcha* for the larny* kittes ek sê*.'

KLAP (klup)
Hit, slap (Afrikaans). Slap, partake in, perform an act. 'Ek sal jou a snotklap gee.' (I will hit you hard enough to make the snot fly.) 'Let's klap another Klippies*.'

KLIPPIES AND COKE
Brandy and Coke. Named after Klipdrift, a popular brandy.

KNOB
Idiot, dolt. 'Don't be a knob by dropping in* on me bru*.'

KNYP (k-naip)
Pinch.Bite the bullet. When your bladder is full, and you can't go to the toilet, you knyp.

KOOK
Beginner who gets in everyone's way. A kook is not necessarily a grommet*, although a grommet can be a kook. Kooks can be all ages. Grommets are kids.

KOTCH, see bark the dog

KOTSBLANKET
Fountain of puke resembling a blanket.

KOWIE
Port Alfred. From the name of the river that runs through it.

KREEF (kree-erf)
Cape spiny lobster. The nutrient-rich waters of the West Coast are home to millions of these delicious crustaceans. Make friends with a local and go kreef diving, or bait them with a lobster pot (the kreef, not the locals). The daily bag limit is four. Season starts in November for four months.

KUDU
A large antelope that is often the subject of macho posturing in bars.

KUSSED, kus, kished
Exhausted, tired. 'I am kussed out/
kus after that six-hour session*.'

L
LACERATE
Hot surfers rip, shred, carve, tear,
and lacerate. All slashing or cutting
motions can be applied to a surfer
who is going off in cooking* waves.
Also shred, rip, tear, carve.

LAMMIE (lum-mee)
Welt. A lammie is a kind of welt
caused by hitting someone with
the middle knuckle of your middle
finger. School kids give each other
lammies, usually on the forearm. A
proper lammie becomes a bump
immediately. From the Afrikaans word
'lam', which means paralysed or lame.

LANK
All-encompassing adjective
describing lots of something. 'There
are lank people in the water.' 'I dig
him lank.' 'He's lank thin.'

LARNY
Fancy. 'He's such a larny.' 'You are
wearing larny clothes.' 'Why are
you dressed so larny?' 'We went
to a larny party that had caviar for
pudding.' For coloured people in the
Cape, it means 'Friend'. 'Hoesit* my
larny!'

LAS (Luss)
1. Cancel, leave it. 'They stopped the
   fight when he was told to las it.'
2. Too much like hard work. 'Getting
   ready for the fancy dress is such a
   las.'

LEGEND, Lej
Hero, good guy, classy oke*. Down
in the Eastern Cape, when the
party is ripping, and everyone starts
getting all soppy and sentimental,
they might start calling each other
'legends'. Also heard when someone
pulls off a lank* clever move. 'Jono,
you legend!' his friends might say.
Can be shortened to 'lej'. 'That
session* was lej, bru*!'

LEKKER
Nice, pleasant, fun, lovely, good,
pretty (Afrikaans). People can be
lekker. Cars can be lekker. You can
have a lekker time. You can feel
lekker. Holidays are lekker. When the
Springboks occasionally win a rugby
match, it's lekker. Of course, a lamb
chop on the braai* is also lekker.

LIGHTEY
Youngster. 'That lightey is a good
surfer, for a grommet*.' (Also laaitie.)

LINE-UP
An area just off the reef or sandbar
where the waves are breaking.
'He was sitting in the line-up.' So
named because at some breaks it
is necessary to align yourself to a
landmark to keep your spot in the
line up. When the swell, rip currents
or winds are strong, you often need
to triangulate yourself with two
landmarks, lest you drift from the
take-off zone.

LIP
Top of the wave when it curls. You
can get hit on the head by the lip,
or you can hit the lip with your
surfboard, a surfing manoeuvre that
involves turning up the face and
connecting the lip. Can be done by
aggressively pushing your board
into the lip, or by allowing the lip to
push your board over as you reach
the top.

LOMP (lômp)
Lethargic or clumsy (Afrikaans).
Descriptive word denoting a lack of
energy. 'He felt lomp after that 12-
hour surf session.'

LOSKOP (lôs-kôp)
Absent-minded, forgetful (Afrikaans).

M
MACK, Macker
Max, huge wave. 'The waves are
macking, bru*.

MADIBA (mah-dee-ba)
The clan name for Nelson Mandela
universally used as a term of respect
and affection. His full name is Nelson
Rolihlahla (Roli-shla-shla) Mandela.

MAJAT (muh-jut)
Low-grade dagga*. 'This kak*
is majat.'

MAKES ON
Makes you stoned. 'Schwee bru*, I
am so on'. Also 'This stuff puts on'.

MAL (mull)
Mad (Afrikaans). 'That ou* is mal'.

MAN IN THE GREY SUIT
Shark. Surfers never use the word
'shark' in the water.

MARCHA
Money.

MARMITE
Not to be confused with its poor
Australian cousin vegemite, Marmite
is a salty yeast and vegetable extract
resembling burnt engine oil mixed
with treacle. It's a protein-rich paste
with a meaty flavour – a by-product
of the fermentation of brewer's yeast
discovered by a German chemist
named Liebig. The Brits made it
commercially viable.

MERT
Drug merchant. 'He went to score a
bankie* from his mert.'

MIELIE PAP, see pap

MIF, same as sif*

MISSION
Hassle, schlep. 'School is a mission.'

MOER (Moer-r)
Hit, punch (Afrikaans). 'I will moer
you if you drop in* on my wave.'

MULL
Prepare dagga* for smoking.

MULLET
This goes beyond short hair on top;
long at the back. Neither does it
refer to bait-fish. A mullet is a person
who is weird, eccentric or insane.
'That ou* is a mullet.'

N
NAFF
Wimp, wimpish. A naff is somebody
lacking backbone. 'Cecil is such a
naff name.'

NAUGHT, naughtus (naw-tiss)
No, Oh no! Used like 'nooit'. 'Naught

bru*! Don't drop in* on me again or I'll moer* you with a picket fence.'

NECK, see bottleneck

NOOIT (noy-t)
Never (Afrikaans). No way, oh no! Also used as an expletive. If you have just heard that a South African won the world surfing champs, you would say, 'Nooit! Are you serious?'

NOUGHT
Asshole, ringpiece. Pronounced the same as naught. 'I fell on my nought.' 'I saw my nought.' 'It's as cold as a polar bear's nought.'

NOW NOW
In a little while. 'We're going surfing now now.' (We're about to go surfing, depending on when the video ends and how long it takes to put on the roof racks, get petrol, and stop at the shop). Now now happens much quicker than just now*. Really.

NUMB
Extremely out of it. 'I got so numb after making a fat number* at Numbers disco.'

NUMBER
Joint. 'Let's make a number.' May have originated in California from the lyric 'One is the loneliest number you will ever do' by Three Dog Night (1969)

O

OBS (o-bees)
Old Brown Sherry. Many a nostalgic surfer will remember the days they lay on the beach with friends around a fire wrapped around a bottle of OBs.

OFF ITS FACE, see ballistic

OKE, OU, (oak, oh)
Guy, chap, bloke. Despite being low on letters, oke or ou are huge words. This word, or its variant, is South Africa's most common word for a man. Probably from Afrikaans 'ou pel' (old mate), but the adjective became the noun after the 'pel' was dropped. 'That ou says he can paddle around Seal Island with one arm.'

ON
Stoned. 'I am so on.'

ON A MISSION
On a quest to complete a task. When you're determined to complete a task, you are on a mission. If you try and persuade your bru* to pull in* to the jorl*, he might say, 'Nooit* bru, I'm on a mission to pass exams.'

ONE TIME
Nice one. You are lank* cool if you say 'One time'.

ONLY
Utility adjective. It does not mean unique as in 'There can be only one', but a utility word meaning lank*, kiff* or very much. 'He was only tuning* him,' does not mean 'He was tuning only him,' or even 'He was just tuning him.' It means 'He was tuning him with great gusto.'

OUTSIDE
An area further out from the shore where the waves are breaking. In small swell, the waves break on the inside. In bigger swell, they might break on the outside.

OVER THE FALLS
The classic surf wipeout, when the lip* of the wave sucks you over, drops you onto the seemingly cement-hard water, and then falls on your head followed by several cycles in a salty washing machine.

P

PADKOS (put-kôss)
Food for the journey, literally road food (Afrikaans). Padkos is usually a few sarmies*, cooldrinks, chips, fruit and maybe a lekker* stukkie* biltong*.

PAP (Pup)
1. Porridge (Afrikaans). Boiled maize meal (mielie pap) is the staple diet of many South Africans. Pap is versatile. It can be eaten as a sweet, soft porridge, or cooked up stiff to be eaten as a starch with a main meal, in which case it's usually referred to as 'pap en sous', meaning pap and sauce (or gravy).

2. Weak, soft (Afrikaans). 'The waves are pap today.'

PARK OFF, park.
1. Chill out. When you park off, you sit down and relax. 'Shall we park off and watch *Riding Giants* for the 40th time?'
2. Sit down. 'Donovan, why don't you park here?'

PARK A TIGER, see bark the dog

PAVEMENT
What Americans call a sidewalk, we call a pavement.

PE
Port Elizabeth, a town near J-Bay*.

PERLEMOEN (perr-luh-moen)
Abalone. A delicious shellfish.

PIP
Head. If you ding your pip, you hurt your head. If you get shacked* off your pip, you get barrelled* off your nut.

PIT
This is where you don't want to be when a huge set is breaking. It refers to the impact zone*, the area where the waves break.

PITJIES (pit-chies)
Dagga* seeds. Occasionally refers to other fruit and vegetable pips.

PLAK (pluck)
Weird state of mind. The Afrikaans meaning is to stick (with glue), but it also denotes a certain mindset. You say to someone with obscure reasons for doing something, 'What's your plak?' (Where are you coming from?) The variation is, 'How's your mind?' This is a distracted, even deranged, state of mind. 'He was on a plak when he dived off the roof.' (He was on a weird trip when he dived off the roof.)

POEPOL (poep-all)
Idiot, twit. 'Don't be a poepol'.

POES
Used in same way as c**t and it means the same thing. 'Don't be a poes'. (Don't be nasty.)

POINT BREAK
A reef that juts out from the land around which waves bend and break.

POMP (pômp)
Bonk, have sex. From the Afrikaans word meaning 'pump'. Literal connotations with farm water pumps and windmills.

PONDOLAND FEVER
After chilling out for any length of time on the Wild Coast, you risk contracting Pondoland Fever. Not a tropical disease, just a general 'Hey like' lethargy brought on by the mind-stewing quality of the local 'herbs'.

PORSIE (paw-zee)
Home, spot, place. 'Should we watch videos at your porsie?'

PULL
Take a drag. 'Can I have a pull bru*.'

PULL IN
Enter. You pull into the barrel* or the jorl*. It can also mean scoring with a member of the opposite sex, as in 'Brian only* pulled into Susan on Tuesday night.'

PULL YOUR WIRE
Masturbate.

PUMPING, see ballistic

PUTS ON
Makes you stoned.

R
RADICAL, rad
Extreme, over-the-top, great. A hot surfer will perform a radical move. If you have just had a good wave, you will say it was rad.

RAT
Not a furry creature with a long tail, but youngsters who surf, many of them beginners. They do sometimes look similar to rats, and are viewed in the same way, if not worse.

REEF BREAK
A surf spot where the waves break on a reef – rock or coral.

RE-ENTRY
Surfing manoeuvre that entails turning vertically up the face, hitting the lip and dropping down the wave either on the face, or over the broken foam.

RHINO CHASER
Not a person who runs after large terrestrial mammals, but a big-wave board, something long enough and strong enough to handle a macking* bomb*.

RING, RINGPIECE
Human sphincter. 'I dropped my rods* and flashed* my ring.' Also used as a more general term for the human bottom. A more descriptive way of saying 'I slipped and fell on my bottom' is 'I slipped and saw my ring.' This has a better ring to it.

RIP, see shred, tear, carve, lacerate Also refers to rip currents. 'He got caught in the rip.'

ROBOT
Traffic light. Peculiarly South African way of describing a traffic light. But then, we only got TV in the mid 1970s.

ROCK UP
To arrive. The more old-fashioned way of saying pull in*. You don't tell anyone you're on the way, you just rock up.

RODS
Trousers. 'I dropped my rods and flashed a brown eye*.'

ROFF (r-rôf)
Rough. Often pertains to an uncouth person or dodgy neighbourhood. 'The perlemoen* poachers in Hawston are quite roff.'

ROOIBAARD (roy-baard)
Superior-grade dagga* cultivar with sticky red hairs on the heads.

ROOIBOS (roy-bôs)
This tannin-free and caffeine-free herbal tea originates from the Clanwilliam area of the Western Cape. Made from the *Aspalathus linearis* bush. Homesick South

Africans buy it from gourmet stores around the world even if they don't like it.

ROOTS
The real thing. 'It's gonna be roots!' It's going to be the real deal. Possibly borrowed from the album *Sepultra Roots*. See cool Port Elizabeth author Hagen Engler's book *Life's a Beach*.

ROP (r-rôp)
Nice, radical. 'That was such a rop wave.'

RUSH
Spurt of adrenalin, thrill. 'I got such a rush riding that 15-foot barrel* at the Crayfish Factory.'

S
SAMOOSA (suh-moor-suh)
Deep-fried triangular curried pie. Originally from northern India, samoosas can be found in cafés around the country.

SAMP
An African food made from whole dried maize, usually eaten with haricot or red beans in a rich gravy stew. Lekker*.

SARMIE
Sandwich. Kids sometimes take a sarmie to school in the morning.

SCALE
Steal. A person who is 'scaly' is a scumbag or a sleazy type, such as a skollie, skelm or skebenga*.

SCHNAAI (sh-nigh)
Rip off, betray, stab in the back. 'He was schnaaied by his brus* when they tipped off the boere* that he had five kilos of rooibaard* in the back of his bakkie*.'

SCORE
1. Purchase. 'Hey bru*, check this bankie* I scored from my mert*!'
2. Acquire, give. 'I scored a luck last night.' 'Bru, score me some wax'.

SCRATCH
Paddle fast. When a big wave looms on the outside*, you scratch to get over it.

SECTION
Part of something, usually a wave, or a joint. When you hit a section called Impossibles at J-Bay*, you get pitted* in an awesome barrel from which you will be lucky to emerge. When you hit the gooey rooibaard* section of a six-blade slowboat* in the Kei, you will be lucky to emerge with wits intact.

SESSION, SESH
A period of time spent surfing. 'It was my second session of the day.'

SET
A group of waves that break one after the other. Swells travel in intermittent sets, with a lull between them.

SHACKED
Tubed. 'Bru*, I got shacked off my pip* during that cyclone swell.'

SHAME
1. Expression of sympathy. 'These piles are lank* sore.' 'Ag* shame bru!'
2. How cute. 'Ag* shame, what a sweeeet puppy.'

SHARK BISCUIT, see doormat
From Australian slang for body-boarder.

SHARP
Affirmation, cool. A popular and trendy word originating from urban black culture that is now widely in use. You also say sharpshoot, or sharp-sharp, pronounced shupshup.

SHORE BREAK
Waves that break almost at the shoreline. Many surf spots end with a close-out* shore break.

SHOT
1. Thanks. You will say 'Shot' when your bru* buys you a brew*. 'Shot bru.' 'Shot a lot Dot.'
2. Goodbye. You will also say 'Shot bru*' when saying goodbye.
3. Yours sincerely. You will end your letter, 'Shot, Peter.'

SHRED, see carve, lacerate

SHWEET, SWEET
Excellent, cool. 'Shweet my bru*!'

SICK
Excellent, radical, good. A sick wave is a really juicy, clean, hard-breaking wave, not a wave that resembles vomit.

SIF
Disgusting. A shortened version of syphilis, sif doesn't necessarily refer to disease, but could refer to a gangrenous coral wound, an overused long drop toilet, a car accident or a chorb*.

SIS
Yuck. 'Sis, man, you just kotched* on my wetsuit.'

SJOE (shoe), shew (shee-you), shewee (shee-you-wee), shwee
Exletive. 'Sjoe bru*, that wave was awesome.'

SKAAM
Embarrassed (Afrikaans). 'Gavin was lank* skaam after he wiped out right in front of his stukkie*.'

SKATE, see skebenga

SKAY
Watch out. If a car is heading for you, and you haven't noticed, you friend will shout 'Skay!' Also 'Chips'.

SKEBENGA (skuh-beng-guh)
Gangster, crook, ruffian (Zulu). 'Skay* Ray, that skebenga is checking* your skedonk*.' (Watch it, Ray, that crook is looking at your car.) Also skelm or skollie.

SKEDONK (skuh-dônk)
A really beaten up old jalopy.

SKEEF (skee-erf)
Skew, bent (Afrikaans). A classic saying heard in bars around South Africa is 'Are you checking* me skeef, China*?' (Are you looking at me funny, mate?) This often precedes a brawl. 'Bru, do you skeem* this stringer is skeef?' (Bro, do you think this surfboard stringer is crooked?)

SKEEM
Think, reckon. 'You skeem?' (You think so?) 'What do you skeem?'

(What do you think?) 'I'm skeeming we surf Seal Point.'

SKELM, see skebenga

SKINDER (skuh-ner)
Gossip (Afrikaans). Usually juicy gossip.

SKITSELS (skuht-sels)
The debris, or detritus, left at the bottom of the jar, or bankie*, after you've used up the best of your dagga* stash. Skitsels are the stalks, pips and bits of leaves.

SKOLLIE, see skebenga
Can be used almost affectionately when talking about a roguish friend. Choose carefully whom you call a skollie. Apparently, derived from 'skoolverlater', which is Afrikaans for 'school leaver'.

SKRIK
Fright, frighteningly ugly (Afrikaans). After being held down for 30 seconds in the kelp at Crayfish Factory, you might get a bit of a skrik. An owl hoot in a cemetery might also give you a skrik. Alternatively, your lover might be a skrik, but that's not so lekker*.

SKYF (skayf)
1. Spliff. 'Let's make a skyf, bru*'
2. A French fry.

SKYFIE (skay-fee)
A slice, or a piece of something, especially an orange.

SLAP CHIPS (slup chips)
Soft and stodgy French fries, ideal for mixing with tomato sauce or vinegar, or both.

SLASH
Piss, leak. 'I'm taking a slash.'

SLIP SLOPS
Beach thongs – the kind you wear on your feet. They're made of rubber and have a strap between your big toe and its partner. Also flip flops.

SLOT IN, slot
Pull in* to a tube*. 'Peter was

perfectly slotted.' (Peter rode the tube perfectly.)

SLOWBOAT
Large joint made with three or more cigarette papers. A six-blade slowboat would be made with six papers.

SLUK (sluhk)
1. Drink. Have a sip of someone's drink. 'Give me a sluk, bru.'
2. To steal. 'I was slukking my dop* when some oke* got klapped* for slukking another oke's dop.'

SLUMTOWN, SLUMMIES
Affectionate nickname for East London, which is near excellent surf.

SMAAK
Like, enjoy, have the hots for. 'I smaak Sam stukkend*.' (I have the total hots for Sam.)

SMOKING, see ballistic

SNAKE
Steal a wave. Some surfers are masters at this. They will paddle around you, heading further out, then suddenly paddle towards the inside* to claim right of way over the wave you were going for.

SNART
Piece of snot stuck to one's face after a duck dive*.

SNOEK
Long narrow fish with sharp teeth found off Cape Town. It tastes great when fresh. Smoked snoek can be eaten as is, which is delicious, or served in a dish called 'smoorsnoek, which tastes better than it sounds.

SNOEP
Stingy (Afrikaans). This is not a fish, but a noun or verb referring to extreme stinginess. 'Solly is a snoep snoek.'

SORRY
Excuse me. While also used for its global meaning, as an apology, South Africans have managed to mutate it further. 'Sorry, can I just get past.' Perhaps it has psychological

roots in the apartheid days, when travelling white South Africans said sorry wherever they went.

SOSATIE (suh-saa-tea)
Kebab. Spicy marinated meat skewered with pieces of tomato, green pepper, onion and sometimes fruit, especially apricot, and braaied*.

SOUTHEASTER, see Cape Doctor.

SPADE, spadework
To court a member of the opposite sex. The verb is used in a number of ways, such as 'Sheila was spading Bruce big time.' 'Bruce will have to put in lots of spadework if he's going to pull in* to Sheila tonight.' Also charf*.

SPAN
A lot, many, much, more. This is mostly a Durban word that is used as an adjective that amplifies things. 'You guys have left out a span of words in your slang dictionary Ek sê*!'

SPAT OUT
Shot out of the tube. Sometimes, when you get tubed, you get spat out with a burst of spray when compressed air caught in the swirling cylinder is suddenly released.

SPEED-BUMP, see booger, doormat.

SPEW, see bark the dog

SPONGE, see booger, doormat

SPOOK AND DIESEL
Cane spirits and Coke.

SQUIF
Crooked. Similar to skeef*.

SQUIRTS
Diarrhoea.

STAUNCH
Dik*, big, strong. 'That prop forward is a staunch ou*.'

STOKED
Totally amped*, revved up, happy. 'The oke* was so stoked after making that wave.'

STOKERFADE
Surf trip that ends with no surf. The amped* excitement and stoke fades when a long drive reveals no surf.

STOP, Stoppe (stôp, stôp-pe)
A sausage-shaped parcel of dope wrapped in newspaper or brown paper.

STROPPY
Cheeky.

STUKKEND (stuhk-uhnt)
Broken, ruined, finished, wrecked (Afrikaans). Variations include 'I'm going to moer* you stukkend' (I am going to beat you to a pulp), 'My heart was stukkend' (My heart was broken), 'I was stukkend last night' (wrecked) or 'I smaak* you stukkend' (I like you lank*).

STUKKIE (stuhk-key)
Little piece (Afrikaans). Sexist term for a person of the opposite sex. Also – of course – a little piece of something.

STYLING
When you're styling, everything clicks into place and you find yourself surfing like Kelly Slater, Tom Curren and 'insert-favourite-surfer-here' rolled into one.

SUKKEL (suhk-kel)
Afrikaans – Struggle, have difficulty with. 'The grommets* are sukkelling in the strong current.'

SURFARI
Surf trip. 'I went on a surfari to Indo.'

SUSS
Savvy. 'Having a bit of suss' is to be quite sharp, knowledgeable or street-wise. 'I have sussed it out' (I have worked it out).

SUT
Exhausted, kussed*.

SWAK (swuck)
Bad, nasty, downer. A disappointed surfer will choon*, 'Swak bru*, the surf is pap*.'

SWAZI REDS
Potent cannabis vintage from Swaziland. Dark red, with sticky furry hairs on the heads. A prime choice for connoisseurs.

T

TAKE OFF
Catch a wave. The take-off zone is the area where you catch the waves.

TAKKIES (tackies)
Sneakers, trainers, running shoes. Often refers to the cheap, hip kind bought in a mass clothing chain called Pep Stores. This word is also used to describe car tyres. If someone has fat takkies they have a souped-up car with wide-brim tyres.

TASSIES (tuss-ees)
A cheap red wine called Tassenberg. You never know what you're going to get when you buy a bottle. It could be a good wine, or it could be plonk. Only the label is constant. For many, Tassies evokes memories of beach parties and a sand-caked babalas*.

TEAR, see carve, lacerate.

TECHNICOLOURED YAWN, see bark the dog

THAT TIME
Nostalgic glimpse into the past. We haven't chooned* each other since that time!

THE MOER IN (moer-r)
Very angry. 'You make me the moer in!'

THROW WITH
Throw at. From how some Afrikaners will translate directly from Afrikaans when speaking English. 'He threw me with a stone,' means 'He threw a stone at me.'

TIGER See 'What kind?'

TING
Thing, joint, zol*. 'Let's make a ting,' you say to your china* on a grassy hill in the Kei*.

TOW SURFING
When surfers are towed into large waves by a jetski you call them tow surfers or tow-in surfers.

TRAP (trup)
Walk, step (Afrikaans). 'My china* and me went for a trap to choon* about the kiff* words we found in this glossary.

TUNE (choon)
To tell, to talk, to provoke. For instance, 'Are you tuning me kak*? 'Tune me the ages.' (Tell me the time.)

TUNE GRIEF
To irritate someone. Whatever you do, if a big oke* in a bar pesters you with macho stories of how he tore off a kudu's head with his bare hands, don't show your irritation by saying 'Are you tuning me grief?' Your relatives will be in grief, indeed. And you won't be around to tune them anything.

V

VAALIES (vaah-lees)
Originally these were holidaymakers from the former province of Transvaal. Now also called Gauties, from Gauteng. People who live at the coast (and surfers especially) consider them to be a lesser breed of person – more interested in making a living than parking off* on the beach and checking* out the waves.

VLOEK (floek)
Swear, swear at (Afrikaans). 'I vloeked Harry and he vloeked me back.' Not to be confused with fluke, also sometimes pronounced 'floek' by South Africans (something happening by accident).

VROT (frôt)
Rotten, putrid (Afrikaans). Something undesirable, smelly, or rotten. It can also mean a paralytic drunken state. 'I was vrot last night.'

W

WAAI (v-eye)
To go or to leave. 'Come, let's waai back to my porsie*.'

WASTED
Paralytic drunk or totally high. 'I was completely wasted at the party.'

WEDGE
A break near a wall, pier or jetty. The waves come in, rebound off the wall and travel sideways into the oncoming swell. This pushes up the wave in the middle, forming an A-framed wedge. If you take off on the wedge, you get loads of speed and can hit the lip with lots of force.

WEST, WAY WEST
Stoned, out of it, far gone. Perhaps a pun on the word 'wasted'. 'Bru*, we ended up way west.'

WETTIE
A drink, refreshment. 'Hey bru*, I'm lank* thirsty, lets grab a wettie.'

WHAT FOR
Aggressive act. 'I gave him what for.' This could be by punching him, or vloeking* him, or chastising him vigorously.

WHAT KIND?
Don't be a jerk. If your friend has just parked a tiger* over the side of your car, you would call indignantly 'What kind?'

WHAT WHAT
Blah blah, yada yada. 'That oke* tuned* me "what what".'

WILDSIDE
Exposed coast, usually facing the predominant swell direction.

WINDMILL, see boatman, egg beater

WOBBLY
Panic attack, fit of rage, nervous breakdown. 'Phillip threw a wobbly after someone drove a Nissan Sani over his new seven-eight custom surfboard.'

WOES (voess)
Vicious, wild, pissed off (Afrikaans). 'Skay* bru*, that baboon looks woes.'

WORSE
Very stoned or drunk. 'I am s-o-o-o-o worse!'

WUSS, WUSSY (woess, woes-see)
Wimp, pansie, naff, weakling. 'Don't be a wuss, it's only a six-foot puff adder that's chewing on your leg.'

Y

YISLAAIK (yuhss-like)
A variation of yissus.

YISSUS, YUSSUS (yuh-siss)
Expression of surprise. From the Afrikaans pronunciation of 'Jesus'. The same as 'My God!' 'Oh Lord'. An expression of surprise, fear or shock.

YO, see yooit.

YOOIT (yoyt)
When a bru* checks another bru across the street, he tunes*: 'Yooit!' If you use this form of greeting, bru*, you are la-a-a-ank* cool. Also ahoy, aweh, howzit, hoesit, yo.

YURRUH (yuh-r-ruh)
Similar to yissus, from the Afrikaans pronunciation of 'Here' (hear-er), meaning Lord, or God.

Z

ZOL (zôl)
A joint commonly rolled out of a piece of newspaper and stuck together with saliva. Many township residents smoke tobacco this way.

ZONKED
Completely stoned.

Letter from the Edge

Decipher this and your blood is truly South African.

Howzit bru,

What's waaing eksê? This page makes me woes. You ous don't have a span of words from Durban! A connection at graft dialled me into your website yesterday, and it made me lag. I am an expat from Durban, with a porsie in Sydney, Oz. It was kief to read this but made me mal that I couldn't choon the ous at graft. Blind ekse.

So I chooned a connection from SA and we skeemed it would be cool to catch up and have a dop. Like all durban ous, we smaak to make a better, so I went for a trap and scored some bankies down the road. We hadn't checked each other since that time so we got fully dronk, made a few tings, and ended up way west. We trapped down the road fully goofed, scored some munchies and scooped a kief chow (no bunnies here, so we had a sosatie). The ou serving us schemed he was way to do, so we vloeked him and ducked.

Just in case, we roasted one more phat one and I went back to my porsie. My stukkie was woes, and charfed me that I'd pulled a blind action.

How's this bru, the surf's been doening it. It's been firing, off its pip. I know I'm chooning you what what, but we are going to klap a mission tomorrow. Pull in eksê. Let's go grind some barrels. If not, hope you okes get a couple. We might end up blasting a few dead bees as well. You check, it's the old story, you get numb and waai surfing.

Shot, Neil

USEFUL WEBSITES

General
www.wavescape.co.za

Miscellaneous / Culture
www.swellguys.com
www.wavehouse.co.za
www.6footunder.co.za
www.surf4sure.co.za
www.sharkspotters.org.za
www.liquidgirls.co.za
www.dungeons.co.za

Events
www.redbullbwa.com
www.goodwave.co.za
www.mrpricepro.co.za
www.oneillsa.com

Bodyboarding
www.sixty40.co.za
www.factory7.co.za

Surfaris, travel and adventure
www.wavescape.co.za
www.surfing-safaris.co.za
www.truebluetravel.co.za
www.jaybay.co.za
www.ttride.co.uk
www.havemorefun.co.za
www.dawnpatrol.co.za
www.binksurftours.co.za
www.beachbum.co.za
www.ansteysbeach.co.za
www.sanparks.org

Surfing administrators / Clubs
www.surfingsouthafrica.co.za
www.salsa.co.za
www.surfkzn.co.za
www.wpsurfing.co.za
www.sonsurf.co.za

Learn to surf
www.learntosurf.co.za
www.surfshack.co.za
www.garysurfschool.co.za
www.kahunasurf.co.za

Surfboards / Shapers
www.geraghtyshapes.co.za
www.surfboards.co.za
www.wavescape.co.za/dream.htm
www.dvgshapes.co.za
www.hh-surfboards.com
www.lazyb.co.za
www.surfblanks.co.za
www.safarisurfco.com
www.biltsurf.com
www.f22industries.co.za
www.peterdanielssurf.com
www.hurricanesurf.net
www.claytonsurf.co.za
www.questboards.co.za
www.33surf.com
www.billeon.com
www.glendarcysurfboards.co.za

Print magazines
www.africansurfrider.co.za
www.swg.co.za
www.bluntmag.co.za
www.zigzag.co.za
www.sixty40.co.za
www.africansoulsurfer.co.za

Surf photography
www.lemonline.net/marqua
www.surfpix.co.za
www.avgphoto.co.za
www.tostee.com
www.chappypix.co.za

Surf shops
www.surfzone.co.za

INDEX

ACKNOWLEDGEMENTS

It is humbling to witness the selfless generosity of individuals who made this book possible. We are a community, and this is, in a sense, a community project.

To Shaun Tomson, your foreword is a reminder to us from someone who knows. If anyone has surfed with him at J-Bay recently, you'll see that he is not just the eloquent spokesperson for our surfing spirit. He lives it.

I am deeply indebted to contributors of photos, cartoons, graphics and information – some scientific, some factual and some frivolous. The energy and message of this book depends on many, as outlined below. A special thanks to gifted picture people, who gave so freely of their time, skill and intellectual property. Take a huge bow, Barry Tuck, Harry de Zitter, Tom Peschak, Michael Dei-Cont, Andy Mason, Tony Butt, Lance Slabbert, Ant Scholtz, Brenton Geach, Pierre Marqua, Ray du Toit, Jared Hartman and Serge Raemaekers.

The contributors of words have added spice to this eclectic mix of culture and science. An original piece by Paul Botha forms the backbone of the history chapter. Tom Peschak adds gravitas to issues around sharks and conservation. The brave life of John Whitmore is poignantly remembered by Tony Heard. Ross Frylinck gives gritty insights into the forlorn splendour of the Diamond Coast. Tongue in cheek, Gideon Malherbe uncovers our surfing addiction. Henri du Plessis provides a profile of a committed exponent of that addiction. Tony Weaver eloquently tackles the challenge of sharing the sea with sharks. Ben Trovato romps through issues around surfing evolution and lifeguards in skimpy Speedos. Darryl Brandreth kickstarts an alternative surfing story. Meyrick Stockigt contributes an unusually fishy tale. Dougal Paterson profiles a top photographer. As the editor who ably pulled the above strands together, Jennifer Stern finds time to write a chunk of the travel chapter.

Huge thanks go to my partner Janet Heard, a Surfers' Corner local, whose eagle eye vastly improves the content. Also to Tyler and Ella for putting up with their frequently stressed-out dad. Thanks to a range of individuals for varied assistance, such as Ross Lindsay, who chased photographs, and gave interviews and insights. Also to Derek Jardine, Tony Heard and Harry Bold for wonderful anecdotes and photos of the 'olden days'. Thanks to Professor Tony Butt for invaluable advice on the perplexing subject of wave mechanics.

Mention must be made of people who were integral to the first *Surfing in South Africa* in 2001, because their input has carried through. Thanks to Craig Sims, Jeremy Saville and the original team at Zigzag, including those who helped with fact-checking, such as Louis Wulff, and others. Also to Ross Frylinck, who pushed me into writing the first book back in the previous century. Thanks to Professor Mark Jury, who originally gave me permission to use spots from his book.

Thanks to Collen Hendrickz and Sandy Shepherd at Juta for your patience and professionalism. Also Patricia Blom, whose wonderful design has enhanced this book no end.

For all sorts of stuff, thanks to the following (and to those who should be here): Nico Johnson, Taryn Cheadle, Tristan Werner, Faeez Abrahams, Nic Hofmeyr, Garth Robinson, Bill Sharp of BillabongXXL, Derek Jardine, Neil Webster, Dion Rolfes, Will Hayler and Linley Lewis of Ticket to Ride, Byron Loker, Chris Bertish, Mike van der Wolk, Peter Deacon, Kevin Levey, Adam Shapiro, Andrew Ingram, Brin Kushner, Callan Emery, Carola Schumann, Chip Snaddon, Damon Crawford, Dan Merkel, Dan Prata, Fleet Numerical Meteorology and Oceanography Centre, Gerbil Treesap, Grant Ellis, Quiksilver ISA World Surfing Games, Gregory Renault, Ian Armstrong, Ian Jamieson, Jacques Descloitres, John Henry, JP Pauling, Julian Wilson, Justin Klusenar, Karen Wilson, Kelly Cestari, Mark Farndell, May Knoetze, NASA-Goddard Space Flight Center, Nic Bothma, Nic Hofmeyr, Paul Speed, Pete Frieden, Peter Deacon, Piet Streicher, Raoul du Plessis, Rudi Kurt, Ryan Lucke, Sean van der Toorn, Shafiq Morton, South African Tourism, Ian Hunter, South African Weather Services, SeaWiFS Project, Goddard Space Flight Center, ORBIMAGE, NASA, Tom Karpinski, Pierre Tostee, and Wayne Monk.

And lastly, thanks to the Wavescape community who have contributed through the years to the website, and hence the spirit and feeling of this book.

BIBLIOGRAPHY

Afri-Oceans Conservation Alliance (www.aoca.org.za)

Anthoni, J F. (2000). *Oceanography: waves.* (www.seafriends.org.nz/oceano/waves.htm)

Bascom, W. (1980). *Waves and Beaches: The Dynamics of the Ocean Surface.* New York: Doubleday

Butt, T. (2002). *Surf Science: An introduction to waves for surfing.* Penzance: Alison Hodge

Coombe, E & Slingsby, P. (2000). *Beard Shavers Bush: Place Names in the Cape.* Baardskeerder.

Cotton, D. (2001). Red Bull Big Wave Africa, *Dungeons '01*

Customweather Inc (www.1stweather.com)

Duxbury, A C. & Duxbury, A B. (1994). *An Introduction to the World's Oceans.* Dubuque:
    Wm. C. Brown Publishers

Global Shark Attack File, Shark Research Institute in Princeton, USA

Illustrated Guide to the Southern African Coast. (1988) Cape Town: AA The Motorist Publications

International Shark Attack File, Florida Museum of Natural History, University of Florida
    (www.flmnh.ufl.edu/fish/sharks/ISAF/ISAF.htm)

Jury, M. (1989). *Surfing in Southern Africa, including Mauritius and Reunion.* Struik: Cape Town

National Aeronautics and Space Administration (www.goespoes.gsfc.nasa.gov)

National Geographic, (www.nationalgeographic.com)

Pank, B. Iziko Museums of Cape Town, in *Océanorama* (France) Jan. 1997

Peschak, T. (2005), *Currents of Contrast.* Struik: Cape Town

Peschak, T. & Scholl, M. (2006). *South Africa's Great White Shark*, Struik: Cape Town

Pezman, S. The Evolutionary Surfer, *Surfer* magazine, January 1978

Pike, S. (2001). *Surfing in South Africa*, Compress

Pinet, P. (1996). *Invitation to Oceanography.* Saint Paul: West Publishing Co

Shark Spotters, (www.sharkspotters.org.za)

South African Surfer magazine, 1966

South African Tourism (www.southafrica.net)

South African Weather Services (www.weathersa.co.za)

Waves, Tides and Shallow-Water Processes (2002) Oxford: The Open University

Poem quotes

pp. 10-11: Bryan W. Procter, *The Sea*, c. 1837

pp. 30-31: Lord Byron, from *Childe Harold's Pilgrimage* 1818

pp. 68-69: Robert Buchanan (p.68) *Horatius Cogitandibus* (st.16)

pp. 80-81: William Shakespeare, *King Lear* (III, ii)

pp. 114-115: Lord Byron, from *Childe Harold's Pilgrimage* 1818

pp. 132-133: Aeschylus, *Prometheus Chained* (l. 95)

pp. 142-143: Steve Pike, *www.wavescape.co.za*

pp. 254-256: Samuel Johnson. Quoted in: *James Boswell,*
    Life of Samuel Johnson, 18 March 1776 (1791)

CREDITS

Pictures

p.5, Barry Tuck; p.6, Barry Tuck; p.9 (bottom), Pete Frieden; p.9 (top), Dan Merkel; pp.10-11, Brenton Geach; p.13 (top), Andy Mason; p.13 (bottom), Ross Lindsay/Heather Price; p.14, Harry Bold; p.15 (left), South African Surfer; p.15 (right), Derek Jardine; p.16 (top, middle), Derek Jardine; p.16 (bottom), Harry Bold; p.17, Harry Bold; p.18 (right), Garth Robinson Collection (photographer unknown); p.18 (left), South African Surfer; p.20, Harry Bold; p.22, Faeez Abrahams; p.23, Zigzag; p.25, Faeez Abrahams; p.27 (top), Grant Ellis/Quiksilver ISA World Surfing Games; p.27 (bottom), Lance Slabbert; p.28, Nic Bothma; pp.30-31: Nic Hofmeyr; p.33 (top), Andy Mason; p.35 (top left), Nic Hofmeyr; p.35 (top right, bottom right), Barry Tuck; p.35 (bottom left), Steve Pike; p.36, Steve Pike; p.37 (right) Ian Armstrong; p.37 (top), Tostee. com/Red Bull Photofiles; p.38, Kelly Cestari; p.40, Steve Pike; p.41, Gideon Malherbe; p.42, Gideon Malherbe; p.44, GQ magazine; p.45, Ian Jamieson; p.46, Chip Snaddon; pp.48-67, Harry de Zitter; pp.68-69, Al McKinnon/BillabongXXL. com; p.70, South African Surfer; p.71 (top), Andy Mason; p.71 (bottom), Grant Ellis/Red Bull Photofiles; p.72, Grant Ellis/Red Bull Photofiles; p.73, Shafiq Morton; p.74, Piet Streicher; p.77 (top, middle left), Jared Hartman; p.77 (middle right, bottom), Grant Ellis/Red Bull Photofiles; p.78, Michael Dei-Cont; pp.80-81, Jared Hartman; p.83 (top), Andy Mason; p.83 (bottom), Pierre Marqua; p.84, Grant Ellis/Red Bull Photofiles; p.85 (inset), Fleet Numerical Meteorology and Oceanography Centre; p.86, Tony Butt; p.87 (top left), Tony Butt; p.87, South African Weather Services; p.88, NASA-Goddard Space Flight Center; p.89 (left), 1stweather.com; p.89 (right), Al McKinnon/BillabongXXL.com; p.90, Tony Butt; p.92 (top), South African Weather Services; p.92 (middle, bottom), Fleet Numerical Meteorology and Oceanography Centre; p.93, Pierre Marqua; p.94 (top), Pierre Marqua; p.94 (insets), Fleet Numerical Meteorology and Oceanography Centre; p.95, Steve Pike (from original by Tony Butt); p.96, Tony Butt; p.97 (top), Michael Dei-Cont; p.97 (below), Tony Butt; p.98, Sean Collins/BillabongXXL.com; p.99, Jacques Descloitres, MODIS Land Group, NASA Goddard Space Flight Center; p.100, TIF SeaWiFS Project, NASA/Goddard Space Flight Center, and ORBIMAGE; p.101 (top left) 1stweather. com; p.101 (top right), South African Weather Services; p.102, Tony Butt; p.103, Callan Emery; p.104 (top right), Steve Pike; p.104 (top left), Tony Butt; p.104 (bottom), Pierre Marqua; p.107, NASA; p.108 (top), Rudi Kurt; p.108, Steve Pike; p.109, Pierre Marqua; p.110 (top) Andrew Ingram, Cape Argus; p.110 (bottom), South African Weather Services; p.111 (top left), 1stweather.com; p.111 (top right), Julian Wilson; p.112 (top), South African Weather Services; p.112 (inset), Fleet Numerical Meteorology and Oceanography Centre; p.113 (top), Ryan Lucke; p.113 (bottom), Brin Kushner; pp.114-115, Tom Peschak; p.117 (top), Andy Mason; p.117 (bottom), Tom Peschak; p.118, Tom Peschak; p.119, Tom Peschak; p.120, Tom Peschak; p.121 (top), Steve Pike; p.121 (bottom), Tom Peschak; p.122, Tom Peschak; p.125 (bottom), Steve Pike; p.125 (top), Tom Peschak; p.127, Tom Peschak; p.129, Tom Peschak; p.130, Tom Peschak; p.131 (top left), Karen Wilson; p.131 (top right, bottom left), Serge Raemaekers; p.131 (bottom right), Tom Peschak; pp.132-133, Barry Tuck; p.135 (top), Andy Mason; p.135 (bottom), Barry Tuck; p.136-137, Andy Mason; p.138, Ant Scholtz; p.139, Steve Pike; pp.142-143, Lance Slabbert; p.145, Andy Mason; p.147 (bottom), Michael Dei-Cont; p.147 (top), Pierre Marqua; p.149, Barry Tuck; p.151, Tom Peschak; p.153, Ray du Toit; p.154, Ray du Toit; p.156, Ray du Toit; p.157, Ray du Toit; p.159 (top), Steve Pike; p.159 (bottom), Tom Karpinski; p.160, Piet Streicher; p.162, Steve Pike; p.163, Steve Pike; p.165, South African Tourism; p.167 (top), Dan Prata; p.167 (bottom), Shafiq Morton; p.169 (top), Lance Slabbert; p.169 (middle), Michael Dei-Cont; p.169 (bottom), Peter Deacon; p.170, South African Tourism; p.172, Michael Dei-Cont; p.173, Michael Dei-Cont; p.175 (top), Barry Tuck; p.175 (bottom), Grant Ellis/Red Bull Photofiles; p.176, Lance Slabbert; p.177 (top), Steve Pike; p.177 (bottom), Barry Tuck; p.178, Michael Dei-Cont; p.179 (top), Steve Pike; p.179 (bottom), Michael Dei-Cont; p.180, Steve Pike; p.181, Barry Tuck; p.182, Pierre Marqua; p.183 (top), Michael Dei-Cont; p.183 (bottom), Pierre Marqua; p.185 (top), Michael Dei-Cont; p.185 (bottom), Ryan Lucke; p.186, Michael Dei-Cont; p.188, Piet Streicher; p.189, Ryan Lucke; p.191, Raoul du Plessis; p.192, Tom Peschak; p.193, South African Tourism; p.197 (top), South African Tourism; p.197 (bottom), Gerbil Treesap; p.201, Mark Farndell; p.202, John Henry/Ticket To Ride.co.uk; p.205, Barry Tuck; p.206, Gregory Renault; p.207, Ant Scholtz; p.208, Carola Schumann; p.211, Barry Tuck; p.212, South African Tourism; p.214, Wayne Monk; p.217 (top), Serge Raemaekers; p.217 (bottom), Damon Crawford; p.218, Serge Raemaekers; p.220, Serge Raemaekers; p.221, Serge Raemaekers; p.222, Serge Raemaekers; p.223, Serge Raemaekers; p.225, Meyrick Stockigt; p.226, Serge Raemaekers; p.227 Serge Raemaekers; p.229, Paul Speed; p.230, Sean van der Toorn; p.233, Barry Tuck; p.235 (top) Adam Shapiro; p.235 (bottom), Barry Tuck; p.236, Barry Tuck; p.237, Barry Tuck; p.239, Lance Slabbert; p.240 (top left), Justin Klusenar; p.240 (top right, bottom right), Lance Slabbert; p.240 (bottom left), Barry Tuck; p.241, Lance Slabbert; p.242, JP Pauling; p.243, Barry Tuck; p.245, Barry Tuck; p.246 (top left and right), Barry Tuck; p.246 (bottom), Ant Scholtz; p.247, Barry Tuck; p.248 (bottom), Barry Tuck; pp.248-249 (top), Barry Tuck; p.249, Steve Pike; p.251 (top), Tom Peschak; p.251 (bottom), May Knoetze; p.252, South African Tourism; p.254-255, Steve Pike; p.256, Andy Mason; p.270, Barry Tuck

Words

p.21, Tony Heard; pp.25-26, Darryl Brandreth; pp.41-43, Gideon Malherbe; p.44 Henri du Plessis; p.47, Ben Trovato; p.49, Dougal Paterson; p.123, Tom Peschak; p.126, Tony Weaver; pp.129-130, Tom Peschak; pp.138-139, Jennifer Stern 'What to do when the surf is flat'; pp.152-155, Ross Frylinck; p.225, Meyrick Stockigt; p.238, Ben Trovato